Identity and Memory

Identity and Memory

The Films of Chantal Akerman

Edited by
Gwendolyn Audrey Foster

Southern Illinois University Press
Carbondale and Edwardsville

"Girl talk: *Portrait of a Young Girl at the End of the 1960s in Brussels*" was reprinted in *Framed: Lesbians, Feminists, and Media Culture,* by Judith Mayne (University of Minnesota Press, 2000).

"Invented memories" was reprinted in slightly different form in *Endless Night: Cinema and Psychoanalysis, Parallel Histories,* edited by Janet Bergstrom (University of California Press, 1999) under the title "Chantal Akerman: Splitting."

Library of Congress Cataloging-in-Publication Data

Identity and memory : the films of Chantal Akerman / edited by Gwendolyn Audrey Foster.
    p. cm.
  Originally published: Trowbridge, Wiltshire, England : Flicks Books, 1999, in series: Cinema voices series; with new pref.
  Filmography: p.
  Includes bibliographical references and index.
    1. Akerman, Chantal—Criticism and interpretation. I. Title: Films of Chantal Akerman. II. Foster, Gwendolyn Audrey.

PN1998.3.A435 I33 2003
791.43'0233'092—dc21
ISBN 0-8093-2512-8 (cloth : alk. paper)
ISBN 0-8093-2513-6 (pbk. : alk. paper)   2002030594

Printed on recycled paper. ♻

The paper used in this publication meets the minimum requirements of American National Standard for InformationSciences—Permanence of Paper for Printed LibraryMaterials, ANSI Z39.48-1992. ∞

Reprinted from the 1999 edition published by Flicks Books.

Contents

Preface

With the publication of the American edition of *Identity and Memory: The Films of Chantal Akerman,* the career of this celebrated auteur is perhaps at its highest point. With a substantial body of work to her credit, discussed in detail in the numerous essays in this volume, Akerman is without doubt one of most important and innovative filmmakers working today. Since this collection first appeared, Chantal Akerman has created several additional works in her typically prolific style, shooting two projects on video for French television and a 35mm feature film created on a seven week shooting schedule. In 1996, Akerman created *Chantal Akerman by Chantal Akerman,* a video meditation on her life and work, in which she directly addresses the camera for the first half of the film, reading from a prepared text. In the video's second section, Akerman reviews her career as an artist with clips from her films, as if coming to terms with her own cinematic past.

In 1999, Akerman completed *Sud,* a breathtaking experimental documentary about the horrific murder of African American James Byrd Jr. in Jasper, Texas, who was beaten and dragged to his death from the back of a pickup truck by three white men. The film begins with Akerman's signature long takes, as she drives through the town documenting the people and the landscape of Jasper. No narrator tells us what to think or what we are about to experience. Akerman intercuts interviews with Caucasian and African American members of the community, who speak about the horrible crime, with long sequences of an African American church service and images of the Texas countryside. By letting the protagonists speak for themselves, Akerman evokes the bleak reality of racism that made Byrd's murder possible. The film ends with an almost unendurably long tracking shot from the back of a car, looking back impassively at the three-mile stretch of road where Byrd was dragged to his death.

Sud is less than roughly seventy minutes long, yet it has the impact of films such as Alain Resnais's *Night and Fog* (1955) or Henri Georges Clouzot's *Wages of Fear* (1953). It is minimalist in its number of shots and sequences, but this only makes the overall impact of the film all the more compelling. Akerman uses silence and ambient sound to draw the viewer into a subjective state of understanding. As a documentarian, Akerman never involves herself in the events she witnesses but rather documents the people and places of Jasper impassively, nonjudgmentally, as if to present to her audience a tapestry of human cultural experience, placing the spectator at the scene of the crime. *Sud* is thus a remarkable mixture of realism and intentional distancing technique, which leaves the viewer speechless, angered, and sad. It is a lyrical tribute to the barbarism of race-based crime and America's continuing deep-seated racism.

In 2000, Chantal Akerman released the feature-length fiction film *La Captive (The Captive),* an elegant adaptation of Proust's "La Prisonniere," book 5 of his epic work *Remembrance of Things Past. La Captive* has been critically hailed as a masterpiece and topped most of the New York film critics "Ten Best" lists for the year. However, the film has yet to be released theatrically in the United States, although it was a substantial hit in Europe and is now available on DVD. Shown at the French Film Festival at the Walter Reade Theatre in New York in 2000 with the director in attendance, *La Captive* drew immediate praise for its masterful capturing of obsessional love, sexual obsession, and passion. Stanislas Merhar's performance as Simon, a bored, wealthy young man in the grip of an erotic obsession he can neither understand nor control, is understated and stunning. Simon's love-object, Ariane, impressively played by Sylvie Testud, is ultimately unable to deal with the continuing pressure of Simon's attentions.

La Captive opens with a poetic sequence of images showing Ariane at the beach, frolicking with her friends. Ariane is attracted to both women and men, especially Simon, but obviously bored and unhappy in her ultimate role as Simon's reluctant yet ultimately compliant prisoner. The relationship between the rich, indolent Simon and the seemingly willing Ariane is doomed from the start, yet Akerman takes her time with this desperate scenario, allowing the characters' obsessions to gradually unfold before the viewer's eyes. Akerman composes *La Captive* in her trademark long takes, sometimes with a slowly tracking camera, and alternatively with a series of static set-ups that confine the characters within the performance space they inhabit. The film simmers with sexual tension and elegance and is fitting proof that Akerman continues to be one of the most important and influential filmmakers working today.

As the essays in this book ably demonstrate, Akerman's films are at once audacious and original, displaying a feminist vision that is uniquely her own. In all of Akerman's work, we see an obsession with memory and identity that continues to haunt both the director and her audiences. In the years to come, Akerman's work will undoubtedly continue to expand in new and unexpected directions, whether in video installations, feature films, or documentaries. This volume captures the filmmaker at the height of her creative powers, demonstrating both her enormous influence on contemporary cinema in the United States and Europe and her inexhaustibility as an auteur, as cinema moves into the twenty-first century.

Gwendolyn Audrey Foster

Acknowledgments

For their help in creating this volume, I wish firstly to thank the various contributors, who brought a deep understanding of Akerman's work to their various assignments, and who completed their essays promptly and with great precision. Matthew Stevens of Flicks Books and Brian McIlroy lent support during the early stages of this project. Dana Miller, Wheeler Winston Dixon, and the members of the Department of English at the University of Nebraska-Lincoln also assisted in numerous ways in the completion of this volume. I would also like to thank Bruce Jenkins of the Walker Art Center for providing additional research materials which were of great use in creating this text. My greatest debt, of course, is to Chantal Akerman, for creating these beautiful and mysterious films, and for her continuing commitment to revitalising and reshaping the muse of the moving image.

Identity and Memory

Introduction

Gwendolyn Audrey Foster

The essays in this volume explore the work of Chantal Akerman, one of the most important filmmakers of the late-20th century, whose films have had a profound impact on feminist discourse within the cinema, and within avant-garde film as an international discipline. Born in 1950, Akerman came to the United States after leaving film school in Belgium. One of her first jobs was as a cashier for the 55th Street Playhouse, a porn theatre in New York City. In an interview with Gary Indiana, Akerman noted that "I worked at the 55th Street Playhouse...as a cashier; and...I [amassed] $4,000 and made *Hotel Monterey* [1972] and *La Chambre* [*The Room*, 1972] with that".[1] Claiming that she was profoundly influenced by Jean-Luc Godard's *Pierrot le fou* (1965), Akerman established her style even in these early efforts. In *Hotel Monterey*, for example, people move in and out of the frame of a stationary camera. Already Akerman is expressing an interest in the transient nature of modern urban life, with an emphatic eye towards spaces that underscore the discord of mobility – hotels, train stations – and the people who move within these spaces.

Je tu il elle (*I...You...He...She*, 1974) is Akerman's breakthrough feature-length film, composed of long blocks of static black-and-white takes, reminiscent of the films of Andy Warhol. Asked about Warhol's influence on her work, Akerman noted that she had seen only *The Chelsea Girls* (1966) and *Eat* (1963), and commented that "a critic said I have something from Warhol and something from Robert Wilson, that I'm a mixture of that. Probably Warhol is a big, big originator...but it wasn't because I saw it; it was something that was there. I think my films are more sentimental."[2] Akerman's impassive camera documents the solitary life of a single woman lost in a modern industrial world. The scene of this woman, naked and alone, desperately eating sugar, is remarkable for its intensity, as is the footage of her desperately arranging and rearranging the meagre furniture in her apartment. The woman then hitchhikes, and gives an offscreen hand job to a truck driver. Feminist critics have scrutinised this scene, sometimes missing the camp humour inherent in such a treatment of sexuality. Next, the woman makes love to another woman, in a sequence that has similarly attracted a great deal of attention from feminist critics. Because the camera records the action in a scientific manner, the scene has often

1

been noted for its self-conscious display of dehumanisation and lack of visual pleasure.

However, as Andrea Weiss points out, this "absolutely uneroticized lesbian lovemaking scene must be credited for its courage in 1974, especially given that it includes the filmmaker in the scene and rejects art cinema conventions governing lesbian sexuality".[3] The camera positioning is specifically meant to de-aestheticise the onscreen lovemaking, by making us aware of our offscreen voyeurism. The naturalistic use of sound also underscores the scene's break from Hollywood and art-house depictions of sexuality. However, not all critics have found the scene to be without eroticism. I find the scene more erotic than conventionally constructed sex scenes because of Akerman's embrace of natural sound and image, and because of the tension that develops in watching such a radically different approach to the sexual body, in much the same way that I find pleasure in Warhol's films. As Judith Mayne notes, "one could hardly find a contemporary woman's film more saturated with authorial signature than *Je tu il elle*".[4] It is perhaps the difficulty of the avant-garde re-representation of the female body that makes this film so memorable. The fact that the main woman character is played by the filmmaker herself tends to move the critic into a discussion of subjectivity beyond the realm of the film frame.

Female identity and subjectivity are at the centre of the thematic core of *Jeanne Dielman, 23 quai du Commerce, 1080 Bruxelles* (1975), Akerman's film of routine daily activities of a Belgian housewife and prostitute. As Teresa de Lauretis argues, in *Jeanne Dielman, 23 quai du Commerce, 1080 Bruxelles*, "the narrative suspense is not built on the expectation of a 'significant event'...but is produced by the...hesitations between real-time gestures as common and 'insignificant' as peeling potatoes, washing dishes, or making coffee...What the film constructs – formally and artfully, to be sure – is a picture of female experience".[5] The routine existence of Jeanne Dielman is punctuated by a scene in which the woman suddenly kills a client with a pair of scissors after having sex with him. The almost unendurable long take of the woman sitting at a table for several minutes after the murder (doing absolutely nothing) discourages audience identification, even as it builds tension in the same way as do the sex scenes in *I...You...He...She*.

News from Home (1976) and *Les Rendez-vous d'Anna* (*Meetings with Anna*, 1978) exemplify Akerman's continual risk-taking anti-cinema. In *News from Home*, Akerman lets the camera stare at urban spaces while an offscreen narrator (Akerman) reads letters from a mother to an absent daughter. Akerman utilises the monotony of the mother's voice to create discord and disharmony, rather than using narrative plots designed artificially to construct human dilemma. *News from Home* can be read as an astute commentary on the artificiality of mainstream cinematic narrative conventions. Similarly, *Meetings with Anna* uses sameness to create drama. In this film, the camera follows a woman filmmaker who travels through depeopled spaces – hotels, train stations, underground railways. She meets a man desperate for companionship. Rather than conform to conventional heterotopic narrative closure devices, the woman leaves the man.

Meetings with Anna can be identified for Akerman's signature long takes, avoidance of close-ups, naturalistic sound, lack of mainstream narrative, and self-inscription as woman director. Sexual encounters are unfulfilling, and the film encourages a cerebral audience identification, rather than a "pleasurable" passive audience experience. *Toute une nuit* (*All Night Long*, 1982) continues the theme of solitude, as it follows the monotonous sexual encounters of one particular night, as suggested in the film's title. Couples do *not* get together in *All Night Long*. Marsha Kinder describes the challenges posed by this film:

> By denying us a single unifying story, by frequently pitting word against visual image and non-verbal sound, by discouraging us from identifying with any of the anonymous characters, by denying us a single unified subject position... *Toute une nuit* makes us change the way we read a film.[6]

Akerman's *Nuit et jour* (*Night and Day*, 1991) departs significantly in style from these earlier films. The film is much more commercially-oriented and narratively constructed. The film centres around the life of Julie, a young woman who lives in Paris, and who makes love to one man by night, and another man by day. At the end of the film, Julie walks away from both lovers. The film is stunning in terms of cinematography and the use of colour and framing. Critics have noted the lack of anger and intensity of *Night and Day*, in comparison with Akerman's earlier work. Nevertheless, *Night and Day* can be read as a significant feminist statement. The central protagonist explores her sexuality and simply walks away from the men without suffering, or even choosing, one of them. Akerman here regenders the love-triangle film, in which a male hero chooses between traditionally binary opposites of good and bad women. Since then, Akerman has continued to create new and unexpected films in a variety of performative structures. This volume considers both early and later works by the filmmaker, and gives careful consideration to Akerman's continual development as an artist and a social force within the cinema. Akerman's films will continue to challenge with both their technique and their complex feminist discourse.

The essays in this volume consider Akerman's key films in a number of different lights. Maureen Turim's essay, "Personal pronouncements in *I...You...He...She* and *Portrait of a Young Girl at the End of the 1960s in Brussels*", explores "the highly abstracted fictions" that Chantal Akerman constructs in her film, *I...You...He...She*. This phrase also resonates with Akerman's use of the personal pronouns. While it is possible to see the "je" of the title as the woman whose writing block is coupled with obsessive sugar-eating from a paper bag in the first segment of the film, "il" as the truck driver whom the woman meets in the second segment, "elle" as her woman friend of the third segment, and the "tu" as floating amongst them as a shifter of their intercourse, these personal pronouns also recall the hesitation about writing dramatised in the opening sequence. It is as if an author, in writing this story, could not decide on the voice of narration. This "indecidability" couples with a minimalist abstraction and an artificiality to flirt with autobiography in the highly structured segments that comprise this film. Turim's discussion of *I...You...He...She* leads into a consideration of Akerman's more recent effort, *Portrait d'une jeune fille à la fin des années 60 à Bruxelles* (*Portrait of a Young Girl at the End of the 1960s in Brussels*, 1993), and demonstrates how these two widely disparate films share common concerns in Akerman's vision of the cinema.

Of Sandy Flitterman-Lewis' text, "What's beneath her smile? Subjectivity and desire in Germaine Dulac's *The Smiling Madame Beudet* and Chantal Akerman's *Jeanne Dielman, 23 quai du Commerce, 1080 Bruxelles*", the author notes that, "[i]f one of the projects of a feminist counter-cinema is the exploration and representation of female subjectivity", a way to address the issue of feminist alternatives is to analyse the work of women filmmakers who have specifically designated the representation of feminine desire as their terrain. *La Souriante Madame Beudet* (*The Smiling Madame Beudet*), made in 1923 by Germaine Dulac, and *Jeanne Dielman, 23 quai du Commerce, 1080 Bruxelles*, made 50 years later by Akerman, provide excellent points of departure and comparison, both filmmakers being preoccupied with questions of cinematic language, narrativity and "the feminine". Both films are firmly situated in the domestic realm, and take as their focus women whose lives are marked by the oppressiveness and repression of the household order. In each film there is a critical moment, linked to the sexual experience of pleasure/*jouissance*, which results in an act of murderous revolt. Yet, importantly, the approaches, methods and critical *démarches* of the two filmmakers diverge in crucial ways; for Dulac, *The Smiling Madame Beudet* represents the exploration of individual psychology; on the other hand, we might say that Akerman's focus in *Jeanne Dielman, 23 quai du Commerce, 1080 Bruxelles* is less on individual character than on the social inscription of desire, an interest in psychoanalysis as opposed to psychology.

In "The feminine side of New York: travelogue, autobiography and architecture in *News from Home*", Jennifer M Barker argues that a reading of theories of women's autobiographical writing against theories of cinematic narration and enunciation illuminates the complexities of Akerman's attempt to illustrate the "non-presence" of narrative subjectivity in *News from Home*. The film's image track focuses exclusively on public spaces and nameless crowds; the soundtrack combines Akerman's own voice with her mother's written words. In this sense, Akerman's own subjectivity is constructed not through a linear telling of her own history, or through a focus on her own "presence", but rather through the juxtaposition of the "body" of the city in which Akerman lives, with Akerman's reading of her mother's lonely ruminations, in the form of the frequent letters she sent to Akerman from Brussels. By writing her life through a writing of urban spaces and another's words, Akerman locates subjectivity at the intersection of the public and private, thus articulating cinematically a notion of subjectivity that is both post-structural and somehow beyond the paradigms offered by literary theory for understanding the "Self".

In "Echo and voice in *Meetings with Anna*", Ivone Margulies offers a discussion of the mode of verbal address and performance in Akerman's *Meetings with Anna*. The theatricality in *Meetings with Anna* – the oblique frontality of the characters, as well the extended dialogue-qua-monologue format of their minimalist verbal exchanges – is typical of a particular strand of European antinaturalism (Bresson, Duras, Straub/Huillet and Rohmer) which Margulies examines. More importantly, she explores the ways in which the protagonist of *Meetings with Anna* exercises her option to remain single in the face of multiple encounters with men. Margulies suggests that the particular poses assumed by the characters in Akerman's film as they listen or speak to each other are more than a formal issue; that, in fact, Anna's option to remain single is an integral factor in the film's effect of hyper-theatricality.

Catherine Fowler notes of her essay, "*All Night Long*: the ambivalent text of 'Belgianicity'", that it positions the film as a bridging moment between Akerman's "1970s cinema of anti-seduction and her 1980s and 1990s cinema which incorporates a more direct address of narrative and its various pleasures". Fowler suggests that, as a liminal film, *All Night Long* offers a space for a meeting of the "fleeting locations of Akerman's cinema, whether formal or aesthetic (avant-garde, art cinema, European auteur cinema) geographic (New York, Paris, Belgium) or thematic (the mother, time, space, rituals, gestures)". Such a meeting is dependent upon the critical "blankness" of Belgian cinema and the "non-identity" Brussels, which thus allow other identities to dominate the film: "How does Akerman's treatment of Brussels, her city of birth, compare to her treatment of New York, where she has said she feels most at home, or Paris where she now lives?" What sort of a relationship emerges between Akerman and Belgium?

Janet Bergstrom's essay, "Invented memories", deals with Akerman's relationship to Jewish identity, focusing on her films *Histoires d'Amérique (American Stories/Food, Family and Philosophy*, 1989), *D'Est (From the East,* 1993) and *Golden Eighties/Window Shopping* (1986). Akerman's dream as a filmmaker has been to make an historical pageant about "the diaspora of the Eastern European Jews". She has discussed this dream-film in the light of many other projects that she hoped would be stepping-stones to its realisation. Akerman's relationship to her own Jewish heritage is complicated by the fact that her parents, displaced Polish Jews who settled in Belgium, refused to discuss their past with her, especially her mother's experience in a concentration camp in the Second World War. Because of this, as Akerman has explained in a number of interviews, Akerman feels compelled to "make up" a past to substitute for theirs. *American Stories/ Food, Family and Philosophy* is the closest Akerman has come to making a film of rememoration. It features structural dynamics common to Akerman's films: the title (*Histoires d'Amérique*) is in French, but the film itself is in English; the film takes place in the United States, but is peopled with displaced Europeans. *American Stories/Food, Family and Philosophy* is one of the most important of Akerman's films for understanding the evolution of her film work, and it speaks to compelling contemporary issues of Jewish identity and representation. Bergstrom will continue her consideration of Akerman's work in her forthcoming volume, *Like a Road Movie*.

In "*Night and Day*: a Parisian fairy tale", Ginette Vincendeau considers *Night and Day* from the point of view of its evocation and reworking of the Nouvelle Vague, in particular through the film's representation of the city, and Akerman's depiction of the amorous relationships that form the nucleus of the film's narrative. Vincendeau also considers Akerman's more recent film, *Un Divan à New York (A Couch in New York*, 1996).

My essay, "The mechanics of the performative body in *The Eighties*", examines the manner in which Akerman playfully deconstructs the auditions held for her musical comedy, *Golden Eighties/Window Shopping*, as the text of the film that became *The Eighties* (1983). In this poetic contemplation of the mechanics of the performative body, Akerman exposes the simulacrum of the female body as it is constructed in the musical comedy film, queering the performative body in an anti-narrativistic yet pleasurable montage of aural and visual passages. Songs, lines of dialogue and fragments of choreography are repeatedly rehearsed, as Akerman demystifies the process of the filmic and syntactic construction of the heterotopic musical, while simultaneously offering a meditation on the scopic zones of the body. *The Eighties* thus motions towards a hyperreal cinema of embodied pleasure across the limitations of the cinematic apparatus, rearticulating the bodies and voices of Akerman's performers into a confrontational displacement of our expectations of the traditional musical and/or narrative film.

In "Girl talk: *Portrait of a Young Girl at the End of the 1960s in Brussels*", Judith Mayne examines Akerman's film, with particular emphasis on the interrelationships between sexuality, authorship and female adolescence. Lesbian desire in *Portrait of a Young Girl* occupies a central yet paradoxical place. In that sense, the film echoes other films by Akerman, from *I...You...He...She* (in which, despite its status as the most "explicitly" lesbian of Akerman's films, lesbian desire remains both visible and marginal) to *Meetings with Anna* (in which Anna's various heterosexual and familial encounters are problematised by her desire for another woman, who makes a somewhat ghostly appearance as a disembodied voice on Anna's answering machine). *Portrait of a Young Girl* also takes Akerman's preoccupation with lesbian desire and cinematic authorship in new directions by focusing on the specific historical period of the 1960s, understood both culturally (particularly insofar as adolescence is concerned) and cinematically – through references to a wide range of films, particularly those associated with the New Wave, from *Cléo de 5 à 7* (*Cléo from 5 to 7*, 1961) to *Vivre sa vie* (*It's My Life*, 1962). Finally, in "Bordering on fiction: Chantal Akerman's *From the East*", Kristine Butler deconstructs Akerman's 1995 video installation, presented at the Walker Art Center and elsewhere. It is, above all, a cinema of waiting. Akerman focuses on moments preceding or following an event: she films train stations, snowy streets at dawn, people walking, standing, waiting. The drama, if there is one, is outside the frame. This is a cinema of inaction: what has happened, or what will happen, is elsewhere. Akerman's cinematic style is uniquely suited to the demands of a museum installation as a space made for wandering. In her past work, Akerman has developed a film language in which the lateral movements of the camera suggest the wandering of a subject at once spectator and participant. *From the East*, although it is informed by Akerman's cinematic work, is not simply a film, but rather an event: "The very personal movement of each museum-goer, who walks, sits, looks or does not look, listens to out-of-sync noises and dialogue, leaves or does not leave, creates the movement of the installation itself".

In all these essays, we see the figure of Akerman constantly moving into new ground in her work as a filmmaker, unwilling to repeat past accomplishments, thoroughly involved in reinventing both herself and the medium she has chosen as her tool of expression with each new work. It is hoped that, in these essays, the reader will find a number of new and unexpected insights into Akerman's increasingly important body of work as a filmmaker, and that the viewer will be guided to a deeper appreciation of her films and her constantly shifting concerns as an artist over the past twenty years. Whatever Akerman attempts in the future, one can expect it to be simultaneously transgressive and celebratory, as she continually pushes back the representational and narrative boundaries of the medium of the moving image in the last moments of the 20th century. As she moves beyond film into the realm of performance art and video installations, Akerman in all her work urges us to meditate and contemplate the various manifestations and permutations of the manufactured moving image, with or without a narrative structure, using music or natural sound, silence or dialogue, a static camera or one that joyously participates in the action. Akerman's films are both revolutionary and invigorating; they are also the work of an uncompromising and dedicated practitioner of the cinema.

In her considerations of alterity, sexuality, subjectivity, performativity, mother-daughter relationships, Belgianicity, Jewish diasporic identity, female subjectivity, lesbian identity and other concomitant issues, Akerman creates a cinema which is at once engaging and rigorous, merging issues of identity and memory with the quotidian pursuit of an expanding everyday, or commonplace, consciousness.

Notes

1   Gary Indiana, "Getting Ready for *The Golden Eighties*: A Conversation with Chantal Akerman", *Artforum* 21: 10 (summer 1983): 57.

2   Ibid.

3   Andrea Weiss, *Vampires & Violets: Lesbians in the Cinema* (London: Jonathan Cape, 1992): 114.

4   Judith Mayne, *The Woman at the Keyhole: Feminism and Women's Cinema* (Bloomington; Indianapolis: Indiana University Press, 1990): 129.

5   Teresa de Lauretis, *Technologies of Gender: Essays on Theory, Film, and Fiction* (Bloomington: Indiana University Press, 1987): 131.

6   Marsha Kinder, "The Subversive Potential of the Pseudo-Iterative", *Film Quarterly* 43: 2 (winter 1989/1990): 16.

Personal pronouncements in *I...You...He...She* and *Portrait of a Young Girl at the End of the 1960s in Brussels*

Maureen Turim

"Personal pronouncements" is a phrase I have chosen to use to speak of the highly abstracted fictions that Chantal Akerman constructs in her films, *Je tu il elle* (*I...You...He...She*, 1974) and *Portrait d'une jeune fille de la fin des années 60 à Bruxelles* (*Portrait of a Young Girl at the End of the 1960s in Brussels*, 1993). This phrase resonates with her use of the personal pronouns in the title of her first feature, *I...You...He... She*; in fact, the descriptive phrase, "Personal Pronouncements", was used as the English version of that title for the film's initial US release, although today it is far better known by the original French title. My reason, however, for evoking this phrase is the succinct way in which it conjoins autobiography and enunciation to point towards a revelation of the intimate.

In some sense, all writing and personal filmmaking border on autobiography, even when placed in the third person, or filmed without direct reference to the filmmaker's body or life; the game here – since Akerman acts, as well as writes and directs – is to play with the first person of written fiction and yet to avoid autobiography in favour of fiction. The direct first-person voice-over that would cement autobiography is replaced by first-person articulations belonging instead to a character writing letters, and the voice-over readings of parts of these letters are playfully edited into a performance piece designed to emphasise indirect over direct discourse.

Yet, even as the self is disguised by these ruses of language, the body of the author dominates the images; the body, too, participates in disguise, acting and fiction, but it is also repeatedly offered in its nakedness and, at least metaphorically, stripped of any disguise other than its own revelation. The body here is young and sensuous, sculptural, yet without refinement; soft, yet evincing strength, rather than a passive voluptuousness. The breasts are large and the hips wide, yet the body remains strikingly adolescent. It is a bit awkward, unsure of its own allure, in no sense coy, and certainly not stereotypical of female bodily display. It is not the heterosexual female body of so many known images, but it also, especially denuded, lacks signs of androgyny – at least in the usual sense of a body that lies at the ambiguous borders of body classifications, or blends them, suggesting a feminised masculinity or a masculinised femininity. And yet, in the sense that it reminds one of the body of the Italian actress, Anna Magnani, sensuous and tough, female and strong, it is a body that eludes gender stereotypes to define its own presence.

Like this body that troubles us as an unusual image, an uncertain sign that nevertheless reveals the autobiography in the physicality of self-portraiture, Akerman's filmmaking allows for ambiguity and oscillation. It is at once a display, an acting out, and a disguise. By "acting out", I mean not only the process of enactment by actors and actresses, but also "acting out" in the psychoanalytical sense of the portrayal of unconscious wishes through actions, a concept I have evoked elsewhere to discuss Oshima's *Koshikei* (*Death by Hanging*, 1968).[1] To act out (*mettre en acte, ageren*) is a psychoanalytic construct indicating actions taken by a subject in the grip of his or her unconscious wishes and fantasies. These repetitive gestures return from a repressed past that is precisely not remembered. The gestures appear absurd until the underlying psychoanalytic logic is revealed. In Akerman's film, the revelation of her character's unconscious desires is shadowed by the hint of a revelation of an authorial, personal, autobiographical unconscious, as the space between fictive character and authorial voice is alternatively collapsed and expanded in the film's unfolding.

Consider how the film's main character, the "je", traverses three distinct sorts of spaces over the course of the film, spaces that divide the film into large narrative segments which I will summarise briefly before closer examination later. In the first segment, this woman writes in her room. In the second, she hitchhikes, but the space of her journey is confined to one shot of the highway, shots in the cab of a truck whose driver picks her up, and shots in the bars, restaurants and a bathroom at which they stop. In the third segment, she visits a former lover, whose apartment is the setting – hallway, kitchen and bedroom, primarily – of this entire segment. Each of the three segments remains detached from each other, stressing their autonomy. The relation of these segments one to the other, remains left to speculation and suggestion.

So central and obvious is this tripartite structure that nearly all those who critically address this film start with an explanation of it. Jean Narboni, in a provocative theoretical reading of the film, emphasises circular structures inscribed in the three segments, and the film's escape from the first three persons of singular verbal address: "Discourse in the fourth person singular, which is neither the histrionics of subjectivity (the 'I'), nor the despotic quality of interpellation and of demand (the 'you'), nor the objectifying horror of the non-person (the 'he/she')".[2] He sees the segments mounting through numerous restagings of specular lures coupled with provocations offered by the looks of others, and culminating in the long third sexual sequence, a confrontation with "pornography, and its *ruin*".[3] Judith Mayne, in her excellent and challenging essay, "Mistresses of Discrepancy", sees each section as "turning centrally on the separation between the woman as a narrating subject and as an object", viewing the film as significant "in terms of female and lesbian authorship in the cinema".[4] She is reluctant to characterise the narrative progression from segment to segment as a movement from isolation of the self through a hesitant heterosexuality to a triumphant lesbian sexuality. Such an allegorical reading would reduce the film to a linearity that it seems to disallow, according to Mayne, as "the structure...is not linear".[5] Françoise Audé has offered a different developmental reading of the film, in which she proposes the links between the segments to be a movement towards separation.[6] According to Mayne, this analysis is one troubled "with more than a tinge of homophobia", as it reads the film as demonstrating the "necessity for separation and departure by taking the conclusion of each segment as definitive, including the departure from the lesbian lover in the third segment, "done surreptitiously while the other sleeps".[7] Without a doubt, the debate here is one that ultimately hinges on the fundamental question of connecting structures to meanings. We might well ask how such a daring intervention into filmmaking form and structure, as proposed by *I...You...He...She*, affects interpretation. The time that has passed since the emergence of structuralism both in filmmaking practice and in narratology perhaps will permit us a renewed investigation and new angles on both structures and meanings in this film. What I propose to do here is to pursue further examination of this structure from a perspective that is decidedly post-structuralist. The questions framed by a three-part structure – progression, linearity, oppositions – will be foregrounded in this essay. Akerman's more recent film and her installation work will serve to provide further retrospective rethinking of the earliest film work.

To return to the first, long scene of the film, our main character, played by Akerman herself and unnamed until the closing credits when she is identified as "Julie", voices the words she is depicted writing. As Mayne analyses, this voicing is not necessarily in sync with the image. Sometimes the words anticipate an image, sometimes they seemingly contradict it, and sometimes they simply offer other information. Let me stress that, as a result, any apparent directness of address is ironically undercut; we have voice/image counterpoint, rather than matching, illustration or redundancy. For example, we first hear her direct opening statement, "Je peint les meubles en bleu le premier jour" ("I paint the furniture blue the first day"), then, after a long delay, the additional statement, "en vert le deuxième" ("green, the second day"). The actions narrated by these phrases are never seen. We never see any painting, nor any colour changes – which, in any case, in the film's black-and-white format would have to be indicated by shifts in a grey scale.

Nevertheless, these pronouncements in voice-over about colour changes of the furnishings establish a pattern of mutability. This mutability *does* receive expression in the image, but through other means, by furniture being shifted around between shots, especially between the first two shots. The montage of these two shots seems at first glance to be a simple 180° camera shift on Julie at her desk, but turns out, as we think about the second shot in relationship to the first, to have involved moving every piece of furniture in the room, so that the desk itself is turned 180° while the camera is in the same place.

Furthermore, blue and green ("I paint the furniture blue the first day...green, the second day") are perhaps chosen as an intertextual reference to a scene in Michelangelo Antonioni's *Il deserto rosso* (*Red Desert*, 1964), in which the troubled and sensitive female protagonist, Giuliana (Monica Vitti), shows her empty shop front to an old friend of her husband, Zeller, who has come to this site out of a curiosity provoked by his first meeting with her, and perhaps as the first step in a seduction. Giuliana's state of mind, her psychoanalytic alienation, portrayed through innovative shifting colour schemes throughout the film, expresses itself here through an indecision on the colour scheme for the walls of this shop. She has painted the walls with large blocks of various colours, whose flat rectangular shapes provide abstract geometric backgrounds as Giuliana wanders through the space, remarking that perhaps the ceiling should be light blue, then, after a pause, that the walls should be green. Even if entirely coincidental, this connection between the two films suggestively links two female protagonists who are obsessive, engaged in an uncertain exploration of their sexuality and their personal desires, and whose spontaneous actions seem dictated by inner recesses that harbour their reactions to a disturbing world. Equally, a connection is to be made between the conceptual filmmaking adopted by both films, in which set design becomes a sign of narrative self-consciousness, including functioning as a reference to the virtual aspect of a film set. Set design presents itself as a singular inscription that imposes itself on other possibilities. In both scenes, the filmmakers remark on how they may fix in any given frame only one of the many possible spatial configurations and set designs, and refer to the mutability of composition and design as temporality progresses, and montage or camera movement shifts the scene. Such ludic turns from shot to shot, phrase to phrase, continue in *I...You...He...She*, as the letter is presented as being written over a period of a month, a process we witness through selected moments as a performance piece which could be entitled "the month-long writing of a letter". This deliberate staging marks – but only through the most indirect of indices – the psyche and motivations of our main character.

It is through such fluctuations of revelation and concealment, such plays with the form of representation, that the film so self-consciously marks what a personal pronouncement might be.

This reflexive presentation of filmic writing is first indicated by the title sequence that presents, in cursive writing, the French singular conjugations as they might be traced on a primary school blackboard. We might make the association with the learning of language, the learning of sexual difference, the long, repetitious process of coming to knowledge and coming of age. It is an association with learning how to write, how to move from speech as enunciation to its graphic traces, with all the poetics of contradiction and incommensurability which that implies.

That is what the first segment of the film offers, a staging of a difficulty with writing, a hesitation with a commitment of pencil to paper, and of self to permanent record of an enunciation. It stages this through a minimalist style of denuded *mise en scène*, one that actually progresses towards increasing evacuation of objects in the image, as if to provide the most distinct frame for repetition. Obsession is given the formal design of a set of framed repetitions. For, in presenting Julie, a woman whose writing block is coupled with obsessive sugar eating from a paper bag in the first segment, the film begins to portray a "je", a subject, through her actions witnessed externally, seen as a montage of postures. It is possible to see Julie as the "je" of *I...You...He...She*, as we know Julie is played by Akerman, and we know that Julie writes to a "you" using the first-person pronoun. Yet, equally, we know that this sequence is a performance piece, that any self seen here is being enacted. A strategy that delineates selected moments from a month through its voice-over, yet stages an image that does not simply coincide with this delineated temporality, makes us aware not only that film might be seen as staged performance, but also that performance in its most basic and philosophical sense is at issue here. The formal discrepancy internal to the representation is significant, not to be brushed aside as a mere rawness or a "chic" style, which nevertheless offers realism as it has been.

I will shortly examine in more detail exactly how this staging occurs, and what its implications might be. Firstly, however, let us look at the general relationship of this segment's structure to what follows, for, like many minimalist and structural works, this film benefits from repeated viewings and differs with each viewing or retelling. A first look at its structure will help map the film's complexity, the moves it makes, and the games it plays. For nothing here is as straightforward as a first watching of its action or a simple retelling of its "plot" might imply.

As I have discussed, the film divides into three distinct segments that connect to each other as a journey of the main character, Julie. If she is "je", then "il" could be the truck driver whom she meets in the second segment, after hitching a ride on the highway. "Elle" might be Julie's former lover, the woman friend she arrives to visit in the third segment. We might say, therefore, that "je" travels from self-isolation through the intercession of "il" and to "elle", or, extrapolating further, that the film traces a movement of "je" from a claustrophobic self-imposed month-long solitary confinement to a random encounter with "il", to the goal of her journey, a reunion with "elle". We might even connect "elle" with the unnamed person to whom the letters are written. Yet, each time one describes this film, one shifts and reconstructs its representations, as we shall see; this bare-bones structural version of the film is a stripping of it down to its elemental and symbolic pronominal quest, but it immediately invites a symbolic interpretation, reading into the image, monologues, dialogues and sounds an investment that carries its own presuppositions.

If we accept this version of the film as a transversal of pronouns, the "tu" floats, never assigned, only used in conversations, and never directly addressed in the letter. So, in a larger sense, my use of "might" in the above paragraph is meant to indicate how all the pronouns remain only indirectly assigned, recalling the hesitation about writing dramatised in the opening sequence. It is as *if* the author in writing her story could not decide on the voice of narration. So she films. So she performs. Or, to be more precise, she offers artificial enunciations as the filmic performative. I wish to emphasise once more the artificial stagings of this film, often misleadingly described by critics as if the film presented only a straightforward *cinéma-vérité* realism, captured "sur le vif" ("in live action"). Let us say rather that the pronominal indecidability couples with a minimalist abstraction and an artificiality to flirt with autobiography in the highly structured segments that comprise this film.

In this context, the third person, the "il-elle" of the pronoun sequence here seems to suggest not only male-female differentiation, but also Julie's potential bisexuality, her choice of a love-object or sex partner of either gender. In addition, it activates a fluctuation of identification for characters within the representation, and for the audience in relation to the characters represented. Clearly, a lesbian audience might identify with or project themselves into different aspects of Julie's journey more than a male heterosexual audience would, but we must note, concomitantly, that the film never seems to address a particular audience, never employs codes meant to offer it a privileged identification; this may account for Mayne's hesitation in calling the film a "lesbian film".

Such indecidability finds reflection in Julie's hesitation in the writing of the letter, a scene that offers itself as an elaborate visual pun on "filmic writing". Although pared down in a quite different manner to that of Robert Bresson's films, Akerman's film has much in common with his notion of "l'écriture filmique",[8] and with prior notions of filmic writing that have had a long history in French film theory. There are particularly rich echoes of *Un Condamné à mort s'est échappé* (*A Man Escaped*, 1956). The cell of Bresson's condemned political prisoner might be seen as replaced here by a self-imposed prison, while his valiant efforts to scrape his way to escape and his continued participation in the Resistance are replaced here by an obsessive reworking of a letter, an obsessive pattern of eating. This displacement from a will to escape to food eaten obsessively connects to other Bresson films. The eating from the bag of sugar, coupled with the later demand of sandwiches, is similar in effect to the jam Marie eats straight from the jar at the poacher's hut in *Au Hasard Balthazar* (*Balthazar*, 1966), and to Mouchette's relationship to food in the film that bears her name. Once again, as in the intertextual reference to Antonioni, the female protagonist here connects to Bresson's teenagers through their shared strained relationship to desire and their sense of a detachment from a world they seem to find oppressive on a quotidian basis. Such systematic litotes in Bresson and Akerman grows in significance once one considers its function in the portrayal of desire. Through the studied filmic and narrational means by which desire is indirectly rendered in these narratives, it becomes filtered through a dark lens, a "soleil noir", in a manner that evokes Julia Kristeva's analysis of depression and creativity, and especially writing.[9] Julie's desire eludes any inscription into consciousness, in its flirtation with displacement onto obsessive behaviour (eating sugar), and in its expression through the random encounter (the truck driver) or the indeterminable goal (the renewal of a relation with the former lover, no sooner consummated than ruptured).

Let us consider further how feeding is linked to desire. Desire for nurturance, linked to desire for breast, is metonymically displaced throughout the film. The focus on the sugar bingeing, and later on the two sandwiches demanded before any desire for sex is addressed presents orality as a leitmotif connecting the segments beyond their physical trajectory as a journey. These food incidents hint at the psychic economy of food obsessions such as bulimia. Here, however, the focus of such disorders is abstracted from any detailed or realistic consideration, instead operating as indices of the psyche in the most intriguingly understated, if insistent manner, a manner that lets visual representation, repetition and temporality speak. In fact, the insistence on the movement of food from hand to mouth (and this in relationship to pen on paper) is one of the most studied visual actions of the film.

As such, this movement makes a fascinating comparison to the unseen "hand job", the sex scene in the truck in part two, between Julie and the truck driver – presented discretely visually, but vividly verbally, through his running commentary. Here Akerman seems to give us her version on an Andy Warhol film from the Factory period of temporal continuity and sexual exploits; as in Warhol's *Blow Job* (1963), the act is represented in continuity, traced in its effects on the face of the subject receiving the sexual stimulation of his organ which is understood as reaching its climactic activity through the actions of a partner whose touch is kept offscreen.

"Bouge ton main" ("move your hand"), he says after apparently taking her hand in his to place it on his penis. It is as if activity on her part needs to be commanded, as he gives step-by-step verbal instructions and continuous feedback as to the effects which her touching is having on his body, as in "il va sortir de sa peau" ("it's bursting"). The portrayal of the truck driver here seems to draw on the attractions of a working-class male mystique canonised by Marlon Brando and, in imitation, Joe Dallesandro, and we are told earlier that Julie was drawn to his looks in her voice-over statement: "I saw his beautiful neck, his red hair and I felt like kissing him". This, however, is said in the marked absence of any initiating action on her part.

Silence opens up space in which he talks, and she becomes an analyst, listening without comment to the truck driver's narrative of desire. Offering a male monologue of self-revelation, unsolicited, he tells the story of meeting his wife and his thoughts on being a father. He chronicles the meeting of his wife in anonymous sex, followed by a period of intense sexuality, then by the waning of sexual desire when they had children. His jealousy over his infant son's erection is stated without any self-consciousness or embarrassment; he can reveal what would seemingly be the darkest recesses of his psyche, and do so directly.

The fantasies that accompany his masturbation while driving form the next revelation. He offers two images that arouse: a wet cunt or a woman in a corner crying. These paired images recall the sex and desire monologues in Godard, such as the long monologue by the hairdresser in *Deux ou trois choses que je sais d'elle (Two or Three Things I Know About Her*, 1966), or the monologue by the wife as she sits on the edge of the desk at the start of *Weekend* (1967); we have here the same proclivity for the "inadvertently" poetic juxtaposition of verbal images, ones which, even when they do not come at the end of the monologue, create a pause and a moment of reflection on speech as writing, especially when framed through a film.

After the sex and its monologue coda, Julie's face and her body language seem to indicate that she is vaguely grateful for his daring to command the sex, and she seems at least respectful of his verbal self-exposure. Her fascination with him becomes evident in the long bathroom scene where she watches him urinate and shave, but it is a fascination that, framed by the florescent light and the electric razor, seems paradoxically detached. The bathroom segment offers detached fascination in the same oxymoronic tone that one associates with Warhol, recalling the long bathroom scene in the film he made with Chuck Wein – *My Hustler* (1965). In *My Hustler*, the entire second part consists of a shot in which John MacDermott stands before the mirror, shaving, combing his hair, and rather obsessively washing his hands, while Paul America occupies the space behind him preparing to shower and waiting for his turn at the mirror. The film extends duration, presenting all the moments of delay. As a result of the elaborate exchanges that can occur in this time, the scene in *My Hustler* endows obsessive bodily care with its full meaning as seduction. However, in *I...You...He...She*, while the faces of Julie and the truck driver are momentarily doubled in the bathroom mirror, this proves to be the extent of their coupling, as the second segment ends abruptly to cede to the arrival at the lover's apartment. Due to this abrupt ending, their encounter retrospectively acts far more as a transitional journey than as an adventure in its own right. Its transitional nature may be seen in relationship to the earlier segment, which now is more clearly recast as lonely and passive, even depressive.

Sloth, inaction and the self-justification typical of certain forms of depression were, after all, intermittently foregrounded in the earlier segment. Julie's voice-over tells us "Je me suis couché le sixième jour" ("I slept the sixth day"), and later, "Je jouais avec ma respiration et puis, j'ai oublié de continuer ce jeu" ("I was playing with my breathing, and then I forgot to continue to play this game"). Inactivity, idleness and forgetfulness are connected to an external justification; with some apparent relief, Julie notes that "il a neigé, la vie reste bloquée" ("it snowed, activity was suspended"). "La vie reste bloquée" literally translates as "life remains blocked", which suggests, in itself, her state of inactivity, although the enunciation continues to indicate an external cause, and tells us that she must wait until snowstorms stop, a full four days. But when the weather changes, Julie has not. Her passivity remains pronounced in her manner of narrating her activity: "Il a cessé de neiger. Je me suis trouvé nue" ("It stopped snowing. I found myself nude"). Akerman returns to such images of laziness in her sloth episode of the all female-authored compilation film, *Seven Women, Seven Sins* (1986). There seems to be something personal, autobiographical, as well as obsessively repetitious in Akerman's evocation of a woman lying about, unable to pull herself away from a bed, coupled to darker motivations for reclusiveness than simple laziness. Embedded in these images rests the dread of an outside world that requires that the self rise to engage with it.

Depression as enclosed in this room compares to that voiced by the young French woman during the basement incarceration by her parents in the flashback to post-Second World War Nevers in Alain Resnais'

Hiroshima, mon amour (1959). We can hear the direct and studied minimalist voice of the scriptwriter of that film, Marguerite Duras, echoing throughout Akerman's film, but never so closely as in the line "quand je me levais la tête brusquement il y a des gens qui marchaient dans la rue" ("When I raised my head suddenly there were people who were walking in the street"), which compares to Duras' character's pronouncement that, after a period of oblivion, suddenly she became aware of sounds and people moving on the street. While Duras' character is put into the basement by her parents out of shame over her secret affair with a German soldier, as punishment both for her love affair and for her raving obsession with the loss of this love, Akerman's Julie imposes her own restrictions of movement. The insanity in *Hiroshima, mon amour* is proclaimed from a position of retrospection by the character years later: "J'étais folle, une fois, à Nevers" ("I was insane, once, in Nevers"). In *I...You...He...She*, depression, not insanity, is the issue, and even depression is only indirectly indicated. Nevertheless, both scenes flirt with the surface of a disturbed self, and Julie's incarceration becomes all the more disturbing, as it is self-imposed with its causes left undetermined, only hinted at through the anxious letter-writing. Julie methodically pursues communication in the form of a letter-writing destined always to be rewritten and never to be sent. The only revelation of self she seems capable of committing consists of the merely physical. She can be nude or, more literally, "find herself nude" in the most passive sense, and she can flirt with looking at herself in a mirror and even with exposing herself to a stranger, but all these bodily manifestations of denuding are only displacements of pronouncements of self-revelation that remain illusive. "I wrote three pages, then six pages to say the same thing", she tells us chronicling her letter-writing impasse, which later takes the form of spreading sheets of paper out on the floor, arranging and rearranging them. This writing impasse, this authorial action of paradoxical passivity, sends the audience a letter contained between the lines of Julie's unwritten missive. The self is revealed indirectly, if at all, under the guise of a fictive performance, but, as I began to suggest earlier, perhaps the images created by this performance are paradoxically far more revelatory a stripping than might be assumed.

Let us turn, therefore, to the third segment, the unannounced arrival at the lover's apartment. Space here is determinant, as the barriers between the two women, unspoken, manifest themselves by the rigid distances maintained through their restrained body language in approaching one another. This discomfort and lack of embrace are echoed in the difficulty negotiating the space between the elevator and the apartment door. It is a space visited twice, first quickly, on entering, then returned to as a site of renegotiation, when Julie precipitously decides to leave, taking her former lover's statement of rejection literally as an immediate and unequivocal demand. Standing there in the potentially public space of the landing, with the elevator opening to end the encounter, they reconsider Julie's departure and then re-enter the apartment with the promise of some exchange, some attempt at intercourse, slated to start with the sharing of food, if not conversation, sex, love or reconciliation. Thus, the scene places great insistence on a simple snack, on a slice of bread spread with Nutella (a chocolate-hazelnut spread associated with children's breakfast), but accompanied by wine; then Julie demands, simply, "J'ai soif" ("I'm thirsty"). All communication between them is dominated by the table, by eating, the food exchange substituting for words of substance, while the only words offered refer only to the food. We have only the absence of conversation, in any usual sense, and instead the iteration of a refusal – "you may not stay". This assertion is overturned without verbal exchange, by a touch, an awkward, pressing hug, the embrace of an adolescent saying "no, hold me", insisting with the body on direct communication and insinuating overwhelming need.

The wordlessness continues. A long sequence of the two in bed, nude, rolling over and over each other, wrestling with the touch of their bodies, accompanied, as Narboni notes, by the accentuated sounds of the sheets, the movement. The sex is awkward and beyond words. Kisses are not exchanged, breasts not touched, limbs not stroked, only the rollicking foreplay of an almost unintentional meeting of these women's bodies fills the duration of the bedroom encounter. Only when they arrive at orality, at the former lover's embrace of Julie's labia, does the segment move from a quasi-wrestling match to a defined sex act, but, even so, the usual codes of sexual portrayals in filmic images are so avoided that viewers are left with a singular depiction of sex. This singularity is less that of women, of lesbian love, than that of a style of filmic writing that traces the awkward through to its own poetics, that refuses any romanticism in the flirtation with the physical, that troubles one's tactile imagination, one's imaginary and identificatory insertion into touch-portrayed as touch-felt. Yet, in a cut to a new angle, a close shot from behind the head of the bed on their faces as they embrace, the film finally offers just the vivid images of flesh, of proposition and willing juncture that had been withheld. Yet, we never enter the land of joyous bodies, soft words or dreams. The sex act ends, and the scene culminates in a wordless departure the morning after. Julie rises, dresses and leaves.

I see this sex sequence as breaking with a still prevalent stereotype of lesbian sexuality at the time of the film's production, the "best friends and dearest lovers" model of an ideal feminist lesbianism. This model pictured lesbian relationships as always emotionally articulate, because women supposedly could more easily talk to each other, especially about feelings. By presenting lesbian bodies in an inarticulate sexuality, but one that also resolutely avoids the codes of lesbian sexuality as pornographic display for a third party, coded as a heterosexual male, the sequence writes lesbian sexuality into a particular consonance with the previous two sequences of the film, and perhaps with them alone. By this, I mean that if we have a halting encounter, the trans-segmental catechises suggests that it is because this embrace is so endowed with desires that overflow its participants' volition and the ability of the protagonist to write herself into another's life. Julie arrives unannounced because a letter could not be written and could not be sent; the body arrives at the destination of the errant letter. Or, following Narboni's insistence on the film's circularity,[10] an insistence founded on its first line, "Et je suis partie..." ("And I left..."), which he reads as referring to Julie's departure at the end, the missed communication is *both before and after* the encounter, as well as circulating through it. The body is, in turn, nearly mute, able only to ask for food and drink, able to ask for a touch only with an awkward gesture; unable to sustain an embrace, figuratively, into the conversation that *must* follow if the embrace is to be renewed, reinscribed and reinscribable. Unlike the moon goddess condemned wistfully to night-time visitations alone, she will not be back tomorrow. Her film ends. This ending on departure has a finality, even if we do take the structure as a circular enunciation, for we always return to the departures that incessantly end each segment. The film demonstrates Julie leaving, finally, each and every space. Nor should we forget that the actual screening of the film culminates in the wordless departure the morning after. This very phrase, "the morning after", suggests the apocalyptic, as well as space and time after a sexual encounter; the ending that is here suggested is at least the suspension of a narration, because at this point there is nothing said and, perhaps for the time being, nothing remaining to be said; the departure says it all.

Let me submit that gender is far more troubled here, and less a polarisation of clear opposites than earlier commentators saw. This is perhaps connected to the trouble which Judith Mayne recognises when she hesitates to name Akerman into the category of lesbian filmmaker, for one senses the articulation here to be that of an outsider to any known (or, put differently, her own) gender identity, either as relayed by the other, or as confirmed by the sister-self. If the truck driver – a man of the road, the quick sexual impulse, of muscles and of the phallus in need of stroking – offers a form of typical masculinity, the lover offers a stereotyped femininity, marked in interiors, food and a submissive body that says "no", but complies. Julie is a troubling third being, wandering through their spaces as a stranger, an alien. She makes no demands of masculinity, yet complies with its demands with bemused indifference; she makes a consistent yet indirectly spoken demand to femininity, with the emphasis here on the *indirect* and on the absence of further direction that the departure exemplifies. This film dares to explore a gap in identity, the alienation from a narcissistic affirmation, but to do so in a manner that will not permit a *simple* psychoanalytic decipherment. Litotes, understatement, leaves the film viewer with images that refuse the plenitude of interpretive completion and certainty. One must approach such a film with psychoanalysis only gingerly, cautiously avoiding any overreadings and fixities of symbolisations that are, in any case, always traps, even in the case of the most obviously coded films.

The film's play with symptomatic behaviour does tempt the analyst to come up with a "diagnosis". For, as I discussed earlier, the film is fraught with depressive symptoms, oral fixations and mutism. It offers a *mise en scène* replete with what Narboni eloquently terms the "mirror-door-windows",[11] the glass door to Julie's apartment in the first segment in which she looks at herself, only to realise it is a transparency through which she can be seen. Finally, it becomes an opened door through which she leaves, and it remains open, in complete disregard to protecting anything like personal property. One could align this mirror via Lacan's theorisation of the mirror stage with a troubled passage through primary narcissism.[12] So the traditional psychoanalytic diagnosis might read: oral fixation and primary narcissistic difficulties linked to creativity and homosexuality, but stumbling on a lack (castration fear, or female lack-in-being). One would only have to show how the links made between depressive symptoms, homosexuality and creativity in Didier Anzieu's contribution, "Vers une métapsychologie de la création", in *Psychanalyse du Génie Créateur*,[13] or in Julia Kristeva's *Soleil Noir: depression et mélancholie* might be reconceived to transform their analysis of the male homosexual artist for the creative personality who is both homosexual and female.

Yet, there is as much of a problem with such diagnosis, even if we should not ignore its inscription in the film. For, even if such developmental connections are put in the best possible light, as suggestively explaining the work, rather than reductively framing the artist, they draw on – or at least do not entirely escape from – an history of pathologising homosexuality as a deviant or, at least, aberrant form of sexuality, expandable by a difference in developmental schemata. Read as tracing a connection between the oral and the desire for unification with the maternal, the film would be reduced to an external confirmation of a diagnosis, assumed to have a general valence.

We should remember that if the film flirts with the desire to display the body, it is a desire that it *self-consciously treats as unconscious*. In other words, the film works as a contemporary intervention precisely because it offers its own reading of the unconscious (and that of an authorial voice making a personal pronouncement behind it). Unconscious motivations become both something which the film does not "know" and, conversely, knows well. Let me suggest that such a film troubles the symbolisation of the psyche and its interpretation in a manner parallel to Maya Deren's *Meshes of the Afternoon* (1943), another film about rooms and time, although more about dancing than writing (or, perhaps, insisting on dance as writing). If, as I have suggested elsewhere,[14] Deren (who was the daughter of a psychoanalyst) knew and refused the possible psychoanalytic interpretations of her film, Akerman follows in her footsteps, which are forever spliced together across the distant spaces of dreams and cinema. She follows by insisting that the cinematic portrait of the self will always fulfil and escape any singular psychoanalytic interpretation, teaching us instead something about methodology in psychoanalysis. Stated differently, "the portrait of the artist as case history" is a superannuated approach, and one that is bound to ignore how a film confronts a too certain desire simply to decipher, to know. Instead, it asks its tracing of psychoanalytic material to be a challenge and a speculation on psychoanalytic methodologies.

For feminism and for lesbian consciousness, the significance of such a demonstration of creativity and self-portraiture beyond confinement to symptomology is of crucial importance, especially when the films dare to show the unresolved struggle of being a woman, or of being a lesbian, of expressing and of acting on desire. The goal for the long term seems to be to avoid fulfilling a traditional analyst's sense of who one is, in order to challenge the theory to accommodate the shifting politics of newly possible identities, ones that can only emerge as a culture becomes ready to let them be and develop, rather than suppressing them or turning them into the already known. Perhaps films can never start directly with that goal, or they will miss it by trying to keep it too closely in sight (an overly didactic emphasis, a too self-conscious project that may forget its own unconscious). Perhaps the impulse towards creating such challenging works needs to be a mixture of a highly personal revelation with an artistic self-consciousness, the kind of mixture which Deren and Akerman sustain.

It is in this context that *Portrait of a Young Girl* poses a fascinating return to adolescent sexuality and friendship as a fully philosophical inquiry. The psychoanalytic here is figured in its relationship to doubt and alienation, in which contact with others appears burdened by an urgent necessity of survival. The film traces the day and night of three teenagers in Brussels, as Michelle skips school, meets a French Army deserter named Paul, and goes to a "boum", a private dance, with her girlfriend. A scene in bed with Paul, and the later repeated choosing of her girlfriend as partner at the joyous and sensual centre of a circle dance echo the truck driver and former lover sequences of *I...You...*

He...She, by giving us a similar, if more exuberant, encounter with a male superseded by the non-verbalised choosing of a female partner.

Throughout this day, Michelle struggles with suicidal impulses that she expresses through what she reads, writes and says. Her violence towards the self is clearly connected to a violent rejection of the father and the family. In a scene that closely recalls the fragmented and negated process of writing of the first sequence of *I...You...He...She*, Julie sits in a café writing letters in her father's voice meant to excuse her absences from school; these letters form a paradigm of possible excuses, from sickness to a death in the family; this exploration of possible reasons for absence follows the logic of the declension of the pronominal in *I...You...He...She*. Here the game of possible articulations ends with the inadvertent statement of unconscious wishes, self-consciously displayed: the death of the father, or the death of the self.

Here, however, political context is more directly manifest than in *I... You...He...She*, as resistance of military service provides Paul's need for Michelle and for Brussels. A political and historical reading of Lacan's seminar, "L'Envers de la psychanalyse",[15] originally presented in 1969-70, offers an intriguing source to compare to this revelation of the self, its relationship to psychoanalysis and to politics. Lacan draws connections between elements borrowed from existential philosophies in his thought and the events of May 1968. Akerman similarly demonstrates her character's affinity for Kierkegaard, as Michelle quotes from memory a long passage on the meaning of self and suicide while standing with Paul in a bookshop, and she brings this existential preoccupation into conjunction with the war in Vietnam, shown in its echo in a European context. Here, in Europe, students resist another army, or even just refuse to go to school, as an internalised reaction to global forces. That such resistance is coloured by sexual identities still in formation, uncertain, nascent, tentative, barely knowing the voice of their own desire, makes Akerman's strategy of a simple film of a day of encounters and conversations rich beyond its surface, especially the last shot in which all resolution is left to a silently executed, spatially-rendered encounter-exchange between the triangle of two young women and a man.

It is this triangle and the return to simplicity, to the minimal (after more elaborate films such as *Les Années 80* [*The Eighties*, 1983] and *Golden Eighties/Window Shopping* [1986] seemed to indicate that Akerman had finished with simplicity), that invite the comparison with *I...You...He...She*. In my view, an understanding of the relationship of psychoanalysis to this filmic and narrative form enables the films to resonate fully, establishing their significance to the history not only of filmmaking form, but also of feminism and lesbian studies in their implications for cultural studies. For what we have in both Akerman's first film and her most recent work is an attention to adolescence and young adulthood as a period in which the self retraces all its prior knowledge of the other and the universe in the process of actively exploring sexual desire. The stripping of the body to its naked vulnerability before initial sexual encounters and the writing of one's first letters, or, conversely, the silent first gestures, professing or demanding sexual love, are here given their full weight, in a cinematography (including a sound envelope) that insists on the act, the gesture and the duration of moment. Akerman frames the external elements of an interiority she holds in reserve, suggesting its complexity as a demand for respect. These films are among the most sensitive coming-of-age stories told from the perspective of a young female in contemporary culture.

Nevertheless, there is a profound difference between the two films, which is worthy of note. *Portrait of a Young Girl* is a far more straightforward continuation of New Wave filmmaking, of tracking shots following perambulating dialogue, coupled with interior scenes of exchange, verbal, sexual and other closely examined activities. *I... You...He...She*, on the other hand, introduces into film the aesthetics of performance art in a manner similar to Yvonne Rainer, and recalling not only such US performance artists as Carolee Schneemann and Joan Jonas, but also several European artists. Many pursued in the 1970s a rendering of performance in the framed image, photography and film, but especially in video even as video first emerged as an art form. Compare the letter-writing sequence that opens *I...You...He...She* with a performance from 1975 at the Krinzinger Gallery, Innsbruck, entitled "Thomas Lips", by Marina Abramovic (a Dutch artist originally from Yugoslavia). The two-hour performance began with Abramovic seated nude at a table slowly eating a kilo of honey from a silver spoon, but progressed through a series of actions including the cutting of a five-pointed star on her belly and a session of violent self-flagellation. Once Abramovic begins performing as a duo with Dutch artist Ulay, their series entitled "Relationwork" resonates strikingly with the scenes of couplings in Akerman's film. Their performances stage repetitive motions and poses of extended duration, such as "Relation in Space" (July 1976, Venice Biennale), in which the pair repeatedly walk past each other, touching, until, at increasing speeds they collide, and "Interruption in Space" (January 1977, Kunstakademie, Rinke Klasse, Düsseldorf), in which each first walks towards a wall, then runs at it, hitting it straight-on. In "Relation in Time" (October 1977, Studio G7, Bologna), they sat motionless, back-to-back, tied together by their hair.[16] Abramovic and Ulay's work on duration, the symbolisation of the lack, or perhaps the transcendence, of communication, the insistence on an audience submitting to witnessing the torturous performed before them is far more intense and exaggerated than Akerman's work. Comparison to such performance art places Akerman's film in an entirely different context, one in which it seems but a mild incarnation of a zeitgeist of such extremely torturous enactments.

For all the insistence of film reviewers on Akerman's confrontational minimalism, she offers a narrative poetics far more fluid and visually graceful than contemporaneous performance art. Nevertheless, Akerman's connection to such artists is one of exchange, as shown by the reflection of Akerman found in the work of another young Belgian female artist, Marie Audré, whose video works bear close resemblance to the filmic images of Akerman, both as "narratives of desire" and "romances of the everyday", and as investigations of framing and temporality. Audré's 1982 video, *Galerie de portraits*, and her 1987 *Bruxelles, une ville en été* in turn seem to find their reinscription in Akerman's *Portrait of a Young Girl*. Performance, film and video not only become parallel modes of expressivity of postmodern portraiture, but also reach a point where double voicing of work in film and video, such as Akerman's film, *D'Est (From the East*, 1993) and the video installation drawn from the same images, become increasingly common and significant, a tendency that perhaps has its own legacy in the way in which performance and environmental art embraced documentation in photos and video, then began to use video as integral to their conceptual projects.

My point here is to place Akerman in a larger history of art that is more inclusive than just that of film history, so that we might see her personal *pronouncements* as personal *portraits* in a significant crossing of visual and verbal art forms inherent in her reinvigoration of cinema. The utterance and the gesture are given similar weight, as is silence and the gap between any gestures or words whatsoever. It is in such a space where each signifier gains its own prominence, in a space of minimalism that maximises all elements of representation into a heightened inscription that her tender poems about self and existence, glancing off the promise and disappointments of others, gain their beauty.

Notes

1 Maureen Turim, *The Films of Oshima Nagisa: Images of a Japanese Iconoclast* (Berkeley; Los Angeles: University of California Press, 1998).

2 Translated from the French: "Discours à la quatrième personne du singulier, qui n'est ni l'histrionisme de la subjectivité (le 'je'), ni le despotisme de l'interpellation et de la demande (le 'tu'), ni l'horreur objectivante de la non-personne (le 'il/elle')". Jean Narboni, "La quatrième personne du singulier *(Je tu il elle)*", *Cahiers du Cinéma* 276 (May 1977): 10-11.

3   Translated from the French: "porno, et sa *ruine*". Ibid: 7. Emphasis in original.

4   Judith Mayne, "Mistresses of Discrepancy", in *The Woman at the Keyhole: Feminism and Women's Cinema* (Bloomington; Indianapolis: Indiana University Press, 1990): 131.

5   Ibid: 132.

6   Françoise Audé, "Le Cinéma de Chantal Akerman, la nourriture, le narcissisme, l'exil", in Jacqueline Aubenas (ed), *Chantal Akerman* (Brussels: Atelier des Arts, 1982): 151-165.

7   Mayne: 243n7-244n7.

8   "L'écriture filmique" ("filmic writing") is Bresson's term for what Alexandre Astruc called the "caméra-stylo". See Raymond Bellour, *Alexandre Astruc* (Paris: Seghers, 1963), and Robert Bresson, *Notes on Cinematography*, translated by Jonathan Griffin (New York: Urizen Books, 1977).

9   Julia Kristeva, *Soleil Noir: depression et mélancholie* (Paris: Gallimard, 1987).

10   Narboni: 13.

11   Translated from the French: "miroir-porte-fenêtres". Ibid.

12   Jacques Lacan, *Le Moi dans la psychanalyse* (Paris: Editions du Seuil, 1982).

13   Didier Anzieu, "Vers une métapsychologie de la création", in Didier Anzieu, Michel Mathieu, Matthew Besdine, Jean Guillaumin and Elliott Jaques (eds), *Psychanalyse du Génie Créateur* (Paris; Brussels; Montreal: Bordas Dunod, 1974): 1-30.

14   Maureen Turim, "Childhood Memories and Household Events in the Feminist Avant Garde", *Journal of Film and Video* 38: 3/4 (summer/autumn 1986): 86-92.

15   Jacques Lacan, *L'Envers de la psychanalyse* (Paris: Editions du Seuil, 1991).

16   Marina Abramovic, *Artist Body* (Milan: Edizioni Charta, 1998): 129-215. See also Thomas McElvilley, "Marina Abramovic/Ulay", *Artforum* 24 (January 1986): 52-55.

What's beneath her smile? Subjectivity and desire in Germaine Dulac's *The Smiling Madame Beudet* and Chantal Akerman's *Jeanne Dielman, 23 quai du Commerce, 1080 Bruxelles*

Sandy Flitterman-Lewis

Nothing lovelier can be found in Woman, than to study household good. (John Milton)[1]

Often nothing tangible remains of a woman's day. The food that has been cooked is eaten; the children that have been nursed have gone out into the world. Where does the accent fall?...It is difficult to say. Her life has an anonymous character which is baffling and puzzling in the extreme. (Virginia Woolf)[2]

If one of the projects of a feminist counter-cinema is the exploration and representation of female subjectivity, both Germaine Dulac and Chantal Akerman must certainly be placed at the forefront of this endeavour. And significantly, their focus on feminine self-definition also provides us with suggestive and even provocative models of cinematic resistance to the dominant narrative fiction film. Dulac (*La Souriante Madame Beudet* [*The Smiling Madame Beudet*, 1923]) and Akerman (*Jeanne Dielman, 23 quai du Commerce, 1080 Bruxelles* [1975]) each creates a work that asserts the centrality of women's consciousness at the same time that it emphatically challenges the hegemony of the Hollywood feature film. Yet, each director chooses very different modes of resistance that entail distinct ideas of character, plot and action, as well as notions of temporality, editing and discursive form. As a consequence, each director proposes divergent definitions of spectatorial desire. The fact that these films were made some 50 years apart, in very different aesthetic and ideological circumstances, can give us the necessary historical context in which to analyse and evaluate the kinds of solutions found by each director to problems of representation of the feminine. Dulac, whose context is shaped by the radical formal innovations of the first avant-garde in France, wants to disrupt those conventions of the mainstream film that prioritise both masculine narrative logic and external dramatic action. Yet, while maintaining her aesthetic theories of Symbolist fusion and musical composition – or even perhaps because of these – Dulac's exploration of her heroine's inner world leaves a number of narrative elements relatively intact. On the other hand, tempered by several decades of global feminist theories of unconscious signification and sexual difference, Akerman's film directly confronts the most basic structures of the cinema – as well as the unconscious mechanisms underlying them (visual pleasure, gendered spectatorship, narrative causality, identification and fantasy) in order to articulate a totally new language of cinematic desire.

However, there are some striking similarities between the two films, parallels that establish *The Smiling Madame Beudet* as the undisputed ancestor of Akerman's film. Each film is named for its female protagonist, a heroine whose critical moment of *jouissance* (suggested as a phantasmic symbolisation of unconscious desire) results in an act of murderous revolt – and thereby provides each text with both its climax and its central enigma. These moments are associated with each woman's smile, but these are smiles so subtle, so evanescent, that Leonardo da Vinci's famous smile (in another time and another form of representation) is immediately called to mind. However, while Mme Beudet's smile is prepared for by the film's title (or rather, hinted at, since the title is clearly ironic), Jeanne's "smile" can only be read from the chiaroscuro of her enigmatic expression, a highly ambiguous portrait that repeatedly evokes mutually exclusive meanings. Nevertheless, to speak of these smiles is already to consider the films at the level of a reading, making interpretive parallels when more obvious ones abound.

Custom crooned its soothing rhythm

Both films take place within the frozen perimeters of domestic space, automatically qualifying them, generically, as "women's films". And each director reveals this feminine-encoded space to be a veritable prison cell, traversed by the familiar signs of custom that evoke, by each film's close, the stifling domesticity that has turned these women into robots, monsters or both. Dulac's film (made in 1921 and released in 1923) concerns a latter-day Madame Bovary (Germaine Dermoz), whose only escape from the overbearing vulgarity of her fabric merchant-husband (Alexandre C Arquillière) is her extraordinarily rich fantasy world. Two days in the life of this mismatched couple result in averted tragedy. A sensitive lover of poetry and music, Mme Beudet (whose first name is never disclosed), having begged out of an evening's entertainment in town, finds her beloved piano locked. At a loose end, she reads, reflects and dreams, then distractedly loads the gun that M. Beudet often puts to his head in a gleeful parody of suicide. The next morning, overcome by guilt and fear, Mme Beudet desperately tries to empty the gun before the sadistic joke can be repeated. However, not only does she fail, but also, for the first time, M. Beudet aims the gun at his wife instead. The film climaxes and resolves ironically, as the egotistical brute misinterprets the loaded gun as his wife's attempt at suicide. His renewed appreciation of her is matched by her disbelieving resignation and (with the resumption of her provincial housewife's role) by the implicit closing off of any future flights of imaginative fantasy.

In Akerman's film, the oppressive husband is replaced by an equally representative figure of patriarchy, the teenaged son Sylvain (Jan Decorte) who, despite a rather deadpan acceptance of his mother's household regime, functions as the masculine presence that defines both the terms and the limits of a world that Jeanne (Delphine Seyrig) has doggedly tried to make her own. The title, *Jeanne Dielman, 23 quai du Commerce, 1080 Bruxelles*, is as deceptively thorough as the film's narrative procedures. The precision of its details – name, exact address, specific location – gives the illusion of heightened objectivity while revealing very little real information. It thus gives us everything and nothing at once, all we need in order to identify this woman, nothing that we must have in order to understand her. In *Jeanne Dielman*, the two days of Mme Beudet's world become three, as the camera records every action in the life of this widow who incorporates prostitution into her daily routine: preparing breakfast; sending her son to school; making the bed; shopping; having sex; getting paid; cooking dinner; listening to the radio after the meal; taking a walk; brushing her hair; and so on. And when the inexplicable suddenly erupts (in the form of a murder near the film's end), the camera maintains the same distance and objectivity used to record the household routine.

On further reflection, however, not every action receives cinematic representation. In fact, the camera is selective, maintaining the false modesty of an ellipsis for the first two of Jeanne's weekly customers. We see only the pecuniary frame of these encounters: In the hallway, hat and coat are taken; literally moments later (the indeterminate time marked by a single brief shot of the closed bedroom door), hat and coat are returned in exchange for cash. However, this pattern is broken by the third customer, who is actually seen inside the bedroom (the first and only time this depicted space is penetrated by someone other than Jeanne), where the aftermath of sex and the ensuing murder are privileged with visibility. The plot, such as it is, involves the daily rhythm of Jeanne's household routine (beginning with dishwashing after pre-preparation for supper; reception of the client of the day; bathing; scrubbing the tub; making the bed; greeting Sylvain; and so on); the disruption of this routine by an unknown event occurring with client number two (an uncovered soup tureen; tousled hair; overcooked potatoes; unoccupied moments and confused hesitations, indicating that Jeanne's timing has been thrown off); the consequences of this ruptured schedule (waking up an hour early and sending Sylvain off to school; inventing activities to fill the time; arriving too early at unopened shops; losing her regular seat and missing her regular waitress for afternoon tea; returning home late); and Jeanne's methodical yet seemingly arbitrary stabbing of client number three (done with the same blank energy that characterises all her tasks, and punctuated by seven minutes of silence as Jeanne sits at her dining-room table in the growing darkness of the evening).

It is obvious that the literal "action" (or lack of it) of the two films is similar. Even the pattern of "events" which moves towards some type of attenuated yet irrevocable climax is shared by both, each redefining the central narrative terms of plot, character and address along the way. And both films replace conventional action with reflective, meditative rhythms, contemplative structures implicitly aligned with both women's time and a feminine mental universe. Yet, to point in this way to each film's evocation of female subjectivity immediately brings up a complex of representational issues – how can that elusive interiority be represented at all, since, by definition, it is unrepresentable? Or, to suggest another problematic, even if we acknowledge that Dulac's avowed project is the cinematic depiction of her character's mental processes (thoughts, memories, dreams, fantasies, hallucinations), Akerman has made no such claim. In fact, her stance is resolutely external, to such an extent that most writing about her work takes as given the hyperrealist, minimalist evocation of reality's surfaces.

Dream along with me...

Yet, this is exactly the point at which the two films can be most fruitfully compared, as much for their similarities as for their differences. When each of these women filmmakers is considered in the context of her male contemporaries, Dulac and Akerman share a common concern with dimensions of female subjectivity and desire. In their films, the intersections of cinematic language, narrativity and feminine consciousness that articulate questions of sexuality and representation establish Mme Beudet as the true spiritual mother of Jeanne, her modern daughter. However, the strategies for achieving such feminist representation differ, corresponding to the types of cinematic resistance that characterise each woman's era. In short, the emphasis on depicting unconscious processes, as opposed to evoking the unconscious through organised structures of the gaze (or their challenge), can be said to parallel two kinds of textuality that emerged along with the cinema's first efforts to represent subjectivity.

Given the centrality of the viewing position in the cinema's history as a discursive form, these textual strategies can also be seen as two contrasting modes of spectatorship, two modes of viewing that, interestingly, correspond to divergent visual structures in European and American cinemas. Since the earliest days of filmmaking, French and German directors experimented with ways to translate the mind's activity onto the screen. They emphasised the content of the representation, either by using subjective distortions produced by technical devices, or by finding metaphoric equivalents in the image itself. In any case, a means was sought that would allow the image on the screen immediately to suggest mental processes or effects of visual perception. *The Smiling Madame Beudet* is a stunning example of this tendency, for Dulac's attempts to create a cinematic equivalent for the internal monologue of prose fiction results in something unique for its time – an entire fiction film that is a celebration of the cinema's unrivalled capacity to render subjectivity directly, without the mediating distortions of verbal language. Dulac uses a virtual anthology of cinematic techniques in order to depict this inner world; more than half of the film's 40 minutes are devoted to the cinematic representation of Mme Beudet's dreams and desires. Dulac is as certain of the content of these imaginings as she is of her character; she uses these representations to place the viewer right inside the consciousness of this woman, whose only real life is the one she dreams. Writing about her ideal of a purely cinematic stream of consciousness, Dulac states: "Movement, interior life, these two terms are not incompatible. What is more active than the life of the psyche, with its reactions, its multiple impressions, its swells, its dreams, its memories?".[3]

The other tendency, which came to be associated with the Hollywood model of the fiction film, allows viewers to occupy a position so close to a film's characters that it replicates the process of subjective identification without recourse to the visual representation of mental activity. This involves what is known as the "point-of-view" system – the organisation of a series of looks (from camera to characters, between characters, and between spectator and screen) that binds the spectator simultaneously into the cinematic fiction, its characters, and the imaginary universe that they imply. This orchestration of vision, a process intrinsic to cinematic narration since its inception, structures the spectator's desire in relation to the image, and, as such, constitutes the central meaning-structure of cinematic discourse. Jean-Luc Godard, one of Akerman's avowed mentors, sums it up with characteristic economy: "If direction is a look, montage is a heart-beat...Cutting on a look is almost the definition of montage, its supreme ambition as well as its submission to *mise en scène*".[4] Indeed, in *Jeanne Dielman*, Akerman gets to the heart of the matter by challenging these very mechanisms of vision and identification – in a film that studiously avoids classical editing patterns just as it redefines the virtual pivot of the point-of-view system, the shot/reverse-shot structure. At first, it might appear that Akerman's strategies of externalisation which foreground the "look" deny the very subjectivity that Dulac wants to represent. But, in fact, it is precisely in terms of female subjectivity, its definition and alternative representation, that

Akerman's film achieves its most important innovations.

Much has been made of Akerman's static, distanced camera. In this film in particular, the 200 minutes of minimalist, real-time depiction of Jeanne's daily activities suggest at once the heightened realism of the "objective" documentary camera and the frontal stance of early cinema's pioneers (a stationary camera position that frames each action in a theatrical proscenium by replicating the position of the theatre-goer in the audience). In speaking of this pervasive, unnarrativised look which structures *Jeanne Dielman*, Akerman asserts her position as authorial source:

> You *know* who is looking; you always know what the point of view is, all the time. It's always the same. But still...[i]t was not a neutral look...I didn't go in too close, but I was not *very* far away...[T]he camera was not voyeuristic in the commercial way because you always knew where I was. You know, it wasn't shot through the keyhole.[5]

Since the Hollywood model of the fiction film literally depends on the effacement of the camera/author's position in order to maintain its illusionary effects, Akerman's strategy defines an oppositional stance that is continually reinforced with each static shot of the film. By asserting that the logic of vision which organises the shots and disperses the gaze is emphatically hers, she foregrounds her own "view", and thus intervenes (persistently but unobtrusively) in the fictional world of the film. Yet, in order to do this, she foregoes any obvious strategy that would call attention to itself in a facile reflexivity. She makes her intervention at the level of the organising gaze and, in doing so, reformulates one of the three articulated components of cinematic vision, the look of the camera/author.

But it is not only this paradoxical presence of the organising look that characterises Akerman's intervention into traditional visual structures. As noted, at the centre of the cinema's identificatory meshwork is the shot/reverse-shot system, the volley of looks that joins the viewer to the fictional characters and their subjective identities. Here, too, Akerman provides a lucid explanation for her elimination of the point-of-view shot so crucial to the binding operations of the fiction machine:

> It was never shot from the point of view of the son or anyone else. It's always me. Because the other way is manipulation. The son is not the camera; the son is her son. If the son looks at his mother, it's because you [the director] asked him to do it. So you should look at the son looking at the mother, and not have the camera in place of the son looking at the mother.[6]

Thus (with one incredible exception, to which I will return), the viewer never watches Jeanne through the defining filter of a created character. Akerman chooses to replace this fiction with a construct from social reality, a more general application that is both shared and intimate, one that is taken from daily life and childhood memory. In the commonest and most iconic image of Jeanne, she is seen from the back as she stands at the sink washing dishes.[7] Second to that is a category of images of Jeanne doing other housework, running errands, shopping, and so on. Thirdly, there are those images of Jeanne in intimately solitary moments of her domestic routine, such as scrubbing the bath-tub or brushing her hair. In all these, the position of looking evokes a generalised childhood view of a mother's actions, reasserting the regularity of these repetitive tasks and the (simultaneously maternal and) domestic scene in which they are performed.

But these are also looks that, through their sustained duration, invite the viewer's speculation about Jeanne's thoughts – she has to be thinking something – as she accomplishes each task. This is not the case with that other housewife, Mme Beudet, whose every idea, daydream and fantasy are rendered in detail by Dulac's inventive portrayal of her internal world. Jeanne herself is something of a blank screen (due in no small part to the brilliant physical acting of Delphine Seyrig, who makes every representation a lived activity); the flatness of the scenic space, the mechanical rhythm of the movements, and the monotony of the depicted environment all make Jeanne a visual equivalent of the film's tone. And it is partly because of this pervasive mood of obsession-tinged serenity that the spectator enters into a game of construction and attribution regarding Jeanne's mental universe.

Yet, Akerman goes beyond what the term "game" implies, because the stakes for feminism are much higher. By creating a female protagonist whose desires escape articulation, she encourages viewers to supply their own fantasies in tandem with what they imagine to be Jeanne's. This process accelerates, becoming more complex as Jeanne's enigmatic actions and their consequences grow increasingly disturbed. Instead of the directly rendered motivation of Mme Beudet, we are given hints, small clues that tell us that even the most trivial mistake can instigate a universe of trouble. In this way, Akerman does not so much deny female subjectivity as find a way to render it, paradoxically, by remaining on the surface of things. Simple explanations for Jeanne's actions no longer adhere as the actions themselves seem increasingly, and frustratingly, irrational. We cannot know what Jeanne's desires are, and yet we must think about what they might be; the viewer's contemplation is unavoidable.

Does she or doesn't she?

But it is ultimately with the film's agonisingly cryptic climax that its issues around narrative, sexuality and meaning crystallise. With a complex of undecipherable narrative occurrences, Akerman achieves an extraordinary – and unprecedented – kind of viewer engagement, for these moments unfailingly give rise to numerous mutually contradictory readings, each in its turn asserted with a sense of interpretive authority. Even the designation of one single climactic moment is fraught with complexities; it is, in fact, almost impossible to establish the absolute truth of the "event". Simply comparing a few summaries of the film's action can illustrate this point. Some critics speak of a crucial occurrence behind the bedroom door with customer number two; others say that the defining moment does not occur until near the film's close. Others agree that something important has happened with the second client, but it cannot be specified, while still others disagree as to the exact meaning of the critical moment near the film's end. The dynamic fluidity of the reading process underscores what is perhaps the most important element of the film's feminism: its meaning is intrinsically bound up with each viewer's subjectivity, thus placing the spectator at the very centre of the film's meaning process. But this is not simply any kind of gender-neutral viewing presence; one's knowledge of (or interest in) women's experience, whether directly lived or only imagined, necessarily comes into play with each interpretation. Thus, every single reading of the film's action unavoidably hinges on some dimension of the feminine, because each one of these complex narrative moments is strategically, if subtly, shaped by questions of female sexuality. In a stunning alternative to the spectator of classical Hollywood cinema (who occupies a masculine position, regardless of gender) Akerman posits a female viewing subject, one whose very comprehension of the film depends on feminine affinities.[8]

A closer look at these specific narrative moments will illustrate the connections between female pleasure and meaning that form the basis for this alternative kind of spectatorship. As previously noted, the fact that something (unrepresented and therefore undefinable) has happened with client number two is revealed through minute slips in the action, traces of some disorienting force that has injected chaos into Jeanne's well-regulated life. Her failure to replace the lid on the soup tureen where she keeps her "earnings" is the first sign; electric lights left on, forgetting to greet Sylvain at the door, indecision about what to do with unaccustomed crises, all add up to something amiss. Time, which has been so carefully mastered by Jeanne's efficient schedule, now seems to unravel, leaving wide gaps unfilled.

The first chain of consequences to result from this unexplained lapse involves overcooked potatoes; even here our speculation is engaged, as the reason for the ruined vegetable could be anything from extra time with the second customer to a languorous bath. In every case, we must imagine Jeanne's thoughts and actions, while the only uncontroverted fact is that her world cannot incorporate this excess of uncertainty. Starting to cook a second batch of potatoes involves more unforeseen elements: there are no more potatoes, new ones have to be bought; extra time is taken with less precision in the preparation; the meal itself has to be interrupted while Jeanne and Sylvain wait for the potatoes to cook. As they sit in silence for what seems an interminable while, Akerman delivers one of the most hauntingly and unexpectedly beautiful sequences in the cinema. A stationary shot of Jeanne, seen from the opposite end of the table (the preferred camera position of this film, exquisitely shot by Babette Mangolte), lasts for almost two minutes, as her reflective expression and tousled hair give subtle hints of a memory that makes a barely perceptible smile appear. This, of course, turns out to be foreshadowing for the seven-minute sequence that ends the film, but the meaning here is retroactively determined and only adds to the complexity of possibilities supplying Jeanne's reverie.

The second "knot of speculation" centres on what can be considered the film's visible climax, the penultimate sequence (when we finally witness Jeanne and her client in the bedroom) and the last seven minutes of the film (the single, static, crepuscular shot of Jeanne at the table). The sequence opens with a shot of Jeanne at her mirror, unbuttoning and then systematically folding her blouse. Then there is an overhead shot of Jeanne on the bed as she rests, writhes, and struggles to push away the dull weight of the man on top of her. This is the first truly ambiguous expression in a sequence that will become known for its indecipherability. There are other firsts here too – the first time the camera discloses the physical intimacy of Jeanne and a client; the first semi-overhead shot; the first image of Jeanne being watched by someone else; or her own awareness of being watched. The next thing that we see is Jeanne buttoning her blouse as the client sprawls back on the bed, in view through her dressing-table mirror. And then, in a shot which paradoxically maximises its disturbing effect while dedramatising its violence, the mirror discloses the man on the bed as Jeanne grabs a pair of scissors and stabs him. The abruptness of the act and its understated depiction have a dramatic impact on the viewer, and this is amplified by the immediacy of the contemplative shot that follows.

Female sexuality in this context of uncertainty is not the familiar spectacle of debased eroticism that pervades our culture from swimsuit editions to blockbuster films, representations that hinge on the visible binaries of patriarchal power and their concomitant exploitation of the feminine. Rather, it is a notion of sexuality as inseparable from

35

meaning, an engagement with signification that disturbs fixed categories and definitions while it establishes the problematic of female pleasure as central to any account. Regardless of the interpretation of specific instances in the film (which is the climactic moment? what does it signify?), the pivotal event that determines the course of the fiction is elided or, at best, only provisionally established through its traces, one interpretation among others. Because this crucial moment is unrepresented (unrepresentable?), questions of female sexuality and desire are intrinsic to each interpretation. There is simply no avoiding it: in order to discuss the film's meaning at all, one has to consider female sexuality as a term of meaning.

All readings of the film must turn on the very meaning of women's pleasure; to posit an interpretation means, at the very least, establishing female sexuality as a terrain of debate. Does Jeanne experience orgasm or does she not? Does this happen with client two or three? If the latter is the case, does her expression signify pleasure or its opposite? If, again, the latter is the case, does this mean that pleasure has been experienced with the second client and not with the third? Or does Jeanne's face tell us that there has actually been orgasm with both second and third customers? Is the resulting violence out of a sense of frustration or violation? Is the experience of pleasure something Jeanne longs to repeat, or, after a second orgasm, is it a sign of the ultimate colonisation of her most intimate self? In what ways can her action of murder be seen as an attempt to retake control? In what ways is it consistent with her character as it has been established, or is it a total surprise? Is this a cry of futile self-defeat or one of liberation?

All these readings, and more, can be substantiated with textual evidence, and, importantly, whether one takes one particular view or its opposite, all interpretations must start and end with a feminist inflection. Therefore, it is precisely around an "unrepresentable (or, at best, ambiguously representable) desire"[9] that *Jeanne Dielman* builds its climax, leaving the viewer endlessly to contemplate that which cannot be seen. And this contemplation inevitably raises questions, proposes answers, and raises more questions about femininity itself; to interpret the film is to engage with the classic enigma of culture. In this way, Akerman is able to appropriate – for the viewer – that articulation of desire and vision that defines the cinema, in a film that exemplifies, in her words, "la jouissance du voir" ("the ecstasy of seeing").[10]

What's beneath her smile?

Two women smile in two films by women – or do they? Both Jeanne Dielman and her precursor, Mme Beudet, leave us with as many questions as we can ask, establish uncertainty where cultural assumptions assert the opposite ("these are 'women's films', their

36

meaning is obvious"), and reveal to us the infinite complexity of women's lives, thoughts and dreams. Both Akerman and Dulac use strategies of indirection, silence and productive doubt to enable us to explore women's cultural roles and their subjective selves. In doing so, each in her own characteristic way reinvents the cinema. Dulac dares to imagine what female subjectivity might be, then uses all the resources of cinematic expression to convey a reality previously ignored or culturally effaced. Yet, as substantial as her assertion of a female imaginary is, she relies upon oblique suggestion to depict Mme Beudet's pleasure in her fantasy world. In this way, using the image as both a touchstone and a starting-point, she allows the viewer's participation to mesh with the attributed experiences of her heroine.

Akerman's strategy is even more indirect, for, asserting nothing and suggesting everything, she lets the enigmatic shadows and lowered eyes of her heroine's face evoke multiple and transforming complexities of thought. Akerman is very careful to prepare the viewer for this interpretive play by constructing stages in Jeanne's contemplative mode that gradually, seductively, invite our reading. Once the viewer becomes adjusted to Jeanne's bland, automatic expression as she goes through her household routine, the slightest variation stimulates conjecture. Thus, after client number two, a barely perceptible, but significant luxuriating expression replaces Jeanne's monotonous stare; every household chore potentially becomes a sensuous adventure, every surface an intriguing site. Nowhere is this suggestion more condensed than in the mealtime scene of waiting (for the potatoes). This is the first we see of Jeanne in unoccupied time; the frontal shot provides us with a distanced but enticing vantage point, and the expressive play of facial features begins. It is almost as if this is the first moment of contemplation that Jeanne has ever had, and we can just about see the thoughts dancing across her serene face. And, although the more dramatic instance of Jeanne in contemplation occurs in the last seven minutes of the film, it is here in the suggestive prelude that the shadows of a smile appear. This is exactly as it should be, for to have Jeanne smile after the murder would anchor the free play of thought in a conventional (and obviously predetermined) reading. Here, however, in the presence of her son and the familiar space of the meal, Jeanne is free to let a variety of indeterminable movements insinuate the possibility of a smile on her face.

This is not to say, however, that the last seven minutes of the film are devoid of such a possibility – on the contrary. Even though darkness absorbs the details, and the only light source is the aquatic flickering of the blue neon sign outside, this single shot evokes numerous possible interpretations and equally conflicting emotions. More a climax in its own right than a denouement (which its languid, silent rhythms make it seem to be), this image of Jeanne at the table with time to spare resumes all the identificatory issues that would characterise epiphanic, climactic thought. As the viewer experiences this time along with Jeanne, a multitude of possibilities present themselves: small traces of expression, of wonder, dullness and doubt, of confusion, rationalisation and panic. And just enough of a hint of a smile to throw every sense of certainty away. This character, who is only seen in surfaces, suddenly gains incredible depth by virtue of the viewer's attributions. We imagine "what she's thinking", put ourselves inside her head; every question circulates around sexuality – undefinable, uncontainable, unstable – and no response is posed. Akerman has inverted the terms of identification, or invented new ones. A depth of experience and feeling is attributed to this character whose interiority the film had worked so hard to deny, and the result is a redefinition of subjectivity in terms of the cinematic gaze.

A final comparison of a single image from each of the two films can suggest their affinities and shared concerns while demonstrating the truly exemplary status of both in the articulated issues of vision, femininity and cinematic desire. At the same time, the differences traced at the start of this essay between two sets of strategies and corresponding eras can find expression in this consideration of how each director treats the situation of a woman at the mirror. In *The Smiling Madame Beudet,* the heroine absently brushes her long hair as she determines her opportunities to unload the gun. Sitting at her dressing-table, she contemplates, in remorse and desperation, how to slip undetected into her husband's study. Dulac gives us a breathtaking image, as Mme Beudet's face, lavishly surrounded by her flowing hair, is replicated in her triple mirror. This reiteration of the woman's face, framed and enhanced by the multiple borders of the mirror, reminds us that the image is always a mode of representation, and, as such, can never stand in for the real person. Where Mme Beudet's nascent smile had preceded a moment of fantasy, her expression now reveals the utter absence of both. The vacant, tormented expression is a prelude to the concluding image of the film – the bourgeois couple in the dingy provincial street, locked into their world by habit, consigned to a life without imagination. But Dulac's images have left the viewer with an array of expressive possibilities for the conception and articulation of female desire.

Akerman's approach might at first seem to contradict this optimism, but her reworking of traditional cinematic codes reinstates it with force. In a film that denies the reverse-shot of dominant fiction, she finds a way to assert its centrality, and also the possibilities to disrupt it. For both Akerman and her character, the position of looking has bold consequences. As Jeanne sits at her dressing-table after sex with client number three, she stares absently at the mirror which reveals the john looking at her. In a single image, and without resorting to a cut,

Akerman gives us (1) the man looking at the woman; (2) the woman looking at the man looking at her; and (3) the viewer looking at this mutually responding series of looks from which the most dramatic consequences will arise. This is the first time that the viewer sees Jeanne and what she sees at the same time; this is the first time that the viewer sees what Jeanne sees. In a point-of-view shot that is not one, in a film that avoids the point-of-view shot, in a film that externalises all the action – we have the most intimate interiority portrayed through the gaze. In the film's three and a half hours, this single instant telescopes a dizzying array of looks in a multidimensional display that has, for the narrative at least, dramatic consequences. The viewer, the john, Jeanne, the john, the viewer: a *mise en abîme* of looks that both challenges and installs the mainspring of cinematic fiction.

Germaine Dulac, a pioneering filmmaker for her time, established the viability of women's consciousness as material for cinematic fiction. Akerman, her spiritual daughter, extends this in extraordinary ways. By making the viewer's consciousness central to the meaning of the film, and necessitating that this consciousness emerge from the feminine, Akerman stakes a claim for women's centrality not only to the subject of cinema, but also to its very mechanisms of meaning. Both films do not offer us role models in the traditional sense, complete with preconstituted definitions that shape our thinking. What they offer instead is the opportunity for us as viewers to become our own role models, as we each grapple with what it means to be a woman among competing definitions and received ideas. We must jettison our own presuppositions when confronted with the inexplicable or the challenging. Refusing the conventional mode of empathetic identification, Germaine Dulac and Chantal Akerman present heroines whose very existence challenges the concept of "positive images" with issues and productive problematics about cultural identity, gender and representation. When considering the work of these two filmmakers, there is indeed much about which to smile.

Notes

[1] This quotation appears on the frontispiece of Mrs Isabella Beeton's *Book of Household Management* (1859-60). I would like to thank Gwendolyn Audrey Foster for immeasurable patience, support and inspiration; my sister, Sharon Flitterman-King, for a universe of ideas and philosophy; Chantal Akerman for her kindness in giving me the poster for *Jeanne Dielman*, my muse, twenty years ago when I was just a fan; and, of course, my husband Joel Lewis, who could have used someone with Jeanne's housekeeping skills while I was steeped in trajectories of the signifier.

[2] Virginia Woolf, *Collected Essays*, volume 2, edited by Leonard Woolf (London: The Hogarth Press, 1966): 146.

[3] Germaine Dulac, "Les Procédés expressifs du cinématographe", *Cinémagazine* 28 (11 July 1924): 67-68.

[4] Jean-Luc Godard, "Montage my Fine Care", in Jean Narboni and Tom Milne (eds), *Godard on Godard: Critical writings by Jean-Luc Godard* (New York: Da Capo Press, 1986): 39.

[5] "Chantal Akerman on *Jeanne Dielman*", *Camera Obscura* 2 (autumn 1977): 119. Emphases in original.

[6] Ibid.

[7] In discussions of the film, many people have noted that this image of Jeanne corresponds to their memories of their mothers, and that the familiarity of that position takes them to their childhood homes.

[8] Laura Mulvey maintains that in dominant narrative cinema there is always "a 'masculinisation' of the spectator position regardless of the actual sex (or possible deviance) of any real live movie-goer". See "Afterthoughts on 'Visual Pleasure and Narrative Cinema' Inspired by 'Duel in the Sun'", *Framework* 15-16-17 (1981): 12.

[9] Ibid.

[10] "Chantal Akerman on *Jeanne Dielman*": 121.

The feminine side of New York: travelogue, autobiography and architecture in *News from Home*

Jennifer M Barker

Seeing Manhattan from the 110th floor of the World Trade Center. Beneath the haze stirred up by the winds, the urban island, a sea in the middle of the sea, lifts up the skyscrapers over Wall Street, sinks down at Greenwich, then rises again to the crests of Midtown, quietly passes over Central Park and finally undulates off into the distance beyond Harlem. A wave of verticals. Its agitation is momentarily arrested by vision. The gigantic mass is immobilized before the eyes.[1]

In this passage from *The Practice of Everyday Life*, Michel de Certeau momentarily ascends to the lofty position of an urban spectator, gazing down on the city from an improved vantage point. From his perch, he towers over the city and imagines himself above the fray. He can read the city like a book, perusing the pages spread out before him. He is free even to fancy himself the author of this text, to narrate the city according to his perceptions of it. From this position, his narrative may elide the messy details of the streets below, omitting the smell of the steam rising from the grates, the groans of heavy trucks rumbling through the alleys, the pervasive grey that marks the faces of buildings. In de Certeau's own words, "[t]he voyeur-god created by this fiction...must disentangle himself from the murky intertwining daily behaviors and make himself alien to them".[2]

This mode of observation is in stark contrast to the ground-level observational strategy of Chantal Akerman's *News from Home* (1976), in which the camera travels through the spaces inhabited by its subjects, observing New York City from the vantage point not of towering skyscrapers, but of the city streets and of the subway rumbling beneath the surface of the streets themselves. While de Certeau's fictional observer envisions himself as spectator, architect and narrator of the space he creates according to his own desires, Akerman's image is entirely absent from this film. She is present only in the sense that she occupies the same spaces in which her subjects live and work. Here, the city is produced not by the architect or observer looming from his perch high above the city, but by its inhabitants, by the people walking its streets. The act of dwelling is invested with the significance and creativity traditionally reserved for architecture, and thus a different kind of city is created, a city as dwelling space, rather than as abstract and readable text.

Akerman bypasses the well-known picture-postcard sites and landmarks, and instead seeks out and inhabits the "lived" spaces of everyday life, with which the city's residents would be more intimately familiar. This is not a city of the Statue of Liberty and Central Park, of the United Nations and Times Square, but of subway stations, crowded intersections, and crumbling shopfront buildings. It is no coincidence that there is no long shot of the familiar New York City skyline until the very end of the film, at which point Akerman has already toured the city's more anonymous spaces and is actually departing from its harbour by ferry.

As life passes by Akerman's camera, one senses a reinhabitation of the streets of Manhattan, of the dark spaces left unmapped and unsurveyed by the spectator looking down from the top of the World Trade Center. The city as filmed from this angle, from street level, is not a theoretical text, not the mere grid of lines and curves and intersections conceived by the urban planner. Rather, it is a dwelling in the most intimate, visceral sense of the word. The camera never tilts up to catch a glimpse of skyscrapers disappearing into the clouds above, but remains firmly grounded; this is a landscape of subway tunnels, of alleys, of the hidden places of the city, places just outside the margins of visibility and legibility.

In touring the anonymous spaces of the city, Akerman therefore "fleshes out" not only the marginal spaces of the city itself, but also the kinds of corporeally invested space that are negated by the observation tower. As its title suggests, the film investigates the notion of "home" and origins; the attention paid to urban space and the act of dwelling leads to a discovery of "home" within what appears to be "homelessness". Accordingly, this essay will discuss the film's articulation of the contrasts between architectural and urban spaces and its validation of ignored spaces not only for feminist identity, but also for architectural and feminist theory.

Although many analyses of Akerman's work have focused on the filmmaker's feminist negotiation of identity, in this essay I would like to investigate the ways in which *News from Home* reconsiders not only identity, but also *place*. Through its unique relation to architectural and urban space, and its understanding of the deep resonance between the human body and the body of the city, so to speak, the film charts out new ways of figuring both the city and the autobiographical subject. To explore the ways in which Akerman's feminist project extends to the use of space, I will turn to the work of Elizabeth Grosz, whose approach to feminist theory, particularly her work on architecture and spatial theory, marks a useful turn towards contemporary issues of embodiment, spatiality and phenomenology.

The investigation of theories of subjectivity is a hallmark of Akerman's films and has inspired numerous film analyses on the relevance of the films for contemporary feminist theory. *News from Home* also takes up this theme of identity; in this film, Akerman's own familial relationships are at issue. Over primarily static images of desolate city streets, Akerman reads aloud the letters she received from her mother during her first extended stay in New York City in 1972. Akerman makes no explicit commentary on her mother's words, which are the only words spoken in the film. The letters recount Akerman's unannounced departure from her family and her home town of Brussels, as well as her mother's pained reaction. In letter after letter she implores her daughter to write back, to acknowledge letters and gifts sent with an astonishing frequency, to maintain regular contact with a family who, by her mother's account, misses Akerman desperately. Behind every recounting of the intimate details of family life in Brussels one hears the lamentations of a mother whose connections to her daughter have become suddenly tenuous, stretched to their breaking-point.

Janet Bergstrom and Constance Penley include *News from Home* among a number of films that "have been very helpful in suggesting possible approaches to the question 'who speaks' when what is at stake is the woman's voice/image, particularly in showing the difficulty in asking it: the status of 'woman' (daughter, mother, and so on) is unstable".[3] The film, as Bergstrom and Penley have written, makes

[T]he *I* of the enunciation problematic...the sound track establishes an *I-you* relationship through a mother's letters to her daughter, who has left her family in Belgium to make films in New York. This, and everything else we know about the mother or daughter, we know from the letters, except for the sound of the voice reading them, which we imagine to be the daughter's, and the images we see, which look almost like photographs in the fixity of their hold upon disconnected scenes, streets and subways in New York, with people randomly present or absent, none of them the *you* addressed in the letters.[4]

As Ivone Margulies explains, the fact that Akerman speaks not her "own" words, but those her mother has written to her means that "[t]he voice issues from and is directed at the same place; it echoes from a paradoxical space, both source and end, short-circuiting communication. The pronominal shifters 'I' and 'you' ordinarily signal one subject in relation to another, but here these carriers of subjectivity are shown as precariously rooted".[5] *News from Home*, she continues, "questions the notion of presence, of an evident, unified source for an utterance, at the very moment at which difference and distance seem abolished: the moment of voicing. Addresser and addressee are collapsed, disavowing an essential identity for either".[6]

Brenda Longfellow has focused the analysis of subjectivity in Akerman's films even further, to argue that Akerman's films constitute a series of "love letters to the mother": "Desire in these films circulates around the maternal body, around the variable presence and absence of the mother, around the enduring gaze of the daughter at the mother".[7] The contribution of Akerman's films

> [L]ies equally in their singular attentiveness to the ambivalence and difference that structures the mother/daughter relationship, a difference which informs both the diegesis and the structural articulation of her films...It is precisely the particular structural articulation of her films which functions as the third term, triangulating the mother and daughter relation and framing the films both as a mode of reparation and as evidence of an irreparable divide.[8]

In this film, the mother-daughter relationship becomes the primary means of articulating the intersubjective nature of identity, in that the mother and daughter in this film merge into one voice. By constructing her own autobiography through the reading of her mother's words, by thus paralleling their autobiographical acts, Akerman demonstrates that subjectivity is a function of connections to others, is constructed within a social context, that it arises and articulates itself only through its relation to others.

That imbrication of subject positions seriously "unbalanc[es] the fiction of autobiography", especially since the merging of "mother" with "daughter" occurs specifically in the act of speaking and writing.[9] "[A]utobiographical reference", Bergstrom and Penley write, "serves a complex function, one which draws on a woman's lived experience while, at the same time, complicating the question 'who speaks' by dispersing the origin of the enunciation across many positions; the film-maker, like the filmic system and its characters, is shaped by conflicting interests and desires".[10]

That Akerman speaks her mother's words in English is a sign of the distance between the child and the mother, but Akerman's strong Belgian accent reinforces a shared loneliness. Her mother is, in a sense, "homeless" in the Brussels family home after the departure of her daughter; Akerman is "homeless" in Manhattan. "Here the mother's voice is mediated through the daughter not with a collapse of distinctions", writes Longfellow:

[B]ut with a certain intermingling of subject positions, the 'I' and the 'you', which observe no fixed address of identity. 'Mother' and 'daughter' are always and only effects of a continuous exchange, of a writing/speaking through and with the other. Addressee and addressor unknown, nowhere. At least nowhere in the image.[11]

The epistolary form of *News from Home* and particularly Akerman's own voice-over, which "deprivileges the authorial voice much more profoundly by rendering it feminine, personal, and informal, and by stripping it of all transcendental pretense",[12] accentuate the role played by speech, voice and the soundtrack in her critique of authorship and the autobiographical project. Akerman's voice mingles with her mother's words, and with the alternating silence and noise of the city. The roar of street traffic and the rattling of the subway at times overwhelm the filmmaker's voice and the content of the letters, "momentarily shifting", as Margulies states, "one's interest to the space in which Akerman supposedly reads. Random weaving of attention... bolsters Akerman's subversion of a fixed locus for the 'I'", as well as threatening the continuity of space, as New York's noise battles with Belgium's maternal words.[13] Her mother's words and the sound of Akerman speaking them are horizontalised with the sounds of traffic, so that text becomes rhythm, "concrete materiality".[14]

Although so much of the feminist analysis of Akerman's work has centred on these linguistic issues and the use of the soundtrack to challenge traditional notions of subjectivity, I would like here to focus on another kind of materiality, that of space, to demonstrate that the investigations Akerman undertakes at the level of speech and sound occur as well at the level of architecture, urban space, and dwelling. I am interested in the ways in which her negotiation of female subject positions proceeds through a unique way of representing and occupying space.

Margulies has described what she calls Akerman's "hyperrealist everyday", in which the filmmaker gives priority to details of daily life that are elided by most forms of cinematic representation:

> The label 'Nothing happens,' often applied to Akerman's work, is key in defining that work's specificity – its equation of extension and intensity, of description and drama...The inclusion of...'images between images' begets a spatio-temporal, as well as moral expansion of cinema. The interest in extending the representation of reality reflects a desire to restore a phenomenological integrity to reality.[15]

This essay deals precisely with that "spatio-temporal...expansion of cinema" in relation to the use of space and architecture in *News from Home*, which maintains a focus on the seemingly dreary details of everyday life, as Akerman demonstrates by constructing her own autobiography from written and spoken accounts of her mother's daily life. And just as she acknowledges her personal debt to and engagement in, even if vicariously, the realities of her mother's life as they are communicated through her letters, so she acknowledges her debt to and participation in the mundane realities of the city in which she now lives, realities communicated through the sounds and textures of the city spaces, through her own footsteps and those of others in the streets. The construction of the self becomes a spatial issue; gender relations are written onto the body of the city, shaping it and shaped by it. Through forms of architecture and urban planning, and through forms of *being in* architecture and urban spaces, subjects of the city write and are themselves written in spatial, corporeal terms. Here, living in the city becomes a form of autobiography, in which the subject is acknowledged as grounded in the human body and its resonance with the body of the city.

The use of space and of ways of existing in space as a means of writing the self follows from the fact, demonstrated by the structure of this film, that the very acts of speaking and writing that constitute autobiography are only possible in the context of others. The primary function of writing and speaking is, of course, communication, which implies the involvement of more than one person; writing and speaking are by definition communal acts. Roman Jakobson reminds us that any message, to remain operable, requires "finally, a contact, a physical channel and psychological connection between the addresser and the addressee, enabling both of them to enter and stay in communication".[16] This notion of communication as fundamentally communal casts suspicion on any concept of the autobiographical subject as somehow transcendent, above the mundane realities of life and of other lives.

The connective tissue binding people to one another is, in this case, space and movement, as well as speech. In Jakobson's linguistic theory, the phatic function of language is responsible for the maintenance of the necessary physical channel and psychological connection between addresser and addressee; it takes the form of expressions such as "hello" and "well, well". De Certeau argues that such linguistic communication can occur in space, as well as in language. In his view, "the phatic function...also gambols, goes on all fours, dances, and walks about, with a light or heavy step, like a series of 'hellos' in an echoing labyrinth, anterior or parallel to informative speech".[17] De Certeau compares the movements of pedestrians across the surfaces of the city to the act of writing and speaking oneself:

The act of walking is to the urban system what the speech act is to language or to the statements uttered. At the most elementary level, it has a triple 'enunciative' function: it is a process of *appropriation* of the topographical system on the part of the pedestrian (just as the speaker appropriates and takes on language); it is a spatial acting-out of the place (just as the speech act is an acoustic acting-out of language); and it implies *relations* among differentiated positions, that is, among pragmatic 'contracts' in the form of movements (just as verbal enunciation is an 'allocution,' 'posits another opposite' the speaker and puts contracts between interlocutors into action). It thus seems possible to give a preliminary definition of walking as a space of enunciation.[18]

Thus to walk the streets becomes a means of writing that occurs far below the range of visibility surveyed by the architects and observers looking down from the tops of skyscrapers. These "intertwined paths give their shape to spaces". By walking, by marking out unplanned paths and avoiding others, city residents create a mobile, contradictory, un-"readable" text that resists the attempts of modernist architecture and technology to administer and keep tabs on the movements within its boundaries.[19] "The networks of these moving, intersecting writings", de Certeau continues, "compose a manifold story that has neither author nor spectator, shaped out of fragments of trajectories and alternations of spaces: in relation to representations, it remains daily and indefinitely other".[20]

News from Home embraces de Certeau's metaphor: the subject here dwells in the city spaces as she dwells in "the house of language". The film approaches an expanded, grounded concept of female subjectivity, articulating it by occupying the streets physically, by filming the city's physical inhabitation by people at the edges of the "official" city. The notion of embodiment, both in the human body and in the spaces of the city, is imbued with creativity: one gives shape to space by walking through it. Akerman's camera moves and dwells not in some abstract mapped out concept of a city, but in human dwellings unseen on any map.

Akerman never loses sight of the subject as it lives in real spaces. She examines the act of writing, of articulating a female subject position, in both linguistic and spatial terms. The autobiographical project becomes, in this film, at once spoken, written and inhabited. Her camera embarks on a fantastic voyage wherein the bodies of her human subjects, like her own body, unseen behind the camera, seem in tune with the larger rhythms of the body that is the metropolis itself. Conversely, perhaps, it is the rhythms of the dwellers of the labyrinthine city that lend to the streets their murmur and incessant hum. Akerman lets the streets speak for its subjects, herself included. Sounds of passing cars, horns and rumbling subways swell on the soundtrack as if in answer to her mother's words, speaking for Akerman herself and her fellow New Yorkers.

It is on the surfaces of bodies and streets and the architecture of the city that is manifested what Elizabeth Grosz calls "the constitutive and mutually defining relations between corporeality and the metropolis".[21] To dwell in the city takes on deeper significance, no longer a simple (practical) inhabiting of one place, rather than another. In the scenario Grosz describes, where "[t]he body and its environment...produce each other as forms of the hyperreal, as modes of simulation which have overtaken and transformed whatever reality each may have had into the image of the other: the city is made and made over into the simulacrum of the body, and the body, in its turn, is transformed, 'citified,' urbanized as a distinctively metropolitan body".[22] It is this reciprocity, the deep resonance between body and city, between corporeality and "city-ness" that allows Akerman to cast her autobiography as a "tour" of this city. By tracing the spaces of the city in which she now lives, for which she has left her family and home town, she seeks herself as a subject. The construction of the subject by and in the city is but one aspect of the social construction of subjectivity: just as psychoanalysis examines language as a clue to the subject as constructed in and by it, Akerman looks to the city to understand the subject as constructed in and by the city and metropolitan life.

This imbrication of the body and the city is demonstrated by the long travelling shots in the latter part of the film, in which the scenes Akerman's camera records are determined almost wholly by the rhythms of the city itself: the camera is fixed in the rear seat of a car that moves slowly along a row of shopfront and storage buildings. The camera only rests on one building or another when the car in which it is travelling stops at a red light. The composition and particular subject-matter, whether a gas station or a lamp-post, are dictated by the car's movements, down to the subtle reframing that occurs when the car inches forward ever so slightly.

Similarly, in the scenes shot in the subway, the content and angle of view are determined by the stops the train makes and by the curves of the underground paths. Fixed on the platform, the camera records passengers waiting across the tracks for the next train; their entrances to and exits from the platform are often obscured by trains whizzing by on the tracks near the camera. Shooting from within a train, the camera sees only its own reflection and the occasional station signs when the train stops at each station. In a remarkable pair of long takes, the camera is set up at the rear of a train car, looking down the row of seated and standing passengers. The view alternately includes and excludes the next car, the depth of focus depending entirely on the movement of the train as it hugs the curves of the tracks.

Travelogue and autobiography here become parallel acts of writing the subject as a function of and factor in the city. Akerman's juxtaposition of the genres embraces the principle that "the form, structure, and norms of the city seep into and effect all the other elements that go into the constitution of corporeality and/as subjectivity".[23] It is Akerman's "touristic" approach to the city, her insistence on walking and riding through it, rather than merely observing from a distance, that allows the film to maintain this communion of body and city, of perceiver and perceived. "The tourist", as Giuliana Bruno has written:

> [S]hould be understood as a crucial figuration in the changing relation between subject and object of perception. This figure abridges the distance, and perhaps the difference, between the two as it creates an 'impact' on the world of objects. The touristic gaze essentially questions the 'inhabiting' of place and the space of objects. It modifies the very idea of home, its immobility, its 'real estate,' its 'alien' relation to otherness. Actively engaged in a spatial form of cognition, such a gaze affects the very experience of knowing and remembering. It is symptomatic of the shifting nature of the *vissuto*, an Italian expression that maps the space of one's lived experiences. As a practice, it acts upon the way we construct a narrative of objects, our own narrative, and the narrative of identity.[24]

News from Home manages to dissolve the boundaries of perceiver and perceived, of space and inhabitants, in just this way.

The bodies of Akerman's subjects move through the spaces of this city in near silence, their familiarity with their surroundings spoken not in their expressions nor in their words, as no one speaks in the film except Akerman herself. Rather, "[t]heir story begins on ground level, with footsteps"; their stories are narrated here, in the footsteps, their gestures, their postures, positions and physical movements, which render intimate the spaces of this most public and universally recognised of cities.[25] Consider, for example, the intense exchange between Akerman's camera and one particular male subway passenger. For the most part, the subway passengers acknowledge Akerman's presence only briefly, then turn away and pretend not to notice, although their nervous glances at fellow passengers belie their apparent indifference. In one subway scene, however, a man boards the train and is immediately mesmerised by the camera. He does not sit down and look away, as his fellow passengers do, but faces it directly, his stance almost combative, and stares back. This exchange goes on for an uncomfortably long time, but the camera does not back down. Eventually, the passenger turns and walks away, into the next car, every step of his long trek through the train car recorded by the immobile camera. In this scene, as in others, public transportation becomes an intimate ritual, less a mode of travel than one of communication and exchange.

Akerman's use of the travelogue as autobiography and her recognition of the intersubjective nature of the body and the city yield an investigation of subjectivity that is grounded phenomenologically *in* corporeality, as opposed to fleeing *from* it. Akerman reclaims a space for female subjectivity in the city streets inhabited by her camera and its subjects. Whereas transcendence, as it is represented by traditional (and traditionally masculine) notions of both architecture and autobiography, seeks a flight from the corporeal, *News from Home* seeks out and reinhabits the spaces of feminine corporeality in both the spaces of New York City and in the autobiographical project. The film disturbs the opposition between the corporeal and the transcendent by positing, through the autobiographical form, a subjectivity that is linguistically and spatially resituated in and reconnected to corporeality and "real" space.

Bodies are constantly in communication with the streets through which they walk, the buildings and spaces they occupy. This open register of reciprocity involves, in Grosz's words, bodies and cities "not as megalithic total entities, distinct identities", as the modernist architectural theories of Le Corbusier and Frank Lloyd Wright suggest, "but as assemblages or collections of parts, capable of crossing the thresholds between substances to form linkages".[26] These linkages mark the fundamentally reciprocal relations between the two:

> [B]odies and cities are not causally linked. Every cause must be logically distinct from its effect. The body, however, is not distinct, does not have an existence separate from the city, for they are mutually defining. Like the representational model, there may be an isomorphism between the body and the city. But it is not a mirroring of nature in artifice. Rather, there is a two-way linkage which could be defined as an *interface*, perhaps even a cobuilding.[27]

This conceptualisation of bodies and cities as mutually constructed, reciprocal, fundamentally corporeal, and with margins capable of being transgressed and transformed, challenges the definitions set out by modernist and masculinist architecture. The relationship between the male architect-subject and the city is, in the scenario set out by de Certeau, a one-way street: the world is merely raw material to be moulded by him. He gives his shape to the world and surveys his creations from the pinnacles of the earth. From that lofty philosophical and physical position, the architect thus considers himself the victor in a battle waged with the teeming humanity of the streets below. "To live is to leave traces", Benjamin wrote, and it precisely these traces avoided, written out of the story, by modernist architecture's desire to create a "pure" and purely conceptual city.[28]

The desire to map out spaces from a position high above and safely distanced from them stretches back at least to the 17th century, argues de Certeau, although not until the modern era did technological innovations make possible the realistic achievement of the wish "to be lifted out of the city's grasp. [Here] [o]ne's body is no longer clasped by the streets that turn and return it according to an anonymous law; nor is it possessed...by the rumble of so many differences and by the nervousness of New York traffic".[29] For de Certeau, the World Trade Center stands as an emblem of this scopic desire for abstraction: "The 1370 foot high tower that serves as a prow for Manhattan continues to construct the fiction that creates readers, makes the complexity of the city readable, and immobilizes its opaque mobility in a transparent text".[30]

The tendency to abstraction exhibited not only by modern architecture, with its impossibly tall skyscrapers and boastful observation decks, but also by the twin pursuits of urban planning and cartography (the one mapping the imagination onto space, the other doing just the opposite) thus rescues the proponents of these occupations from the messy and "nervous" daily existence of the masses below. "It transforms the bewitching world by which one was 'possessed' into a text that lies before one's eyes", writes de Certeau.[31] City maps record paths, he continues, but "these thick or thin curves only refer, like words, to the absence of what has passed by...[They] miss what was: the act itself of passing by".[32]

The conceptual city imagined by architects and cartographers becomes a subject itself, "a proper name", in de Certeau's words, at the expense of the millions of human subjects walking the streets below. The elevator ride to the observation deck eliminates these human subjects of the city from the range of visibility; they are mapped out, excluded from the text, leaving only the larger "universal and anonymous" all-encompassing city-subject. Thus, modern technology achieves "the transformation of the urban *fact*", that is, the traces of life in the spaces in which it is lived, "into the *concept* of a city".[33] The city map may itself be visible, says de Certeau, but "it has the effect of making invisible the operation that made it possible. These fixations constitute procedures for forgetting...The trace left behind exhibits the (voracious) property that the geographical system has of being able to transform action into legibility, but in doing so it causes a way of being in the world to be forgotten".[34]

Anthony Vidler locates this distancing of the modernist architect from the "urban fact" of the streets in a deep-seated fear of touch. Indeed, the flight to the heights of skyscrapers is no less than a flight from the carnal corporeality associated with the huddling masses. Le Corbusier, for example, expressed a particularly vitriolic disdain for the carnality of humanity: "Heaven preserve us from the Balzacian mentality of [those] who would be content to leave our streets as they are because these murky canyons offer them the spectacle of human physiognomy!".[35]

This panicked fear of the carnality of the streets results in an architecture that embraces the ideal of transcendence, whereby buildings scale the heavens in an attempt to bring their inhabitants far above the "murky canyons", in which the hordes of humanity swarm and breed. The buildings Le Corbusier envisions transcend all earthly limitations: "Look...towards those widely-spaced crystal towers which soar higher than any pinnacle on earth. These translucent prisms that seem to float in the air without anchorage to the ground...rear their heads one upon the other in a dazzling spectacle of grandeur, serenity and gladness".[36] Transcendence as an ideal implies an escape from all that lies below, in the depths, at the bottom. Thus, the grime of daily existence at street level is invisible and easily dismissed from the heights of the World Trade Center or Le Corbusier's imagined skyscrapers.

The desire for transcendence in architecture finds its counterpart in the desire for transparency, which implies an escape from what lies inside, at the centre. Le Corbusier invokes this principle in the design of his houses, in which "everything...seems to be disposed in a way that continuously throws the subject towards the periphery of the house. The look is directed to the exterior in such deliberate manner as to suggest the reading of these houses as frames for a view".[37] The houses are constructed as windows over the world below. The focus in each room is not on the centre of it, the living space, but on the expansive windows that form the room's border with the outside. The windowscapes of these residential homes recall the observation decks of more institutional and public monuments to man's technological prowess. Le Corbusier's architectural designs attempt to deflect attention away from his own body and the body of the male subject occupying the space in question by emptying out the centre of the rooms and directing the gaze towards the windows, towards the outside. In an analysis of Le Corbusier's representation of his designs through photographs, Beatriz Colomina points out the recurring use of traces of human subjects who are never actually photographed occupying his spaces. The human body is represented always at a remove, through articles of clothing or possessions strewn carefully about the residences. Thus, the pack of cigarettes lying on a table may be read as the emptied sign of a carnal existence whose presence would prove too much for the house itself.[38]

Elizabeth Grosz finds the construction of a conceptual city of the kind described by de Certeau, and the drives towards transcendence and transparency that characterise such efforts, to have a distinctly gendered significance. For Grosz, the very notion of space owes a debt to the femininity of what Plato termed *chora*, a "mythological bridge between the intelligible and the sensible, mind and body", but which Grosz more specifically describes as "the space in which place is made possible".[39] Grosz cites Luce Irigaray's argument that, even where femininity and women are not explicitly evoked in philosophical and architectural texts, they and concepts associated with them serve as repressed foundations for philosophical value. Thus, the none-too-subtle coding (by Plato, and later by Derrida) of *chora* as feminine and maternal allows Grosz to demonstrate that the dark and unmapped places that are eliminated from the range of visibility from the vantage point of the city's skyscrapers are the spaces of femininity itself, deinvested of its bodily forms. This disembodied femininity is used as the ground around and against which modernism builds a "thoroughly masculine" conceptual and social universe.[40] The conceptual city reaches away from its corporeal origins, and, at the same time, it names those contemptible origins "woman".

"[T]his femininity" – that is, the femininity of the spaces fled by modernist architecture – "is not itself merely an abstract representation of generic features...but is derived from the attributes culturally bestowed on women themselves".[41] The city enables subject positions that are distinctly gendered, as well as distinctly metropolitan, through the particular and rigorous division of space and social behaviour:

> The city orients and organizes family, sexual, and social relations insofar as the city divides cultural life into public and private domains, geographically dividing and defining the particular social positions and locations [and establishing] more or less stable divisions, such as those constituting domestic and generational distinctions. These spaces, divisions, and interconnections are the roles and means by which bodies are individuated to become subjects.[42]

Family residences, laundries, schools, and other places identified with women remain at the street level of the conceptual city; skyscrapers and penthouses and observation decks are occupied by the architect, the executive, and the traditionally male *flâneur*. Men "hollow out their own interiors and project them outward, and then require women as supports for this hollowed space. Women become the guardians of the private and the interpersonal...the living representations of corporeality, of domesticity, of the natural order that men have had to expel from their own self-representations in order to construct themselves as above-the-mundane, beyond the merely material".[43]

Grosz suggests that the rigid placement of women within the realm of interiority, materiality and corporeality is, in fact, a displacement. The containment of women within

[A] dwelling that they did not build, nor was even built *for* them, can only amount to a *homelessness* within the very home itself: it becomes [as it does perhaps most explicitly in Akerman's *Jeanne Dielman, 23 quai du Commerce, 1080 Bruxelles* (1975)] the space of duty, of endless and infinitely repeatable chores that have no social value or recognition, the space of the affirmation and replenishment of others at the expense and erasure of the self, the space of domestic violence and abuse, the space that harms as much as it isolates women.[44]

Traditional architectural theory and practice have used *chora*, Grosz writes, as a means of disembodying femininity and building a conceptual universe on the grounds it provides. For Derrida, "it signifies, at its most literal level, notions of 'place,' 'location,' 'site,' 'region,' 'locale,' 'country': but it also contains an irreducible, yet often overlooked connection with the function of femininity".[45] It is a term "[s]leeped in paradox": it enables the becoming of many things, but itself never becomes; it allows the continuation of attributes from the forms to their offspring, and yet it has no attributes of its own. It is located (or, more accurately, dislocated) in "no-man's land", designating "less a positivity than an abyss".[46]

Grosz suggests a rereading of *chora* that may be more constructive for feminist theory. For all the non-presence attributed to it by Plato, *chora* is present in a way that makes it impossible to conceive of anything without it. "The world of objects, material reality in all its complexity, is in fact infiltrated by the very term whose function is to leave no imprint, no trace".[47] It permeates the very things that would seek to rise up and become without ever having to acknowledge their debt to it. *Chora* is "interwoven into the very *economy* of the architectural project itself", which "consists in the distribution, not only of bricks, stone, steel, and glass, but also in the production and distribution of...space, time and movement".[48]

Grosz points out the positive potential offered by *chora* for a reinvestment of space with femininity and corporeality; she imagines a scenario in which "space (as territory which is mappable, explorable) gives way to place (occupation, dwelling, being lived in)".[49] She insists on a project "to return women to those places from which they have been dis- or re-placed or expelled, to occupy those positions –

especially those which are not acknowledged as positions...to be able to experiment with and produce the possibility of occupying, dwelling or living in new spaces, which in their turn help generate new perspectives, new bodies, new ways of inhabiting".[50] One cannot help but remember in this context the remarkable shot in *News from Home* in which a woman sits silently on a chair that is placed, surprisingly, at the foot of a traffic light on the corner of a busy intersection. People rush by this woman on all sides, Akerman's camera fixes her in its gaze, and yet the woman does not move. She sits stoically with arms crossed over her chest, staring back at the camera, her immobility echoed by the "Don't Walk" sign flashing steadily behind her.

It is precisely these previously unacknowledged dwelling positions that Akerman explores and respects. By showing these positions to be inhabited and fleshed out by the people living on the surfaces of the city, Akerman reinstates the material dimension of the city itself. In doing so, she takes up the project urged by Grosz some twenty years later, which is to locate a deep, inhabited female subjectivity in the architectural spaces where it is been denied and disembodied. Her mother's words accompany the images of bodies walking, riding, standing and sitting; femininity is thus reinvested with its corporeal origins through the meeting of sound and image, and ultimately the city is reinvested with both.

The autobiographical form should put Akerman at the centre of the film. In fact, without appearing on-camera, she is the intersection of the maternal, in the form of her mother's letters and their evocation of a complex mother-daughter relationship, and the material, in the form of the city she and the other New Yorkers around her occupy on a daily basis. She is involved at once in intimate relationships with her mother (a relationship of distance, maintained through language, through their inhabitation of one another's memories and imaginations) and with New York City (a relationship maintained corporeally, through their physical inhabitation of one another's bodies). The film is a means of re-evaluating the maternal/material ground for Akerman herself and for the city, which becomes much more than an abstract theoretical project.

The deep connections between the material/spatial and the maternal and between femininity and corporeality are evoked in a remarkable passage from Irigaray, which reads like a paraphrasing of the underlying meaning in the letters Akerman which reads from her mother:

I was your house. And, when you leave, abandoning this dwelling place, I do not know what to do with these walls of mine. Have I ever had a body other than the one which you constructed according to your idea of it? Have I ever experienced a skin other than the one which you wanted me to dwell within?[51]

Akerman reappropriates and reminds us of the maternal body surrounding, permeating all places – the space that makes all possible. By juxtaposing those letters with images of people occupying the spaces of this famous city, Akerman acknowledges that the space her mother inhabits, which is distant and associated with the family home, the private sphere Akerman fled, is not empty but full, valuable and meaningful. Akerman re-evaluates and revalues this maternal body/space; it takes the form of her mother's words, body and city (Brussels) and, at the same time, is transformed into Akerman's own voice and the depths of New York City, its hollowed-out spaces. Although the film is, of course, on one level a personal statement about herself and her mother (an "autobiographical" film), it is, at the same time, an argument about gender relations that proceeds in and through space itself, through the representation, the visual and tactile inhabitation, of New York City as something more than a metaphor, as a real dwelling for female subjectivity.

By acknowledging the imbrication of bodies and cities, the film offers some resistance to the dominant concepts of modernist theories of architecture and space (which, in many ways, correspond to traditional notions of transcendental subjectivity and authorship) in the form of a phenomenologically grounded alternative akin to the touristic gaze Bruno describes. At the same time, by examining spaces and forms of living in space, she validates the places in which women dwell and which are usually considered marginal and anonymous. The film thus suggests an alternative autobiographical and architectural logic, and meets the demands of feminist autobiographical theorists who call for a theory of the subject "that accepts neither ontological nor post-structuralist positions but negotiates a space and a 'subject' between them".[52]

Notes

[1] Michel de Certeau, *The Practice of Everyday Life*, translated by Steven F Rendall (Berkeley, LA; London: University of California Press, 1984): 91.

[2] Ibid: 93.

[3] Constance Penley and Janet Bergstrom, "The Avant-Garde: History and Theories", in Bill Nichols (ed), *Movies and Methods, Volume II: An Anthology* (Berkeley; Los Angeles; London: University of California Press, 1985): 298.

[4] Ibid: 298. Emphases in original.

[5]   Ivone Margulies, *Nothing Happens: Chantal Akerman's Hyperrealist Everyday* (Durham; London: Duke University Press, 1996): 151.

[6]   Ibid.

[7]   Brenda Longfellow, "Love Letters to the Mother: The Work of Chantal Akerman", *Canadian Journal of Political and Social Theory* 13: 1-2 (1989): 79.

[8]   Ibid.

[9]   Margulies: 151.

[10]   Penley and Bergstrom: 299.

[11]   Longfellow: 80.

[12]   Kaja Silverman, *The Acoustic Mirror: The Female Voice in Psychoanalysis and Cinema* (Bloomington; Indianapolis: Indiana University Press, 1988): 214.

[13]   Margulies: 152.

[14]   Ibid: 153.

[15]   Ibid: 22.

[16]   Roman Jakobson, "Closing Statement: Linguistics and Poetics", in Thomas A Sebeok (ed), *Style in Language* (Cambridge; MA: The M.I.T. Press, 1960): 353.

[17]   De Certeau: 99.

[18]   Ibid: 97-98. Emphases in original.

[19]   Ibid: 97.

[20]   Ibid: 93.

[21]   Elizabeth Grosz, "Bodies-Cities", in Beatriz Colomina (ed), *Sexuality & space* (Princeton, NJ: Princeton Architectural Press, 1992): 243.

[22]   Ibid: 242.

[23]   Ibid: 248-249.

[24]   Giuliana Bruno, "Bodily Architectures", *Assemblage* 19 (1992): 107.

[25]   De Certeau: 97.

[26]   Grosz: 248.

[27]   Ibid. Emphasis in original.

[28]   Walter Benjamin, "Paris, Capital of the Nineteenth Century", in

Reflections, translated by Edmund Jephcott (New York: Schocken Books, 1986): 155-156.

29 De Certeau: 92.

30 Ibid.

31 Ibid.

32 Ibid: 97.

33 Ibid: 93-94. Emphases in original.

34 Ibid: 97.

35 Quoted in Anthony Vidler, "Bodies in Space/Subjects in the City: Psychopathologies of Modern Urbanism", *Differences* 5: 3 (1988): 41-43.

36 Quoted in ibid: 42.

37 Beatriz Colomina, "The Split Wall: Domestic Voyeurism", in Colomina (ed): 98.

38 See ibid.

39 Elizabeth Grosz, "Women, *Chora*, Dwelling", in *Space, Time, and Perversion: Essays on the Politics of Bodies* (New York; London: Routledge, 1995): 112, 116.

40 Ibid: 121.

41 Ibid: 116.

42 Grosz (1992): 250.

43 Grosz (1993): 121-122.

44 Ibid: 122. First emphasis in original; second emphasis added.

45 Ibid: 112.

46 Ibid: 114, 116.

47 Ibid: 117.

48 Ibid: 118. Emphasis in original.

49 Ibid: 123.

50 Ibid: 124.

51 Luce Irigaray, *Elemental Passions* (New York: Routledge, 1992): 49.

52 Shirley Neuman, "Introduction", in Shirley Neuman (ed), *Autobiography and Questions of Gender* (London: Frank Cass, 1991): 4.

Echo and voice in *Meetings with Anna*

Ivone Margulies

That is what the time when my mother was alive *before me* is
– History. (Roland Barthes)[1]

Les Rendez-vous d'Anna (*Meetings with Anna*, 1978) displays Chantal
Akerman's filmic trade mark: a simple narrative is structured with such
a heightened degree of visual and aural order that one may miss its
broader ambitions – to place personal and historical issues on an equal,
narrative footing. The film's episodic structure describes Anna's (Aurore
Clément) wanderings as she travels from Paris to Essen and back. She
is a filmmaker with some of Akerman's biographical traits. She is
Belgian, lives in Paris, and has a Polish-Jewish family who escaped the
Holocaust. As Anna travels to promote her film in a small-scale theatre,
"one sees nothing of her activity related more immediately to cinema,
not shooting, not actors nor producers...She has adventures...with
different characters who...tell her their stories, short tales since she is
just passing through".[2] We see her in hotel rooms, train stations,
platforms and corridors, and it is only in the final scene, when she
comes home to her apartment in Paris, that we get a real sense of how
transient Anna's routine is. One of the messages she listens to on her
answering machine details her forthcoming work schedule: "You
should attend the following meetings: Saturday at Lausanne, Sunday in
Geneva, Monday in Zürich. Your hotels are reserved, the thirteenth in
Lausanne...".

The character's nomadism is basic to the film's shape. Anna
encounters five other characters, the meetings following in a block
sequence: Heinrich, a German high-school teacher whom she meets
after her screening at the Roxy, and with whom she has an interrupted
one-night stand; Ida, who moved back from Brussels to Cologne, the
mother of Anna's former fiancé; a stranger she meets in the train,
himself a drifter who intends to settle in Paris; her mother in a train
stop in Brussels; and Daniel, her lover, when she returns to Paris. Each
encounter corresponds to a new scene or sequence, with a clear
division of labour between silence and text, listener and talker, Anna
and the others.

According to Akerman, the protagonist's nomadism and celibacy (in the sense of remaining single) free her to move away from the usual system of possession, from conservative values.[3] Her movement is meant to trigger a larger cultural and historical resonance: "behind...the insignificant events that [Anna] will be told about we shall see the shape of great collective events, the history of countries, the history of Europe and its last 50 years".[4]

This ambitious project takes shape in a film that impresses us first for its bare linear sobriety, for its almost invariably symmetrical shot composition and a camera that stays fixed or tracks the horizontality of trains or the deep space of hotel and train corridors. But it is Anna's countenance that provokes us most. In its emoted opacity, her semi-absorbed attentiveness as she listens to her interlocutors activates a mixed flow of private confessions and European malaise.

In terms of its homogeneous texture, oblique *mise en scène* frontality, and emphasis on denaturalised dialogue, *Meetings with Anna* displays the radical antinaturalism of Eric Rohmer and Robert Bresson.[5] And yet, the film was generically labelled a "European art film", comparable, in its theme and episodic linearity, with 1970s existentialist road-movies such as Wim Wenders' *Im Lauf der Zeit* (*Kings of the Road*, 1976) and *Alice in den Städten* (*Alice in the Cities*, 1974). Given its production history, as well as its relative polish – this was Akerman's first film to be distributed by Gaumont – the film was felt, at the time of its release and in the context of Akerman's trajectory as an avant-garde narrative filmmaker, as something of an aesthetic compromise.[6]

Nevertheless, it is this apparently restrained film that poses a number of issues at the core of Akerman's project.[7] If Anna's wanderings seem to conform to the more conventional episodic mode of the road-movie genre, the film's serial structure is pointedly transgressive. Structured in blocks of encounter-sequences and extended dialogues that operate rather as monologues, the film accumulates as a parade of speeches. These dialogues-qua-monologues list, moreover, in the same breath, intimate revelations and sweeping historical statements. By formally equating minor and major issues, Akerman's minimalist series would seem to support the filmmaker's desire to weave personal and historical matters. While this project is itself an important departure from usual film setting, in which personal situations are played out against the background of pressing historical and political events, it is paramount to investigate the awkward composite generated by Akerman's minimalist aesthetics. As I have discussed elsewhere, Akerman's series promotes an anti-hierarchical structure which produces not actual equality, but its simulacrum.[8] Are we supposed to believe that historical and private issues are equally significant, since they follow in a series? Or is this supposed equation of personal and historical issues meant to distinguish these categories even more sharply, and therefore expose the conventional view of history as a narrative of grand events?

This essay addresses not only the filmmaker's intentions, but also the actual effects of Akerman's formal strategies. It tracks a dual movement: Anna's drifting, maybe at its clearest when she pauses to listen, and the verbal current which her passage disseminates. The filmmaker's project is best understood, therefore, if one is attentive to nuances of the dialogue. Akerman's *mise en scène* and, in particular, her unequal distribution of text are of special interest in a film that pitches two versions of verbal address against each other: *the echo* – the monologues directed at Anna are loaded with past reverberations – and *Anna's voice and her silence*. Because this confrontation unfolds through the open simplicity of a linear trajectory, I want to begin by tracking Anna across the geography it maps.

Akerman's Europe: a minimalist Jewish history

Meetings with Anna is Akerman's film on Europe. It displays the filmmaker's repeated inquiry into the effects of dislocation: "The film is about displaced persons: economic, sexual and artistic refugees... Anna is an exile, a nomad who possesses nothing but the space through which she travels".[9] The film's theme, of a trans-European traveller, and its international cast – Lea Massari, Aurore Clément, Hanns Zischler – further reinforce the film's generic European ground.

Meetings with Anna is also Akerman's most Jewish film. The European ground mapped by Anna is part of a longer trajectory consistently present in the filmmaker's work, a path whose main poles are Eastern Europe and the United States. Several of her films are located either in New York – *Hotel Monterey* (1972), *News from Home* (1976) and *Histoires D'Amérique* (*American Stories/Food, Family and Philosophy*, 1989) – or in Belgium and Paris – *Jeanne Dielman, 23 quai du Commerce, 1080 Bruxelles* (1975), *Toute une nuit* (*All Night Long*, 1982), *Je tu il elle* (*I...You...He...She*, 1974) and *Nuit et jour* (*Night and Day*, 1991). That Akerman has lived in these cities does not entirely explain them as location choices. For the filmmaker's thematic path is symptomatic of a nomadic sensibility attuned to a particular cultural and historical background, and *News from Home*, *D'Est* (*From the East*, 1993) and *American Stories/Food, Family and Philosophy* have insisted on the history beneath this migrant geography.[10] Belgium, for instance, matters less as an European country than as an East-West migratory path towards the United States, a trajectory with a specific significance in Ashkenazic Jewish history. And, although *From the East* is not explicitly about Jewishness, Akerman's sensitivity to the faces, crowds and lines shown in the film reveals her awareness of the parallel image track into which she was tapping. Her referent is clear: "Our imaginary is charged with Eastern Europe. At each face I felt a history...the camps,

Stalin, denunciation".[11] It is always the same thing that reveals itself: images of "evacuation, of marches in the snow with packages toward an unknown place, faces and bodies placed one besides the other".[12] Akerman's interest in this moment of the breakup of the Soviet bloc, triggered initially by her desire to make a film on the poet Anna Akhmatova,[13] further connects Jewish and Eastern European themes: the Pale of the Settlement, where most Jews were living at the turn of the century, and from where the greatest migrations to the United States took place, was located in Poland, at that time a Russian province. Her affinity with this geography is directly related to her own history, her parents having moved from Poland to Belgium in the 1930s.

Meetings with Anna articulates the mix of curiosity and defamiliarisation for a nation (Germany), on the part of a transnational individual (a wandering Jewish woman) in all its intricate, post-Holocaust reverberations. Several scenes reveal the degree to which the film's trajectory – train trips to Essen and then back – is the surface version of another mode of dislocation, one that rather involves an historical dimension.

Anna's relation to German food is a case in point: she loses her appetite at the Cologne station's restaurant; she picks some *petit pois* from a plate left outside a man's room in her hotel; and, after her meal at Heinrich's house (elided), she comments that she ate little because there was too much food. Akerman's wariness converts the German food into an indigestible excess. When scouting for location for the film, she felt that "the food, the German language, were familiar to [her] but [that she] felt towards Germany a sort of a rejection".[14] In another scene, this contradictory relation is graphically demonstrated. Anna crosses a series of train cars as she returns to Paris repeating the film's serial structure – blocks of scenes that succeed each other in a linear fashion. She wanders the entire length of the train, moving from First to Economy Class, to Second Class and then back. We see her looking into each of the Second Class cabins, and then, as she struggles to pass through a crowded corridor in the Economy Class, the camera follows closer to her. Squeezed and blocked from going further, she suddenly turns back, condensing in this scene the mix of interest and estrangement which Akerman herself registers more than a decade later in *From the East*: in the latter film, the crowds' massive movement becomes an image for forced relocation.

Akerman's initial motivation for *Meetings with Anna* was narrower in scope. At first, she wanted to focus on a mother who surprises her daughter with a visit to Paris and discovers her daughter's world. In her writing, Akerman was paralysed with the weight of this encounter. After she created a character who travels, and realised that Brussels (the mother's city) could be represented, at least geographically, as a centre

in the daughter's trajectory between Germany and France, she felt she
could justify the meeting as a momentary return to the mother. By
placing it as a natural stop on Anna's way home, in a series following
three other rendezvous, she structurally dedramatises this encounter.[15]

The film's main problematics – that of individual and collective
displacement – is central to the filmmaker's œuvre, and here it is
attached to another key Akerman question: when the daughter moves
away, does the mother's body remain a centre? And, if not, are the
daughter's movements all the freer for that? Anna's escape from social
ties – from marriage, a fixed sexual preference, having children – is
confirmed at each meeting. Besieged by social and romantic demands,
she responds with a clear detachment. She rejects Heinrich in the midst
of making out, with a remark that seems full of idealism: "We don't
love each other". And yet, when he states his fantasies on meeting her,
she declares, tenderly and off-frame, her lack of romantic illusions: she
tells him how she, too, when lonely, used to confuse love with
physical contact. When she meets Ida, the older woman renews the
sense of Anna's inexplicable singleness. She insists that Anna get back
together with her son (even though Anna has broken her engagement
to him twice). "Don't you want children? With you one never knows",
she states bitterly. And finally, although Anna's encounter with Daniel
reveals a sense of past intimacy, it also displays their divergent feelings
about a common future. When he mentions, for instance, that he
should move to a larger apartment in case he has children, she
candidly asks if he plans to have them.

On the other hand, Akerman's vague and generic references to
history interlace Europe's contemporary crisis (the economic slump
referred to by her mother and Ida; Daniel's existential void) with the
haunting presence of the past, of the Holocaust. Each monologue
pivots around this confluence. Heinrich, the German teacher, takes
Anna to meet his daughter in his house in a neighbouring town, and,
as they linger in the garden, he turns to Anna and makes an
unexpected revelation telling her his life story – his comfortable,
passive relationship with his wife; his wife's relationship with the dark
Turk with whom she has eloped; the pleasure he used to take in
singing *Don Giovanni* with his friend Hans, before he was fired from
his job. He begins to list recent events in German history: "In the '20s
there were the Communists...and then in '33...the war...the peace...the
reconstruction". "And then", he says, "one day my friend lost his job
and I lost my friend, such a nice man. What have they done to my
country?". Heinrich's historical account noticeably elides any mention
of the word "Jew". When he mentions those murdered by the Nazis, he
names only Communists, and one assumes that his friend was a leftist
sympathiser in a West Germany wary of leftists.

The lack of specific reference to the Jews repeats itself at other points, creating, at times, an intimate, delicate effect. When Anna meets Ida, her mother's best friend, their common ground is rather reinforced by the absence of direct references to being Jewish. Ida has returned to Germany after living for 25 years in Belgium after the war. Her comment, "we need to forgive them", is the sum of her remarks on the Nazis. She mentions no camps, only the war. At several points we gather that Anna and Ida share common origins. When Ida mentions how happy she is with her refound language, Anna remarks that she thought she was Polish (in Belgium, she already met Ida, a friend of her mother, a displaced Jew). Ida's knowledge of German – she listens to the train delay announcement and reports it to Anna – is countered by Anna's remark that she understood it (presumably because of the common roots of Yiddish and German languages). Perhaps an even more accurate Jewish identity card is given through Ida's litany of complaints, soft recriminations, all related to the Jewish obsession with having a family.

Slowly, these monologues, echoing one another in their plaintive sonority, construe a troubled portrait of Europe. The crisis extends beyond the past of the Second World War or present-day economics. Daniel is successful, but he is undergoing a crisis of faith. His Judaism is telegraphed in a trite reference to the lost happiness of the promised land of milk and honey. As he bitterly characterises his predicament, he typifies his generation (of 1960s French intellectuals) by moving from a biblical terminology into a disillusioned discourse on the failure of Socialist hopes.

The filmmaker's attempt to create a work in which history and geography do not form the backdrop for individual stories, and instead become temporal and spatial strata of a personal-collective narrative, parallels Gilles Deleuze and Félix Guattari's theories in *Kafka: Toward a Minor Literature*.[16] In this book, they develop new concepts to account for Kafka's dry economical aesthetics, as well as for its collective import. His is an example of a minor literature, one produced by a minoritarian culture from within a majoritarian context, and its "cramped space...forces each individual intrigue to connect immediately to politics".[17] His Jewishness, inflecting his use of German towards a reduced, concentrated form, suggests, for Deleuze and Guattari, the general implications of nomadism (the constant migrations of Jews) for a deterritorialised form of expression. Nomadism is discussed in terms of food and writing. Food is linked to a fixed place, that of planting and harvest, and territorialisation connotes an attachment to family and to conservative values. Conversely, writing – the use of language, and the creative act – results in exile, a deterritorialisation from social conventions (although not all writing is necessarily deterritorialised).

In asserting her own (as well as her character's) transnationalism as a by-product of her Jewishness, Akerman tries to create a sense of identity outside of notions of fixed boundaries, in nomadism. She strongly distinguishes Anna's wanderings from the nostalgic search for identity present in Wenders' films: "Anna's trip through Northern Europe is not a romantic voyage, nor one of initiation or learning...It is her work that makes her travel, but one could almost say of Anna that she has a vocation for exile".[18] Her care in defining her character's Jewish identity as the source of a nomadic fluidity, presents, however, the same problems as the philosophers' notion of deterritorialisation. Their careful distinctions between minor and minority reveal that the notion of identity is still what is at stake. For, even as they describe deterritorialisation as a movement away from one's origins, they need to identify a group from which a minor literature may issue its collective message.[19] These minorities had to make use of a major language as a result of some past, forced relocation (Jews or African Americans, for instance), and it is in part this power imbalance that defines the specific collective charge which their discourse may attain. While Deleuze and Guattari posit values issuing from a minority condition, they caution that displacement *per se* or a minority identity may not necessarily produce a minor literature. The question remains, for Anna and for us, as to what exactly is being produced in her historically displaced nomadism.

We can suggest one of the outcomes of Anna's wandering: the creation of a personal European history. Inflected with Akerman's own ambivalence towards Jewish tradition, Anna's passage is meant both to activate Jewish references and to indicate that a substantial change of gears is taking place.

Meetings with Anna presents several instances in which both the search for and the flight from a fixed identity are present simultaneously. The film combines denial – the word "Jewish" is never mentioned – and assertive pride, as when Anna's refers to the clearly biblical names her daughters would have borne (Judith and Rebecca) had they not been aborted. That they were aborted, as Anna explains, "because it was not the right time", somewhat qualifies the radicality of Anna as a "mutant" being, opting out of familial ties. At the same time, through her scenario, Akerman "aborts" Judith and Rebecca, in a perverse notation of her desire and ambivalence for the continuance of tradition.

Through the character, Akerman asserts her Jewishness and also plays a variation on the wandering Jew. For Anna's spatial crossing delineates, in fact, a temporal, historical gap. As she travels from Essen to Cologne, from Brussels to Paris, the conversations constantly refer to a set of past, worn-out values which seem as alien to Anna as hers are to her interlocutors. If Anna bypasses the issue of national, territorial identity, she certainly confronts – in fact, insists upon – the difficulty of secularisation. The problem posed to a contemporary secular Jewish woman is how to transgress the law, one that is based less on religion than on the permanence of tradition and family values. The yearning to remain single and the acknowledgment of territorialising pressures (to marry, for instance) lead both Kafka and Anna to break their engagements, not "once but twice". Anna's nomadism and singleness – explicable in part through her bisexual preferences – are, in the context of Jewish traditions, transgressive.

But it is rather in small instances of avoidance and resistance, spread out over a few films, that Akerman's conflicted attempt to inflect her Jewish identity with a sense of deterritorialisation is most noticeable. In her video, *Lettre d'un cinéaste* (*Letter from a Filmmaker*, 1984), she verbally asserts her "defiance" of the Jewish proscription of image-creation ("Thou shalt not make...a graven image, or any likeness of anything that is in heaven...or that is in the earth" [Exodus 20: 4]). She is, after all, an image-maker. When, however, the time comes to sign her video epistle, she mollifies her rebellious stance: she considers "Chantal, Chantal Akerman or Akerman *tout court*...My father wanted a boy...let's sign Akerman to give him pleasure". In *American Stories/ Food, Family and Philosophy*, a film composed of vignettes in which stories and jokes are told under the Brooklyn Bridge by recent immigrants from Eastern Europe, Akerman's voice-over starts by telling a tale about remembrance over images of a ferry approaching Manhattan. The tale recounts how each generation displays a progressive loss of memory: from a pious great-grandfather to his great-grandson, there is a growing difficulty in remembering a particular spot for a prayer, and then finally the prayer itself. The filmmaker-storyteller concludes that, since she does not even have a child, the way to maintain Jewish tradition lies in telling tales about remembering a prayer instead. This passage is poignant in its all-too-explicit substitution of fiction (telling stories, making films) for personal (and tradition-anchoring) experience.[20]

The conflict which she experiences between following and ignoring her cultural/religious background becomes an important motive in Akerman's exploration of the representative dimension of individual, banal events. Her mother's letters in *News from Home* exemplify, for Akerman, a minor form of expression, a subculture – of Jewish mothers' addresses – which she dialogically superimposes over her own avant-garde filmic subculture.[21] Personal expression attains a collective resonance through this collage-reply.

In *Meetings with Anna*, the combination of the personal and historical registers is more strained and more apparent. There is a clumsy quality to Akerman's dialogues here, as they force major issues onto intimate revelations. There is a gaucheness in delivery, and the telescoped historical references generate a peculiarly loaded text. Heinrich's speech is especially telling in this regard. The fragmentary

German history which he recounts to Anna contains nothing more than a compendium of generic knowledge, common verities shared not only by Heinrich and Anna, but also by a whole post-Holocaust consciousness. The connecting phrase "and then" ("et puis") makes up the bulk of this list.

Indeed, the film's platitudinous references to grand historical matters are the target of those critics who are confused by Akerman's reductive strategies. Joël Magny, for instance, complains that "it is as if Chantal Akerman could not blend the different messages (too explicit? too insistent? too...) into the banality of the everyday, nor could she neutralise them so as to eliminate their totalitarian character".[22] That the film does not "blend the different messages" is, however, intentional. Rather than a failure in fusing different informational registers, *Meetings with Anna* is another example of the radicality achieved by Akerman's minimalist reductions. The estrangement of Akerman's minimalism results from the formal collapse of two different registers or orders that segue from each other, despite their categorical incompatibility. The film orchestrates variable densities of content – intimate revelations, historical references, contemporary *angst*, as well as Anna's restrained responses – into an "impossible" coexistence. It is this *awkward coincidence*, emphatically promoted by the film, that finally distinguishes Anna from the others.

The forced, uneasy proximity between personal and historical matters is key to Akerman's minimalist writing of a Jewish European history. Akerman's minimalist *mise en scène* – we mostly see Anna and another character; we mostly hear one talking while the other remains silent – supports this general awkwardness in address as the only appropriate form for a thematics of displacement. An exploration of the film's verbal addresses illuminates the nature of Anna's alternative.

A woman's voice

Meetings with Anna moves with Anna. And yet the film's pace hinges more on Anna's pauses than on her motions. As she waits for the reception desk to confirm her placement of a call to Prato, she pauses for a few seconds for what is an extraordinary moment of temporal suspension. Anna's countenance is, at this instant, utterly void so as to let time register.

Other pauses and hesitations, all part of a distended representation of the everyday, are supposed to deglamourise the blond woman's trip. Anna's inspection of the hotel room's bathroom is an example. On the other hand, the choice of a blond Hitchcockian woman was meant as a "distillation, a stylisation": to avoid naturalism, to avoid a "pseudo-real" character, and thus further to defamiliarise Anna as a Jew.[23]

Travelling alone, Anna is naturally quiet. But this silence gives way to an odd prolixity, especially with the hotel personnel.[24] An example of this is her discovery, in the closet, of a tie, which she immediately reports and whose origin she suggests to the hotel's concierge. She describes its colour and fabric, and deduces that it must be from the gentleman who is sitting at the lobby drinking a beer. This and other unwarranted exchanges initiate a progressively uneven dialogue format as the film takes on its overly extended talk-block format.

As I argue in *Nothing Happens*, Akerman confronts cinematic naturalism through her characters' verbal addresses.[25] In *Meetings with Anna*, she typically prolongs each communication, so that the naturalised back-and-forth rhythm of dialogues comes undone. Akerman parades her aversion for the shot/reverse-shot pattern, by also denying its aural complement: the camera remains on both characters, as one character talks and the other listens. The monologues' length creates an instability in the film's verbal *mise en scène*, so that for long stretches of time Anna becomes a relay for the audience. Her passivity as an auditor creates an effect in which words are directed back towards the spectator.

The film's dialogue-qua-monologue structure is not conversational. At the same time that the monologues' extension channels them to an extra-diegetic dimension (in which both audience and character are addressed), they are manipulated, in content and in delivery, to convey redundancy. Akerman searches for a repetitive structure in which the relative distinction of each word or phrase is engulfed by the monologue's monotone. She has stated her interest in transforming dialogue into a litany, a bla-bla-bla, repeatedly writing in "phrases such as 'because' and 'and then' so that the dialogue becomes a refrain" with a rhythm.[26] Her attempt is to reduce the dialogues, both in form and in content to "a psalmody where the meaning of sentences should not really count".[27] The analogy promoted is with a biblical murmur: "And God spake thus, and God spake thus, and God spake thus again...I used to go to the synagogue with my grandfather, and to Jewish school, everywhere it was the same rhythm".[28]

The consistent use of platitudes, the acknowledgment by characters that they reiterate former statements, and the emphasis on a recitational tone confirm repetition – in form and in content – as Akerman's favoured instrument to void signification. All historical references follow Akerman's characteristic use of the cliché – a reminder that content is repeated as form. In her meeting with the stranger in the train, Anna responds with a verbal amen, "So they say", at each of the clichéd remarks about the countries in which he has tried to live: Belgium ("They say it is a country of plenty"), France ("They say it is the country of freedom") and South America (the climate is "hot and humid"). And, in Ida's repeated complaints, one hears the word "again" repeatedly: "I ask you again, for the last time...marry my son".

This type of exchange yields an interesting paradox, however, for the monologues' very length implies a relevance for what is said. If Akerman wants to flatten the dialogue's importance, her reliance on recitation and clichés creates instead a parallel register for verbal reception. Through a vague association with music and chant – songs and religious litanies being shared, collective forms of expression – the film's monologues bridge subtly, and by means of language, the personal and collective registers of one's experience.

Akerman's use of platitudes is therefore reductive only on the surface. Heinrich's speech moves from an intimate revelation of his private life – how his wife left him for a Turk – to history. His talk may not release new information, but his recitation of bookish milestones alongside the traumatic event of his wife's abandonment has the effect of reducing text to tale. And, as we hear this summary version of history, it attains the unconscious force of songs known by heart. This refrain quality, which Akerman calls "psalmodic", and which Deleuze and Guattari identify as the main element in a territorial demarcation (like birdsong or children's limericks),[29] is constant in Akerman's dialogues-qua-monologues: the content of each speech, enveloped by rhythm and repetition, is transmuted into an expression at the service of another, more diffuse signification. Heinrich's informationally null list of grand events, placed in a more private confessional series, contaminates history with a fatigued isolation.

Meetings with Anna's dialogue does not, and is not meant to, convey historical information. Rather, it activates a temporal layer in discourse. The historical dimension, personal and collective, telegraphed in what Heinrich, Ida, the train passenger and Daniel say, creates, in its reduced content, a pervasive sense of weariness, a void that perfectly complements Anna's own stillness as she listens to them. And yet, it is deceptive to equate talker and listener. For these characters' despair is meant as a foil to Anna's self-containment, as she finally passes on.

When, after her fifth meeting, she returns home, she lies down, faces the front and intermittently presses the button of her answering machine. In a miniaturised version of her rendezvous, the disembodied voices remind her of new dates, regret that she is not there, talk about other professional and personal commitments. One of the messages brings us to Anna's own continually missed connection to Prato in Italy. Throughout the film, she has tried to call her woman friend in Italy, with no results. "Anna, dove sta?" ("Anna, where are you?"), says the accented Italian voice.

This absence phantasmically produced by a machine is Akerman's way of condensing the formal economy proposed in the film. The verbal prolixity of each monologue is perfectly matched by Anna's opaque expression. As Anna listens to messages that promise new misencounters, the film intimates, in a perfect closure, Anna's share in this ronde of malaises. Her nomadism is the mechanism that releases the particular European reverberation found in the text – a weariness that envelops the present with history.

And yet, Anna is on a different track. Akerman has suggested that Anna "is on a line of flight, which is not a flight from the world, but rather a manner of anticipating what will become our future, a sort of mutant".[30] Her diverging course is made clear through her attitude as she listens to her various interlocutors. The nature of her attention is questionable, since Anna seems to be always elsewhere as she quietly listens to these stories. At times, the concentration of function – she is solely a listener – creates a sympathetic presence. Mostly, however, this emotion is mixed with a polite but distanced concern.

Although Akerman employs a frontality for the characters in relation to the camera similar to the one employed in classical Hollywood narrative, the overall effect of this position could not be more different. The film's fixed-perspective medium-long shots, coupled with the characters' oblique relation to the camera, elicit a staged distance. At other times, the characters face each other, but their bodies are symmetrically posed in the frame, and they are totally or slightly turned to the front. Whatever their focus of attention within the film, therefore, they create a strong sense of a third, crucial axis – that of the camera.

This dialogical deflection is purposeful. Akerman has explained how Anna's understanding should not be an attempt to erase the difference in another person's statement. To claim to understand "would seem more humane", but it would mean a failed attempt to cover a void in the other's speech.[31]

Her two last encounters, conspicuously different from the others, help explain Anna's "mutant" quality. Akerman has remarked that "the only realist characters Anna meets are Daniel and her mother".[32] She refers here to the more psychologically convincing nature of their monologue style. But Anna also reacts differently. Her emotion seems more focused, and in these meetings we also hear more of her voice.

It is only to her mother that Anna speaks about herself. Her account of her lesbian initiation is superbly simple. As they lie naked in bed, her mother starts: "Tell me" ("Raconte"). And Anna tells of her routine of exhibiting her work, having occasional affairs, spending lonely nights in hotel rooms – information that sums up what we have seen so far. In the middle of this account, she gets more specific: "Once she came to the hotel after a show and we went out for a drink...we kissed...made love...and strangely enough I thought about you". Her mother pauses in silence, and then they start reminiscing about the past: "you were such a well-behaved girl", says Anna's mother.

The suspended question posed by Anna's Italian friend – "Anna, where are you?" – finds in this scene an answer of sorts. Anna's revelation problematises her nomadism, suddenly interrupting, in its intimacy, a carefully controlled series. By establishing an analogy between her mother's and her female lover's bodies, this encounter betrays the source of Anna's romantic fantasies, creating a strong imaginary ground, in Prato/Brussels, for her continual movement. At the same time, Akerman makes clear that Anna's affair is a sign of freedom, rather than an exclusive sexual preference that would explain her wish to remain single.

The second scene involves Anna's arrival in Paris. Daniel comes to pick her up, they go to a hotel (he says he cannot stand his apartment), and, after a long speech on his existential impasse, he asks Anna to sing for him.

Dressed in a white towel robe, Anna stands in the centre of the room, as a television flickers its blue empty light by her side. Daniel reminds her that she wanted to be a chanteuse; she replies that she sings out of tune. After a short pause, she chooses an Edith Piaf song about two lovers who commit suicide. The song's ballad tone contrasts increasingly with the lyrics:

I wash glasses in the back of the café...and in this décor so banal one can cry...It seems still I can see them come...They arrived hand-in-hand, wonder in their eyes...bringing the sun they asked for...a roof under which they could love...in the heart of the city, and...when I closed the door on them, there was so much sun in the back of their eyes that it hurt me...that it hurt me...I wash glasses...la la la...in this décor so banal...la la la they found them body against body, holding hand-in-hand their closed eyes gazing other mornings full of sun they were put to sleep, united and tranquil in a grave-like bed...at the heart of the city...

After the song, the film shifts, for the first time, in its representation of Anna. Anna approaches Daniel and, at his request, lies naked on top of him who remains dressed. Then, after noticing that he has a temperature, she goes out in search of medicine. In the taxi, we see Anna through one of the few close-up shots in the film, as the tears softly roll down her face. The symmetry and parallel movements of train tracks and corridors are substituted for an expressive, sinuous driving through Paris in search of a pharmacy. The film's formal rigour is abandoned, somehow foreshadowing its closure. After she tenderly cares for Daniel, an abrupt cut takes us to Anna's arrival home.

Although this moment stands out in the film, I would suggest that the film's emotional and intellectual core lies in Anna's singing. Sparingly heard throughout the film, Anna's (dubbed) voice is devoted here to soothe the plaintive sing-song heard throughout the film.

Written and performed as worn-out recapitulations, the monologues compare unfavourably with what a woman says, with her voice and her silence.[33]

Consisting mostly of demands and complaints, the monologues acquire an echo quality, as if they are repeated from the past. We know that, for Akerman, these refrains find their exact expression in the religious litany, and that the filmmaker's understanding of history continuously pivots towards the transition from (Jewish) tradition to secular existence. An example of this interest is Akerman's project of adapting Isaac Bashevis Singer's sequel books, *The Manor* and *The Estate*, after she made *Meetings with Anna*. The novels portray specifically the period from 1880 to 1930, the move at the turn of the century from villages to cities, from tradition and religion to secular intellectual concerns.[34] In her film proposal, Akerman explains the book's affective value, and how it animates her relation to history. "I had the impression", she says, "it spoke of me, my family, my history, that it addressed me personally".[35] It is this Jewish European experience that colours Akerman's perceptions of her mother's time, unequivocally marked by the Holocaust; it also inflects the filmmaker's depiction of the existential impasses of France and Germany of 1978, as well as the dissolution of the Soviet Union in *From the East*. In the installation, *Bordering on Fiction: Chantal Akerman's "D'Est"* (1995-96), Akerman's voice reads the passage from the Book of Exodus on the proscription of images in Jewish tradition, bringing the complex nexus of abeyance and transgression full circle. Diasporic movements (provoked, or not, by persecution) intersect a long history of secularisation, and it is this crux that charges Akerman's imaginary.

Formally, the filmmaker's minimalism translates the multiple reverberations of these "great collective events" into personal statements. These temporal ripples (vague in information, but charged with intensity) significantly shape the filmmaker's modernist aesthetics: the monologues' echo-effect allows her to convert meaning into a formal series that eventually accumulates as an affective mass. These reverberations of history also help Akerman thematise, through the character, her own sense of inheritance.

The representation of Anna is necessarily different. Anna may share her interlocutors' space but she certainly does not share their sense of history. Akerman construes this historical frame as an abridged, albeit dense, notation: the monologues addressed to Anna include a post-Holocaust malaise, Jewish traditions and, as a measure of the filmmaker's feminism, a normative patriarchal load. Both Ida and Anna's mother – as well as all the men in the film – unquestioningly display patriarchal expectations. Throughout the film, Akerman gently turns this naturalised form of history against her male characters. Their passivity is a sign that they accept Anna's leaving almost as a deserved response to their own anachronism. As she rejects this legacy, Anna is set apart in a subtle feminist punctuation.

"There is nothing more beautiful than a woman's voice, a woman singing", says Daniel, after he mentions his desire to be ruled by another time, a woman's rhythm, marrying, getting pregnant, and simply following the baby's feeding demands. His fantasy of passivity is answered by Anna's correction – at the start, babies get fed every three hours, and not every two. This remark is once more supposed to check established patriarchal misconceptions. That Anna's singing ensues is significant. As she complies with Daniel's desire to be soothed, her choice of song suggests a perverse twist on the maternal-feminine lullaby-function: an embittered despair leaks from under the "la-la-la" lightness of Piaf's melody, as Anna's voice gently states her resistance to conventional romance and its attendant inequalities.

The film's ending with the answering machine announces another round of misencounters. Its circularity disallows any truly liberating prospect for Anna's wanderings.[36] And yet, what stays with us as we watch the film is an opaque, tender presence. In her semi-absorbed attentiveness, Anna pays her dues to a sense of the past as she subtly traces her own course.

Notes

[1] Roland Barthes, *Camera Lucida: Reflections on Photography*, translated by Richard Howard (New York: Hill and Wang, 1981): 65. Emphasis in original.

[2] Translated from the French: "On ne verra rien de son activité qui relève plus immédiatement du cinéma, ni tournage, ni acteurs, ni producteurs... Comme un marin, elle aura des aventures sans lendemain avec des personnages différents qui vont lui raconter leurs histoires, leurs petites histoires parce qu'elle ne fait que passer". Chantal Akerman, synopsis of *Meetings with Anna*, in Caroline Champetier, "Rencontre avec Chantal Akerman: 'Les Rendez-vous d'Anna'", *Cahiers du Cinéma* 288 (May 1978): 53.

[3] Chantal Akerman, "Entretien avec Chantal Akerman", in Jacqueline Aubenas (ed), *Chantal Akerman* (Brussels: Atelier des Arts, 1982): 17.

[4] Translated from the French: "Mais derrière les petites affaires qui lui seront confiées, nous verrons se dessiner les grandes affaires collectives, l'histoire des pays, l'histoire de l'Europe de ces cinquantes dernières années". Akerman, in Champetier: 53.

[5] Distinctly linear, these filmmakers' narrative contrasts with the programmatic anti-illusionism of Godard's collage aesthetics.

[6] Jonathan Rosenbaum remarks that the film "bypasses the avant-garde to

adopt the rather different familiarity of the 35mm European art film". Jonathan Rosenbaum, "Getting Personal in Milwaukee", *American Film* 4: 10 (September 1979): 66. Louis Skorecki notes that the film's instances of failure are "a measure of the ambition – more clearly commercial than the preceding films of Akerman...more sentimental, a cinema geared to pleasure" ("la mesure de l'ambition – plus nettement commerciale que dans le précédents films d'Akerman...plus sentimentale – d'un cinéma de plaisir"). See Louis Skorecki, "De Handke (La femme gauchère) à Akerman (Les rendez-vous d'Anna): Points de vue", *Cahiers du Cinéma* 295 (December 1978): 38; J Hoberman remarks that, as a film, "Anna is neither as radical nor as challenging as Dielman or Akerman's 'city symphony' *News From Home*... Anna synthesizes aspects of its precursors for more popular consumption". J Hoberman, "MOMA's got a Brand New Bag", *The Village Voice* 30 April 1979: 54; and, finally, Godard uses the epithet "Gaumont" to characterise all he perceives as compromised in *Meetings with Anna*. Jean-Luc Godard, "Entretien sur un projet: Chantal Akerman", *Ça Cinéma* 19 (1980): 5-16.

7   The film's autobiographical import is one such issue. For a filmmaker who has not hesitated in appearing in her work – as voice or body – the use of an actress to play a role so closely referenced to herself seems to magnify the issue of fictional translation. For the filmmaker's objections to such a label, see Michèle Levieux, "Propos de Chantal Akerman", *Écran* 78: 75 (15 December 1978): 50. For a discussion of Akerman's self-representation, see Ivone Margulies, *Nothing Happens: Chantal Akerman's Hyperrealist Everyday* (Durham, NC; London: Duke University Press, 1996): 162-163.

8   Margulies. See mainly chapters 3 and 4, and conclusion.

9   Akerman quoted in Linda Gross, "Emotion Focused Wide Screen", *The Los Angeles Times* 8 November 1979: 30.

10   This geographical-historical nexus is discussed in a chapter on *American Stories/Food, Family and Philosophy* and *From the East* in Margulies: 192-203.

11   Translated from the French: "Notre imaginaire est chargé sur l'Europe de L'Est. À chaque visage je sens une histoire...les camps, Staline, la dénonciation". Akerman quoted in Annick Peigne-Giuly, "Face-à-face avec L'Est", *Libération* 18 September 1993: 37.

12   Translated from the French: "[images] d'évacuation, de marches dans la neige avec des paquets vers un lieu inconnu, de visages et de corps placés l'un à côté de l'autre". Akerman, text on *From the East*, promotional package.

13   For details on Akerman's *D'Est* installation project, see Kathy Halbreich and Bruce Jenkins (eds), *Bordering on Fiction: Chantal Akerman's D'Est* (Minneapolis: Walker Art Center, 1995): 7-12.

14   Translated from the French: "La nourriture, la langue allemande me sont familières, mais j'entretiens quand même avec l'Allemagne quelque chose du rejet". Levieux: 48.

15   Akerman, in Champetier: 53.

[16] Gilles Deleuze and Félix Guattari, *Kafka: Toward a Minor Literature*, translated by Dana Polan (Minneapolis: University of Minnesota Press, 1986). Akerman has referred to this book, as well as to its terminology, in several instances, but especially at the time of the release of *Meetings with Anna*. See Levieux; and Michèle Levieux, "Du Côté de Chez Kafka", *Écran* 78: 75 (15 December 1978): 45-46; Danièle Dubroux, Thérèse Giraud and Louis Skorecki, "Entretien avec Chantal Akerman", *Cahiers du Cinéma* 278 (July 1977): 34-42; Françoise Maupin, "Entretien avec Chantal Akerman", *La Revue du Cinéma/Image et Son* 334 (December 1978): 99-103.

[17] Deleuze and Guattari: 17.

[18] Translated from the French: "Le voyage qu'Anna effectue à travers l'Europe du Nord n'est pas un voyage romantique, ni de formation ou d'initiation...C'est son métier qui la fait voyager, mais on pourrait presque dire d'Anna qu'elle a la vocation de l'exil". Maupin: 101.

[19] Deleuze and Guattari: 16.

[20] Margulies: 195-197.

[21] Levieux: 49.

[22] Translated from the French: "Tout se passe comme si Chantal Akerman n'avait pu, cette fois, intégrer les différents messages (trop explicites? trop appuyés? trop...) à la banalité du quotidien, ni les neutraliser entre eux pour leur enlever tout caractère totalitaire". See Joël Magny, "Les Rendez-vous d'Anna: Le 'non' de l'auteur", *Cinéma* 78: 239 (November 1978): 93.

[23] Maupin: 102. While her first impulse was to chose someone dark for the role of Anna, Akerman decided that a less transparent (Hitchcockian) face was preferable. See Akerman, in Champetier: 55.

[24] Meg Morley has remarked on how "Anna's speech is out of step with the situations". See Meg Morley, "Les Rendez-Vous d'Anna (Chantal Akerman)", *Camera Obscura* 3/4 (summer 1979): 214.

[25] See Margulies: 149-161.

[26] Translated from the French: "moi je l'écris comme une psalmodie, avec des 'parce que', des 'et puis', plein de choses qui font que ce soit rond". Akerman, in Champetier: 55.

[27] Translated from the French: "une psalmodie sans que vraiment le sens des phrases compte". Ibid: 54.

[28] Translated from the French: "et Dieu dit que et Dieu dit que et Dieu dit encore...J'allais à la synagogue avec mon grand-père et je suis allée à l'école juive, partout c'était le même rythme". Ibid. Aware that she cannot exactly recover this rhythm, Akerman writes into her monologues little phrases that transform the entire performance into a litany.

[29] Gilles Deleuze and Félix Guattari, *A Thousand Plateaus: Capitalism and Schizophrenia*, translated by Brian Massumi (London: The Athlone Press,

1988): 312-325.

[30] Translated from the French: "Elle est sur une ligne de fuite, qui n'est pas une fuite du monde, mais plutôt une façon de devancer ce qui se prépare de notre proche avenir, *une sorte de mutante*". Akerman, in Aubenas (ed): 17. The term "line of flight" is a central Deleuzian-Guattarian concept.

· [31] Ibid. She claims that, in a so-called minor literature (cinema), one should not be annulled by an authoritarian voice: "Aurore represents...my character to a degree because she listens, she does not nullify the other, she does not look for a compromise". ("Aurore représente un peu mon personnage, parce qu'elle écoute, elle n'annule pas l'autre, elle ne cherche pas un terrain de compromis".) Maupin: 101.

[32] Translated from the French: "Les seuls personnages réalistes qu'Anna rencontre sont Daniel et sa mère". Akerman, in Champetier: 57.

[33] The simplicity of this oblique address may be compared, in its moving force, to the overall affect experienced in Carl Theodor Dreyer's *Gertrud* (1964), another film whose protagonist's voice (Gertrud was a professional singer), meant to please men, is nevertheless diverted elsewhere. In this favourite film of Akerman's, we watch a similar filmic structure to convey a woman's independent choice: a series of five meetings with three men in which Gertrud rejects them in name of an ideal love. The scenes are structured as extended conversations between two people, in which the characters stare into a blank space in front of them, rarely looking at each other. Their evacuated presence and self-absorption owe most immediately to the condition one assumes when attentively listening not simply to content, but to a mood, a sentiment, a memory. Most significantly, Gertrud's scenes all bear, flashback or not, the quality of a rememoration, its music chamber filmic space installing a "sort of echo...a sound capsule for...past troubles". See André Techine, "La parole de la fin", *Cahiers du Cinéma* 164 (March 1965): 72-73. Both *Meetings with Anna* and *Gertrud* are narratives of independent choice, and, although they use the notion of the echo differently, there is no doubt that a more extended comparison between the two films can illuminate the complicity between modernist and feminist narrative strategies. For extended discussions of Gertrud's musical structure and its implications, see Fabrice Revault d'Allonnes, *Gertrud de Carl Th. Dreyer* (Paris: Editions Yellow Now, 1988): 37-47; P Adams Sitney, *Modernist Montage: The Obscurity of Vision In Cinema and Literature* (New York: Columbia University Press, 1990): 73-80; *L'Avant Scène du Cinema* 335 (December 1984).

[34] Isaac Bashevis Singer, *The Manor* (New York: Farrar, Straus and Giroux, 1967); *The Estate* (New York: Farrar, Straus and Giroux, 1969).

[35] "J'avais l'impression qu'il parlait de moi, de ma famille, de mon histoire... qu'il m'interpellait personnellement". Akerman, "Le Manoir-Le Domaine", in Aubenas (ed): 143.

[36] See Morley: 215.

All Night Long: the ambivalent text of "Belgianicity"

Catherine Fowler

And I left, a small white room, level with the ground narrow
like a corridor, where I remain motionless, attentive, and lying
on my mattress...

Belgium left

With these opening lines in her first feature film, *Je tu il elle*
(*I...You...He...She*, 1974), Chantal Akerman maps out for herself a
cinema which is "condemned to wander".[1] Having blown up Brussels
in her first short film, *Saute ma ville*[2] (*Blow up My Town*, 1968), there
seems to be no option but to leave home, hence the premise of *I...
You...He...She*. In her next few films, Akerman explores other possible
settlements: New York City in *News from Home* (1976), or aspects of
Europe in *Les Rendez-vous d'Anna* (*Meetings with Anna*, 1978). Some
ten years later, Akerman is still wandering, returning to New York for
Histoires d'Amérique (*American Stories/Food, Family and Philosophy*,
1989), and even exploring her parents' Eastern European Jewish
imaginary in *D'Est* (*From the East*, 1993). Meanwhile, she undertakes
a Parisian elopement with *Golden Eighties/Window Shopping* (1986),
Nuit et jour (*Night and Day*, 1991) and *Un Divan à New York* (*A
Couch in New York*, 1996), all of which situate themselves in relation
to French cinema.

What is missing from this itinerary of Akerman's œuvre is a sense
of her relation to that place which originally had to be left: Belgium –
or, more accurately, Brussels. What has also been omitted from this
account are the moments when Akerman does return, namely for
Jeanne Dielman, 23 quai du Commerce, 1080 Bruxelles (1975) and
Toute une nuit (*All Night Long*, 1982). Perhaps one way of suggesting
Akerman's relation to Brussels is to ask why she had to leave the city.
In practical terms, there is a sense in which the small size of Belgium
makes even medium-budget film production difficult. Once Akerman
began to make larger-scale projects, therefore, she had to look outside
Belgium. Besides these practical reasons, however, more clues are
given if we examine Akerman's first film set in Brussels, *Jeanne
Dielman*.

Akerman has called *Jeanne Dielman* "a love film for my mother",[3] and what she depicts in the film is her loving remembrance of her mother's rituals and gestures. Much has been written on the desire for the mother as a key part of Akerman's early films: "If there is a recurring phantasmatic core to the work of Chantal Akerman it lies in the desire to reconstitute the image of, the voice of the mother".[4] However, the full complexity of this desire must be recognised, for the mother does not simply lead us towards a sexually different desire, as Brenda Longfellow suggests.[5] Instead, the mother is used to signify Akerman's Belgian and Jewish identities. Brussels becomes the mother-space, with Akerman's relation to Brussels therefore constructed through her mother. However, *Jeanne Dielman* can also be seen as the film from which each of Akerman's other films seeks to escape, as its image of domestic confinement is swiftly rejected in films which explore the cityspaces mentioned earlier. These films exchange the security and familiarity of Jeanne's daily routine for the rootless sense of alienation and non-belonging of a stranger in a strange city.

Akerman's wandering described above is accomplished only through the exchange of her mother's world, banished to the soundtrack in *News from Home*, for Akerman's own world. By extension, through its depiction in *Jeanne Dielman*, Brussels is cast as the city to be escaped from if one is to escape the life of one's mother. Brussels must be left in order to wander, as well as to be able to film. These two are actually closer than one might think; thus, in the beginning of the scenario to *Meetings with Anna*, Akerman writes: "Anna is a film-maker...we will never really know why...it could be only because that this allows and forces her to wander".[6] To film, therefore, is to travel.

However, *All Night Long* is more difficult to locate within this trajectory of departure, for the Brussels of *Jeanne Dielman* is very far from that represented in this later film. Differences exist in form, as well as in content, with the earlier film's system of anti-seduction being exchanged for an aesthetic which relentlessly seeks to attract the eye with colour, pattern and shape. The repressed Jeanne has been replaced by a multitude of couples, and 23 quai du Commerce is rejected in favour of a variety of locations around the city. With Brussels otherwise left behind, it is interesting to analyse the differences present in a film set at home. In this discussion of *All Night Long*, I will suggest that the film should be seen as Akerman's "home-movie" in a variety of senses, and will explore how the film deals with prevalent themes such as alienation and belonging. I will also want to use my analysis to open up the flow between Akerman and Belgium, between Akerman's cinema and Belgian cinema, in order to consider whether we can extend a reading of Akerman as Belgian beyond *All Night Long*.

All Night Long – a home-movie?

All Night Long is Akerman's "coming home" movie, since it lies as a resting point (as brief as Anna's stop there in *Meetings with Anna*) in between her various wanderings. *All Night Long* is also a home-movie in the "amateur" sense of a film which is meant to record one's home territory, familiar places, friends and family. It is in this sense that the film acquires an unusual status within Akerman's œuvre. *All Night Long* is actually a film between films: after the failure of her project to adapt a film from the work of the Jewish writer Isaac Bashevis Singer, and, in anticipation of the time needed to secure the full budget for her musical project, Akerman attended the Cannes Film Festival in order to try to secure the money for a film about Brussels. *All Night Long* can be seen therefore as a film which stands in for other films, filling their place until they are quite ready. It also acquires a more relaxed status as a film whose cast consists mainly of Akerman's friends and family – including her mother – and which did not have an immediate point of exhibition (except perhaps to those friends).

All Night Long's different status can be extended, since it does not merely fill a gap but bridges it, bringing together Akerman's 1970s cinema of anti-seduction and her 1980s and 1990s cinema which incorporates a more direct address of narrative and its various pleasures. As a liminal film, *All Night Long* provides a space for the fleeting locations of Akerman's cinema, whether formal or aesthetic (avant-garde, art cinema, European auteur cinema) geographic (New York, Paris, Belgium) or thematic (the mother, time, space, rituals, gestures). *All Night Long* thus becomes a showreel of the past and a preparation for the future.

Finally, *All Night Long* can be seen as a home-movie in a more thematic sense, pertaining to its place as the second of Akerman's three city films (the other two being *News from Home* and *Night and Day*). In each of these films, Akerman explores the themes of home(lessness), belonging and the spatial inscription of identity. While each film develops these concerns, the form of each is largely dictated by Akerman's preoccupations at the time. Both *News from Home* and *Night and Day* are extremely conscious of the cinematic history of their locations, and – albeit in very different ways – allow these histories to shape their structure. Through its static framing and "documentary" look at New York City, *News from Home* locates itself alongside the structural cinema of Michael Snow and Andy Warhol. Meanwhile, thematically, the film seems to follow the familiarisation of Akerman with the New York City-space, a process which is formally reflected in the increasing mobility of the camera (from fixed shots to panning to tracking).

By contrast, in *Night and Day*, Akerman creates a fiction which is

79

intertextually playing with a whole history of French cinema set in Paris, from Truffaut's Antoine Doinel trilogy (*Baisers volés* [*Stolen Kisses*, 1968]; *Domicile conjugal* [*Bed and Board*, 1970]; *L'Amour en fuite* [*Love on the Run*, 1979]) to Eric Rohmer's *Les Nuits de la pleine lune* (*Full Moon in Paris*, 1984). These references are made clear both in the dialogue – Julie, the main character, at one point quotes from Delphine Seyrig in *Stolen Kisses* – and in the visual treatment of the city. If, in *News from Home*, Akerman's "staring" tableaux framings suggest a certain fascination with New York City, in *Night and Day* these are replaced by a more distanced attitude invoked by Akerman's position as narrator of the fiction, as well as by the fact that she inscribes herself within these French images only to rewrite them.

Locating *All Night Long* in Brussels

How does Akerman's treatment of Brussels, her city of birth, compare to her treatment of New York, where she has said she feels most at home, or Paris where she now lives? Before discussing Akerman's representation of Brussels in *All Night Long*, it is necessary to make the city visible, for in many, if not most, reviews, *All Night Long* was discussed more for its aesthetic relations to earlier films than for its depiction of Brussels.[7] This is not surprising, as any synopsis of *All Night Long* gives little sense of it as a film about Brussels. Over the course of a hot summer night (the title translates as "all night long" or "all in one night"), couples are seen in various phases of the love affair: meeting, parting, running away together. As a storm brews, so our attention switches to night-time occupations: a man works on his accounts, another tries to sleep. With dawn, reality returns, together with various cuckolding partners. The structure of the film throughout is one of repetition and fragmentation, with short sequences conveying mini-narratives. As this synopsis suggests, the subject of *All Night Long* would seem to be more "love, loneliness, eroticism and insomnia"[8] than the city of Brussels. Furthermore, attention to this content prompts a blanking of the backdrop, and Ruth Baumgarten talks of a "background stripped bare of the rancid overgrowth of pre-determined importances, meanings and drama".[9] It is easy simply to "blank out" Brussels; however, a review by Belgian critic Michel Grodent offers a contrasting view of *All Night Long*:

> The bodies are heavy, they have a certain moistness, a certain density, so Belgian; the landscape, the trams, the clock of Saint-Michel, the Vieille-Halle-aux-Blés, the trams, the rows of houses, the little gardens are 'bruxellois', and Akerman films everything heightening this reality which is familiar to us to the level of cinematic myth. *All Night Long*, this loving tragi-comedy set on

one summer night in Bruxelles, will become, in international and Belgian cinema, like the creation of 'Jef' or 'Amsterdam' by Brel in music.[10]

Clearly, Grodent recognises something in *All Night Long* which other critics do not, and, in doing so, provides the first connection between Akerman and Belgium. I would suggest that what Grodent recognises in the film is Akerman's use of Belgian texts – specifically references, images, and formal and aesthetic systems from Belgian cinema and painting.

Locating the Belgian in *All Night Long*

Grodent's comparison of Akerman's *All Night Long* with Jacques Brel's songs, "Amsterdam" and "Jef", demands further exploration. Initially, Akerman and Brel seem to have little in common, with the former showing little allegiance to Belgium, and the latter making it the muse for his singing. Equally, while Brel sang about all regions of Belgium, from Liège to Brugge and Knokke-le-zoute, for Akerman, Belgium is always Brussels. However, what *All Night Long* and Brel's songs do share – and here one might therefore begin a comparison – is a "melodramatic" delivery. Brel was famous for the hysterical performances of his songs, in which he would often finish with himself (and his audience) close to tears. Singing in French about francophone and Flemish Belgium, he exaggerated his Belgian accent through elongated intonation and the choice of phrases and wordplay which emphasised guttural sounds. It is Brel's operatic sense of the dramatic which *All Night Long* shares, as it uses several means to produce a heightened tension and a sense of constant climax. Yet, having begun this aspect through a comparison with Jacques Brel, I would suggest that a closer point of connection for *All Night Long*, which allows a more visual comparison, is the Belgian painter René Magritte. Accordingly, the heightening which takes place in *All Night Long* can be compared to Magritte's "magical realism".

The stylistic current of magical realism can be traced from the canvases of Hiëronymus Bosch and Pieter Paul Rubens to schools of fantastic literature illustrated in the work of such writers as Franz Hellers, Jean Ray and Michel Ghelderode. It also manifests itself in the successors to the Surrealists, the group known as Cobra, in the work of the painters René Magritte and Paul Delvaux, and later in aspects of Belgian cinema. Suzi Gablik suggests that "[f]or Magritte, painting was a means of evoking a meta-reality which would transcend our knowledge of the phenomenal world".[11] This meta-reality was created by using familiar objects which he combined to create something unfamiliar. Gablik calls this Magritte's "subjunctive mood",[12] and it is this which offers the first point of connection between Akerman's *All Night Long* and Magritte's works.

Magritte's works use a gallery of familiar objects and figures: bowler-hatted men – figures which, for him, signified the Belgian middle classes – umbrellas, apples or pipes. The use of words and phrases (a pipe with "ceci n'est pas une pipe" written underneath; a man standing with "personnage assis" underneath) or the juxtaposition of objects (an umbrella with a glass balancing on top in "Les vacances de Hegel" ("Hegel's Holiday", 1958) means that Magritte's work invites first a look of recognition, then one of alienation, as what seemed initially familiar is thus made strange. Brel's operatic sense of the dramatic is figured in Magritte and *All Night Long* through this subjunctive mood. If Magritte creates this mood through this familiar/unfamiliar dichotomy, in *All Night Long* Akerman accomplishes this through repetition.

Both Magritte and Akerman work with clichés and stereotypes. The initial point of recognition is offered in *All Night Long* via the use of familiar actions and situations juxtaposed against one another. Thus, as the film proceeds, it becomes apparent that many of the sequences are acting out love scenarios, and therefore actions which are familiar from cinema's extensive store of love stories. We recognise the tearful look, the inviting gesture, the twitching curtain, or the whispers in the shadows. I have suggested that, after the initial recognition of the stereotype in Magritte's work, we are made to look again, and the same can be said of *All Night Long*. Akerman accomplishes this second look through her use of repetition, yet the intention of both Magritte and Akerman is the same: to offer an adventure in perception.

All Night Long is, of course, not the first of Akerman's films to challenge aspects of perception. Instead, given her insistence upon figuring the minor, the under-represented and the "images-between-images", one might argue that this has always been her aim. This aim has been linked to feminist and formalist agendas, but rarely has it been given any Belgian roots. However, *All Night Long* suggests that Akerman's interests are shared by Belgian magical realists, and, once we open the flow between Akerman and Belgian texts, further connections emerge.

While the subjunctive mood creates what "could be", it also encourages a certain intimacy between looker and image which contrasts with Akerman's characteristic framing of tableaux and static camera. Much of the subjunctive mood is evoked through Akerman's use of the night, a trope familiar from Magritte, who plays with the concealment which low light offers, and it is this use of the night which lends the film a mood of presence and immediacy. Consequently, the single-couple sequences act like close-ups in which, as in Magritte's images, everyday gestures are enlarged to revue-like proportions, or analysed in intimate detail. Equally, the city is created as a space in which gestures are always grandiose and weighted with emotion, since they are freed from the cold, analytical light of day.

The night provides a space of presence, to which the bodies in the film add a close, intimate atmosphere of contact. This intimate atmosphere is initiated in a scene in which a couple emerge from a house. Their connection to the night is immediately emphasised, as we see their shadows before we see them, and, while the scene includes the sound of an aeroplane overhead and passing traffic, what is predominant is the sound of their shoes on the gravel path. Finally, as the shot cuts to their front door, the couple pass alarmingly close to the camera, and the woman complains about the heat. The effect when watching is such that the spectator, too, is encouraged to "feel" the closeness and heat of the night.

From magical realism, Akerman takes imagery which she uses to dress her Brussels. Although the effect is to insert the city within a familiar Belgian discourse, it could also be suggested that this is a way of distancing the city from the self. Thus far, therefore, Brussels is emerging as a city familiar from Belgian magical realist art, yet with little sense of a relation to Akerman herself. Rather than a complete rejection of any relation, however, there seems to be an ambivalence, present in the intimate/distanced effect of the formal systems. This connection to magical realism can be extended even further into Belgian cinema itself through the work of the filmmaker André Delvaux.

Akerman's cinematic translation of the concerns of Belgian magical realism is not unique, since from art it found its way into the cinema of Belgium's first and most successful auteur, André Delvaux. Delvaux has been making films since 1965 when his debut film, *De man die zijn haar kort liet knippen* (*The Man Who Had His Hair Cut Short*), won international acclaim. What separated Delvaux from preceding Belgian filmmakers was his ability to sustain this success (with some seven other features and numerous shorts). The reason for this seemingly lies in the fact that Delvaux's cinema fits within an art cinema or European auteur model (there is, therefore, a sense in which he paved the way for a Belgian auteur cinema of which Akerman is a part). Although his films were set in Belgium, used Belgian imagery (including magical realism), and often dealt with specific Belgian subjects (the Flemish collaboration with the Germans in the Second World War in *Een vrouw tussen hond en wolf* [*Woman in a Twilight Garden*, 1979]), they reached an international audience. The strangeness of Delvaux's "magical" situations was therefore often accepted as the ambivalence and lack of coherence of art cinema.

Delvaux...is gradually establishing his own unmistakable

world...it is a land of the imagination, an area in which fantasy and reality blend and blur.[13]

As Paul Davay suggests, *All Night Long* and Delvaux share a fascination with gesture and imagination. In his films, Delvaux uses many symbols and images which evoke the work of the magical realist painter Paul Delvaux, to the extent that, in *Belle* (1973), he reconstructs a Delvaux painting as a dream image. Comparisons can also be made with Magritte, since, like Magritte's pictures, Delvaux's films begin with what seem to be ordinary situations: a man is having breakfast (*The Man Who Had His Hair Cut Short*); a couple are meeting for dinner (*Un Soir... un Train* [1968]); or a writer is giving a talk (*Belle*). Through the course of the narratives, however, the main protagonist (in all three cases, a man) finds himself confronted with a situation with which he is not familiar, and a series of strange events ensues.

In each of the above cases, the unfamiliar situation is associated with the Belgian landscape. In *The Man Who Had His Hair Cut Short*, the hero, a former teacher who has just begun a new job as a barrister, is taken on a hot summer's day to observe an autopsy of a possible murder victim. The autopsy, filmed from bizarre angles, begins a distortion of reality which leads to the man believing, later that evening, that he has had an affair with a former pupil. In *Un Soir... un Train*, a lecturer (Yves Montand) has got off a train which had come to a standstill; it then starts again but he fails to get back on. Together with two other men, he wanders the flat, Belgian landscape which is unfamiliar to him, and eventually a ghost town is found. Finally, in *Belle*, a college professor driving home to Spa through the Hautes Fagnes countryside, discovers a wild woman living in a hut. He returns to the woman, bringing her food and gradually compromising his own life as a happily married professional. In each case, it is due to their stay in an unfamiliar area of the Belgian landscape that the protagonists err. It is also through contact with this strange landscape that each loses his sense of the familiar, and his ordinary life as a "happily married family man". Hence the strangeness invoked by the paintings of Magritte and Paul Delvaux is, in André Delvaux's films, associated with the topography of Belgium: "The true Delvaux we find in the finesse and the hypersensitivity of the observation, the truth of the gestures and looks".[14]

To this sense of strangeness may be added a visual system preoccupied with the materiality of objects, spaces and people (their bodies and movements) or, as Paul Davay observes, "the truth of... gestures". Delvaux's films also contain the gestural close-ups which evoke the subjunctive world. In all three of his films mentioned, there are sequences in which time seems to stand still, and a particular moment is raised to a hyperreal state. In *The Man Who Had His Hair*

Cut Short, this happens when the man first goes to have his hair cut, and there are several bizarre close-ups of the clippers as they shave his head. In *Un Soir... un Train*, a meal between the lecturer and his girlfriend is heightened with a close-up of them both eating oysters and then an orange, accompanied by exaggerated sounds.

These moments from Delvaux's films and the close-ups described from *All Night Long* serve both to take the viewer out of the quotidian reality, and to act as indexes to that reality, forcing an encyclopedic look at the gestus of conventions and internalised norms. The work of André Delvaux, René Magritte and Paul Delvaux shares this particular way of seeing – a "double look" which first pierces the everyday, and then makes it appear strange.

Apart from the use of this double look, Akerman shares with Delvaux the mysterious depiction of Belgian landscape. However, she transposes this theme to Brussels. Akerman's portrait of Brussels is thus emerging as one which operates firmly in the imaginary. This imaginary Brussels is visually matched to well-known Belgian texts, and associated with a mystery otherwise reserved for other parts of Belgium. Furthermore, through this indexing of Belgian discourses, an association emerges between Akerman and Belgian cinema, although presently this is constructed largely through her relation to André Delvaux.

Once we turn to the main system of *All Night Long*, repetition, the closeness and intimacy invited by the use of the night are challenged. The repetitive structure of *All Night Long* means that the dominant feature of the film is a multidimensionality and simultaneity of actions. The disconnected spaces and couples therefore form chains of analogies, spinning a complex web of impressions and connections. The full impact of the repetition is only evident, however, once we pay attention to the editing system which privileges the visible, that contained in the image. As spectators, we are made to observe, but the structure of *All Night Long* is such that, very much as in *Jeanne Dielman*, all meaning depends on exactly how observant we are. Through observation, the structure of *All Night Long* emerges as one of visual and thematic connections, patterns, associations, repetitions and, above all, gestures. This "choreography" occurs largely in the dusk part of the film, and involves a matching of looks, actions, spaces and motifs. To return to Magritte, if his combination of different elements prompted the second look, for Akerman this is accomplished by her choreography of matching bodies and gestures which are repeated with a difference.

The first few sequences of *All Night Long* establish a system of "looking" which is replayed with variations. In the first of the "dusk" scenes, a man and a woman are seated either side of a line of tables. Both look off left; the suggestion seems to be that they are both looking at/for the same thing. The woman suddenly sees something, we cut to a man coming into a space previously unseen, and they fall into each other's arms. Scene two: a man and a woman again sit at tables, this time side-by-side. An exchange is taking place: the woman looks at the man shyly/he drinks/she drinks/he looks shyly at her/she looks more blatantly at him/he gets up to pay/she fumbles in her purse/he exits to pay/she stands to do the same/he returns, blocking her exit/they fall into an embrace. The divisions in my account of this sequence are meant to indicate the way in which each of the movements or looks "connects" with the former, and "produces" its successor. Whilst the couple sit at separate tables and do not seem to know each other, a connection is initiated through action, and a pattern of cause/effect ensues.

The scene described earlier, in which a couple brush against the camera, introduces a gesture which is to be extended throughout the whole film. The woman is drunk and leaning against the doorway, as the man opens the door so she starts saying, "I'm scared"; to shut her up and get her inside, the man grabs her elbow and pushes her in. As it is repeated, so this gesture takes on connotations of possession, force and power. Shortly, a man attempts the same gesture to guide a woman inside his house, but she lifts her arm from his grasp and marches in alone. Later, a woman uses this gesture to attempt to persuade her husband/lover to come back to her. Finally, towards the end of the film, this becomes a simple gesture of possession: a man knocks on a door, a woman opens it, the man looks down at her elbow and pulls it saying nothing, the woman closes the door. Repetition moves the initial connotation further. Initially, this gesture takes on the status of standing in for something, almost in the sense of a metaphor; then, with the constant variations, meaning is dispersed and shifted until the signified no longer correlates with the signifier. Two particular scenes towards the end of *All Night Long* rework gestures from the beginning of the night. The first is a repetition of several embraces, but in particular that of the very first couple sequence, in which a man and a woman ran towards each other then embraced with great vigour. In the later repetition, a girl is called outside by a boy, she runs into his arms but he squeezes her too hard, and she complains, "you're hurting me".

The second of these sequences is one of the most powerful in the film. The sequence begins with a man and woman lying side-by-side in bed, both stare above themselves unmoving. Any gesture or connection is disallowed between them; instead, this is one of the few times when words must describe their feelings: "I think we've stopped loving each other". Various scenes are cut in between, but we return to this couple twice more: the second time, the man has got up and is sitting by the window; the third is the most extended. The scene begins with a shot from the outside of the apartment. From three windows in the centre of this building, figures look out at the night. As the wind rises, all three close their balcony doors and retire inside. We cut inside with this man, he is straining to control the net curtains of his window. He walks back towards the bedroom as his wife/lover walks towards him. The man blocks the woman's exit, yet, instead of falling into an embrace, the couple bump straight into each other and bounce off, as if receiving an electric shock. They do not move for several seconds as the storm outside finally erupts, drowning them with thunder and bathing them in a flickering light. Then they slowly move off, the man back to the window he previously closed, and the woman to the window on his left.

This scene could be considered a *mise en abîme* of the whole film. It creates a space in which desire is the point of crisis (in this case, the threatening end of desire). The *mise en scène*: the blue tones of the room, and the shadows and billowing curtains, activating the subjective mood, elevate the moment. Finally, the action of the piece is bodies in space whose connection or, in this case, disconnection is encompassed in a gesture (the knocking together) which has reverberations throughout the film, yet, at the same time, survives as a fragment.

The various elements described above posit *All Night Long* as a film with a two-dimensional structure. While the night and the theme of the couple unify the images of the film, the continual action/connection which is the film's system tends to split this unity, dispersing any meaning in a constant movement away from the concrete. The viewing experience of *All Night Long* therefore becomes one of constant negation in which what is gleaned from each individual image is later taken away through repetition with a difference, variation or contradiction.

In *All Night Long*, Akerman's relation to Brussels is depicted overwhelmingly as one of ambivalence. Although, formally and aesthetically, *All Night Long* refers to Belgian texts, thematically there seems to be more of a distance between Akerman and her home city. The effect of *All Night Long* is to create a city which is spatially fragmented, although temporally bound together. Akerman casts her friends and family in a film which plays out a Belgian "magical" imaginary. On the other hand, a certain ambivalence is assured within this distanced portrait through the film's two-dimensional structure. The use of the night, an editing system privileging visual codes and the magical real all ensure the involvement and closeness of the spectator. However, the formal repetition with a difference then fragments that closeness and displaces all original meaning.

Although *All Night Long* creates a complex image of the Bruxellois, it offers more clarity about Akerman's relation to Belgium and the Belgian. Whether consciously or not, in *All Night Long* Akerman sets in motion a reading of her cinema in relation to Belgian cinema. Specifically, I have discussed her use of a Belgian discourse of magical realism, as well as her reiteration of themes found in the work of André Delvaux. Delvaux's position as father/auteur of Belgian cinema allows Akerman to define herself both within and against such a space. Thus, Akerman can also be seen as a Belgian auteur; however, to Delvaux's male-dominated narratives, Akerman offers the difference of gender, and, within his textual construction of a mysterious Belgian topography, she inserts Brussels.

Chantal Akerman – a Belgian director?

Having begun this essay with Brussels as a blank space in *All Night Long*, a "background stripped bare", I am concluding with more of a sense of its complex content. What is also becoming clear is the fact that the connections between Akerman and Belgium have always been present; however, for several reasons, other identities have dominated. It is worth reflecting upon why Akerman's films have never been read as Belgian, since the nationality of a given director often dictates how she/he is constructed. Thus, it is common for a director to be placed within the cinema of her/his country of origin, and for meaning to be made through comparison with other directors, national genres, themes or obsessions. This is especially the case for a director's early work, yet, for Akerman, this critical location within a national milieu never took place. Early reviews and articles do mention the fact that she is Belgian, yet, once mentioned, this is not pursued.[15]

I would argue that the lack of critical attention to Akerman's Belgian nationality hinges on several factors. The first of these could be the fact that, whereas the films of Belgian directors such as André Delvaux, Jean-Jacques Andrien or Henri Storck often take as their subject an aspect of Belgian history, or figure in their narratives the relation between the Belgians and the Belgian landscape, Akerman does not foreground "Belgianness" in her cinema. In most of the representations of Belgium in Akerman's films, we rarely find any overt sense of Belgium as a country. As far as the two which take place wholly in Brussels (*Jeanne Dielman* and *All Night Long*) are concerned, French or Anglo-American, rather than Belgian, discourses were the main subject of analysis. Thus, the presence of Delphine Seyrig in *Jeanne Dielman* suggested in many critics' minds a deconstruction on the part of Akerman of Seyrig's "European art cinema" connotations.[16]

Secondly, I would argue that the exclusion of "the Belgian" from readings of Akerman's cinema can be partly attributed to the relative blankness of Belgium as a visual signifier, and to the fact that Belgian cinema itself is not strongly represented in Anglo-American film history or criticism. Perhaps the final factor which has determined the lack of a Belgian reading of Akerman has been film studies' agendas. When Akerman began her making films, her careful interrogation of film language became their chief value at a time when film theory itself was trying to come to terms with the workings of the cinematic apparatus. Within this context, Akerman was read not as a Belgian director, but as a female, independent (or avant-garde) director. It is also important to note here that there was little resistance on Akerman's part to the agenda-making which surrounded her films, although this was not the case later when her critical position within a "low-budget feminist" ghetto prevented such projects as her "Gone with the Wind" adaptation of the Singer novel mentioned earlier.

Having suggested that the "Belgian" reading of Akerman's films has been absented, due to various competing agendas, it is only fair to acknowledge that this present essay is itself produced by developments in contemporary film theory. This reclaiming of Akerman's Belgian affiliations must be seen, therefore, within present work on "the national" in cinema as figured in studies of space, place and identity politics. It is present agendas which also reveal the value of replacing the national into Akerman's cinema. As I have suggested from the beginning, Akerman's is a wandering cinema. Thus, in order to explore fully the displacements which it undertakes, it is necessary to consider all spaces of belonging which it crosses. My reading of *All Night Long* has been confined by space, but also by the lack of critical knowledge of Belgian cinema which means that any act of connection between Akerman's cinema and Belgian cinema demands first a large amount of detailed gap-filling. Because of these problems, I have confined myself simply to opening the flow between Akerman and Belgium through the exploration of one particular text. *All Night Long* is the most appropriate place to start this connection, since it is set in Brussels and so evidently mobilises Belgian imagery. While it would be wrong to confine our study of Akerman as Belgian purely to this one film, at the same time lack of space forbids a more extensive study across Akerman's œuvre.

In order to approach an answer to these problems, I have chosen to return to *Jeanne Dielman* as one of Akerman's most well-known films, the first set in Brussels, but for which there has never been a Belgian reading. In briefly rereading *Jeanne Dielman*, I want to suggest how connections between Akerman's cinema and Belgian cinema are present from the start of her work. I also want finally to argue that, although it had to be geographically left, Belgium was carried through Akerman's cinema, formally and thematically.

Jeanne Dielman and "Bruxelles"

Jeanne Dielman displays Akerman's most visible sign of "Belgianness" in its full title – 23, quai du Commerce, 1080 Bruxelles – and evidence of the "blankness" of Belgium and Brussels as cinematic signs is provided by the habitual way in which this title is shortened. Although it is a critical convention to shorten to provide memorability, it also suggests that what is important is not the address, but the woman. The inscription of Jeanne's space in this title has frequently been commented on:

> The full title of the film immediately tells us that Jeanne Dielmann [sic] is defined and circumscribed by the space she occupies – '23 Quai du Commerce – 1080 Bruxelles'.[17]

Yet, there is no comment on the significance of the actual geography which this address describes. Once pursued, this address indicates that Jeanne Dielman occupies a specific space in the city of Brussels, and, if one ignores the area code and takes simply the road, Jeanne is situated in a Brussels neighbourhood which is on the border of francophone and Flemish districts.

As well as "situating" the beginnings of Akerman's cinema in Brussels, *Jeanne Dielman* offers a view of life lived in a city which is divided linguistically, culturally and socially between francophone and Dutch speakers and Walloon and "Flemish"[18] traditions. The sense of division which is invoked by Jeanne's titular address can be extended through textual evidence, in particular in a scene from the first day. After dinner, Jeanne makes her son Stefan read to her. In the conversation which follows, it transpires that Stefan has insisted on going to a Dutch-speaking school. At first, he was teased about his French accent (when speaking Dutch), but now he is beginning to lose that accent. Jeanne, however, is unhappy about her son's choice of school and of language. These nightly reading sessions seem designed to ensure that he retains some French instruction, in this case through reading from Baudelaire's *Les Ennemis* (*The Enemies*). Given the resonance of the film's title, this sequence offers a *mise en abîme* of the divisions of Jeanne's neighbourhood, and clearly situates the film in a Belgian social milieu.

Further Belgian connections exist. While much international attention was paid to the casting of the French actress Delphine Seyrig as Jeanne, there has been little mention of other casting choices. Thus, the Frenchness which Seyrig connotes is balanced by Jan Decorte (as the son) who himself became a filmmaker in Belgium,[19] but most importantly by Jeanne's first client, played by the "godfather"[20] of Belgian cinema, Henri Storck. This casting represents the equivalent to the use of Jean Renoir in French cinema, John Ford in American cinema, or David Lean in British cinema. In other words, through the figure of Storck, Akerman conjures up a whole history of Belgian cinema, within which it is inferred *Jeanne Dielman* should be placed.

Belgium returned

> And I left, a small white room, level with the ground narrow like a corridor, where I remain motionless, attentive, and lying on my mattress...

This essay began with a departure as Akerman set out on a journey which would replace the blankness of Brussels with other landscapes and cityscapes. However, through analysis of *All Night Long* and *Jeanne Dielman*, I have insisted upon the return to that Brussels-space. Such a return offers several prospects: firstly, the filling in of the gaps. Hence readings such as that given to *Jeanne Dielman*, which focus mainly upon elements which were ignored in articles and reviews of the film. It would be easy to treat all Akerman's films in a similar manner – pointing out lost moments. Secondly, I have hoped to show through my analysis of *All Night Long* that a Belgian reading of Akerman's cinema could actually become pivotal, since, once Brussels is reinstated, key themes – home and homelessness, the mother, alienation and displacement – are refocused. While initially any links between Akerman and Belgium would seem to "place" Akerman, she resists the fixing which such an identity might imply through sustaining a sense of ambivalence to Belgium, which is created as both home and non-home, familiar and strange.

Both literally and textually, however, Belgium has to be left behind. It is not that Akerman leaves home; instead, home becomes displaced, and Akerman begins to explore the concept of home through her films. In this rereading, I do not mean to discount the validity of former readings of Akerman's cinema, instead it has been more my intention to show that the "small white room" which Akerman leaves in *I...You... He...She* is not blank but merely invisible.

Notes

[1] From a review of the film by Jill Forbes: "It is no accident that the drama of the diaspora and the persecution of the Jews is as much a sub-text as feminism, or that the woman film-maker is condemned to wander". Jill Forbes, "Les Rendez-vous d'Anna", *Monthly Film Bulletin* 47: 558 (July 1980): 139.

[2] *Saute ma ville* is typically translated as "Blow up My City". The film, which is ten minutes long, ends with Akerman lighting a gas cooker and causing a massive explosion.

[3] Quoted in "Chantal Akerman", in John Wakeman (ed), in *World Film*

Directors 1945-1985, volume 2 (New York: H W Wilson Company, 1988): 4.

4   Brenda Longfellow, "Love Letters to the Mother: The Work of Chantal Akerman", *Canadian Journal of Political and Social Theory* 13: 1-2 (1989): 73.

5   Using the films *I...You...He...She, Jeanne Dielman* and *Les Rendez-vous d'Anna*, Longfellow proposes that the mother/daughter relationship which is figured in each film is Akerman's way of making present "the third woman". Ibid: 85.

6   Translated from the French: "Anna est cinéaste. On ne saura jamais très bien pourquoi...si ce n'est que cela lui permet et l'oblige...à errer". See Chantal Akerman, *Les Rendez-vous d'Anna* (Paris: Editions Albatros, 1978): 17.

7   Examples include: "With *All Night Long*, Chantal Akerman breaks with this will to film, as she herself has said, 'between images'. Instead, she puts her trust in the image." ("Avec *Toute une nuit*, Chantal Akerman rompt avec cette volonté de filmer comme elle le dit elle-même 'entre les images'. Elle investit au contraire l'imagerie.") Catherine Arnaud, "Toute une nuit", *La Revue du Cinéma/Image et Son/Écran* 377 (November 1982): 29; or "There has always been in Chantal Akerman's cinema something repetitive...With *All Night Long*, Chantal Akerman makes repetition the whole structure of her film" ("Il y a toujours eu dans le cinéma de Chantal Akerman quelque chose de répétitif...Avec *Toute une nuit*, Chantal Akerman fait de la répétition la structure même de son film"). Alain Philippon, "Nuit torride", *Cahiers du Cinéma* 341 (November 1982): 26.

8   Ruth Baumgarten, "Couples on camera", *City Limits* 128 (16-22 March 1984): 15.

9   Ibid.

10   Translated from the French: "Les corps sont un peu lourds, ils ont cette moiteur, cette densité, si belges; les paysages, les trams, le clocher de Saint-Michel, la Vieille-Halle-aux-Blés, les trams, les rangées de maisons, les jardinets, sont bruxellois, et Akerman filme tout cela en élevant cette réalité qui nous est familière au niveau du cinéma mythologique...*Toute une nuit*, cette tragi-comédie amoureuse d'une nuit bruxelloise d'été, fera date dans le cinéma international et belge comme la création de Jef ou Amsterdam, par Brel, l'avait fait dans le domaine de la chanson." Michel Grodent, "Avec *Toute une nuit*, Chantal Akerman nous rappelle que nous sommes vivants", *Le Soir* 6 November 1982.

11   Suzi Gablik, *Magritte* (London: Thames and Hudson, 1970): 12-13.

12   Ibid: 9.

13   Paul Davay, *International Film Guide* (London: The Tantivy Press, 1974): 84.

[14] Translated from the French: "Le véritable Delvaux, on le trouve dans la finesse et l'hypersensibilité de l'observation, la vérité des gestes et des regards". Paul Davay, *Cinéma de Belgique* (Gembloux: Editions J Ducolot, 1973): 65.

[15] Examples of Akerman's nationality being mentioned include: "Chantal Akerman, a shrewd young Belgian who is bridging the gap between the commercial film and the structural". Patricia Patterson and Manny Farber, "Beyond the New Wave: I. Kitchen Without Kitsch", *Film Comment* 13: 6 (November-December 1977): 48. Or: "a recent film which examines narrative conventions from a radical Feminist perspective. The film, *Jeanne Dielman, 23 Quai de [sic] Commerce, 1080 Bruxelles*, by Belgian filmmaker Chantal Akerman...". Ruth Perlmutter, "Feminine Absence: A Political Aesthetic in Chantal Ackerman's [sic] *Jeanne Dielman, 23 Quai De [sic] Commerce, 1080 Bruxelles*", *Quarterly Review of Film Studies* 4: 2 (spring 1979): 127.

[16] For example: "Whatever image one has of Delphine Seyrig is bound to be involved with her haute-couture sinuosity, her graceful undulating body and voice. But the Seyrig of *Last Year at Marienbad* and *India Song* does not even resemble the straight-up-and-down puritan, Jeanne Dielman". Patterson and Farber: 49.

[17] Marsha Kinder, "Reflections on 'Jeanne Dielman'", in Patricia Erens (ed), *Sexual Stratagems: The World of Women in Film* (New York: Horizon Press, 1979): 252.

[18] While the Dutch speakers in Belgium are frequently referred to as "Flemish", that term is historically, politically and linguistically contentious. Not only is Flemish a dialect of Dutch which is only spoken in certain regions of Flanders, but also the word carries segregational connotations: referring to the Dutch speakers' struggle against the dominance of the francophones in Belgium. The word "Flemish" also has connotations of the Flemish nationalist movement which collaborated with the Germans during both wars.

[19] Jan Decorte has made only two films, *Pierre* (1976) and *Hedda Gabler* (1980). Descriptions of the films in the Davay's "Belgium" entry in the *Variety International Film Guide* (1977: 75 and 1979: 73) suggest a homage to Akerman, as throughout both films Decorte uses long, still shots and concentrates on the quotidian.

[20] Storck's status as "godfather" is suggested by several factors: firstly, his age (born 1907); secondly, his numerous "founding" activities, which have created a heritage which includes the Centre de l'Audiovisuel à Bruxelles (CBA) and the Centre du film sur l'art (CFA), and committees for the promotion of documentary film; thirdly, the permeation of Belgian cinema with his influence on two levels: professional, as a mentor for such filmmakers as Luc De Heusch or Patrick Conrad; and aesthetic, in the art film genre and continuing documentary strand of Belgian cinema. Finally, while accounts of Belgian cinema are brief and rare, in *all* cases Storck is mentioned.

Invented memories

Janet Bergstrom

Chantal Akerman: Jews have a big problem with the image: you do not have the right to make images, you are transgressing when you do, because images are linked to idolatry.

Jean-Luc Godard: And transgression interests you?

Chantal Akerman: Yes, probably. But that's why I try to make a very distilled cinema where there are no images that are, let's say, sensational. For example, instead of showing a 'public' event because it is sensational, or full of lots of things, I will tell the story of something small nearby.[1]

I. Displacements

Chantal Akerman told interviewers long ago, and then repeatedly as time went by, that the film she really wanted to make would tell the story of the diaspora of the Eastern European Jews. She referred to this dream-project when she was asked about her new films, films that might have been (and may yet prove to be) stepping stones to its realisation – for instance, *Les Rendez-vous d'Anna* (*Meetings with Anna*, 1978). Following that film's release, Jean-Luc Godard conducted an interview with Akerman (an unusual occasion) in which he wanted to find out what exactly she did when she started working on a film (she began with writing; he began with images). It is her relationship to the image to which he keeps returning. To answer him, rather than talk about her current project, she preferred to speak about "another film I have dreamed about making for a long time, a film about the diaspora".[2] Akerman wanted to adapt Isaac Bashevis Singer's two-volume historical novel, *The Manor* and *The Estate*, which follows several interconnected families from 1880 to 1930, particularly in relation to the Jewish religion and traditions or their abandonment, moving back and forth from the Polish countryside to Warsaw and New York.[3] In response to Godard's persistent questions about images, she said that she was searching bookshops for photographs so that she could visualise, for instance, the transition to industrialisation of the Polish countryside. Already, however, she planned to reorient the novel to fit her own preoccupations: "The whole beginning of the book takes place in the country. But I don't like the country, I don't like to film it. So I told myself: 'I am going to put that into a city because I love to film cities.' I love to film them because they have lines."[4] Horizontals, verticals: Akerman imagines the story in terms of the balanced, measured framing that is the cornerstone of her visual style. Nevertheless, we can see from part of the script published as late as 1987 that her film was meant to follow the novel rather closely.[5]

Akerman had to wait nearly ten years before she could make a film about the world which Singer had portrayed so vividly. Her opportunity came when she proposed Singer for a French television series on writers. She went to New York, where Singer had lived for many years in exile as a Polish Jew, to research a half-hour documentary. Unexpectedly, she stumbled upon "a lost world, in a way, a phantom world"[6] through hundreds of letters from immigrants which had been published regularly since 1910 in an "advice column" in the Yiddish newspaper, *The Jewish Forward*:[7] "In the letters readers sent in, they talked about their lives and their problems. There was news, there were jokes, what we call 'Jewish stories.' I was really moved by all these stories. I rewrote them in my own way, fictionalized."[8] She wanted her film to commemorate this disappearing tradition, while keeping it alive in the spirit of Singer's writings: "it seemed obvious to me that it was not necessary to speak about him or his books directly in order to show what he had always written about: memory, identity, the force of life and the torment of exile".[9] To do this, she managed to obtain financing for a feature film, *Histoires d'Amérique: Food, Family, Philosophy* (*American Stories*, 1989).

American Stories is an ambitious, unconventional avant-garde film about displaced Eastern European Jews trying to make a new life for themselves in New York City, their struggle to hold onto a sense of community and tradition, and their confusion about so many things in a non-traditional new world – illness, poverty, death, love, infidelity, longing for families left behind or who had sent them to the United States hoping to keep them out of harm's way. This was the first of Akerman's films explicitly devoted to the subject of Jewish experience. It is presented in a very different manner from Singer's novelistic pageant. Europe is never seen: the film is set on the fringes of New York City, whose skyline we can see across the water in the night sky behind the characters. As in so many of her films, Akerman used realistic description to build up a stylised, distanced narrative:

> To begin with, I had located a lot of places in New York to shoot in. Then I realised that everything was there in an abandoned area under the Williamsburg Bridge: grass was growing in half-decayed houses, as if nature were taking over,

and it gave me the impression of science fiction rooted in the past. The New York sky is in the background, there were smells, noises, bits of colour, graffiti, the very essence of the city. I was in a natural setting, but at the same time in a kind of studio: fiction was born immediately from reality.[10]

American Stories does not have a traditional plot; rather, as its name suggests, it is a collection of stories. The structure is permutational, familiar from Akerman's early films, as well as *Toute une nuit* (*All Night Long*, 1982), a structure heavily influenced by the American experimental cinema that she discovered when she lived in New York in the early 1970s. A series of self-contained vignettes succeed one another: characters stand outdoors, beautifully lit in the night, and address the camera directly, framed by horizontal and vertical lines that give the visual compositions great stability in counterpoint to the stories of uncertainty which we hear. One after another, characters tell us about events in their lives and feelings that weigh on them, as if they have a great need to tell someone. The film audience takes the place of the newspaper audience, and also of the psychoanalyst: the silence of the film audience gives the characters the opportunity to speak before a "neutral listener", that space of release that Akerman has referred to and portrayed elsewhere in other forms.[11] They are mostly young people who talk about situations which their parents' generation might have experienced. They are often worried and do not know what to do, especially without their families to help them, the loved ones still in Europe who may be in danger themselves, with whom they cannot communicate. Akerman calls it a "face-to-face" movie.[12] These monologues alternate with traditional Jewish jokes, which see-saw back and forth between two people. The film is a testimony to the survival of a community built on shared traditions, since, at the end, the characters we have seen separately meet each other at an outdoor dinner, New York visible in the distance. They begin to talk to each other, and immediately they find common ground for animated conversations about subjects that, for them, are inseparable: their families and their philosophies of life. Food, family and philosophy form the basis of an idyllic shared community that did not experience, does not know about, and therefore does not have to bear the weight of remembering, the Holocaust in Europe.

When asked by Godard ten years before *American Stories*, after describing her dream of adapting Singer's novel, Akerman replied that she did feel different from others because she was Jewish:

Godard: How are you different?
Akerman: I don't know, but there is a lot of common ground when I talk to other Jews. We understand each other.

Godard: But do you live according to rituals or traditions? A minute ago, you said that you feel a real shock when you see Jews today who still wear the traditional hats, beards and side curls. Doesn't this shock also come from the fact that they claim to be fundamentally different from everyone else?

Akerman: But the people who are like that aren't claiming anything, they are following rituals they cherish and believe in, that are necessary for them. It isn't a question of claiming something from outside, it has to do with their relationships with each other.

Godard: But what about you? You don't follow these rituals, do you?

Akerman: No, I have lost them.

Godard: Does it disturb you to have lost them?

Akerman: No. The strange thing is that I lost them without really having lost them completely. A lot still remains – in ordinary things, in everyday life, in love.

Godard: And that's what you are going to try to look for in your film.

Akerman: That's what I am going to try to look for, yes. What interests me about this novel is that there was a community that followed its rituals, that had doubts about a god, but doubts from within their belief: they didn't really call their belief in God into question, and so they didn't really question the rituals either. But from the moment they let go of one tiny thing, everything went, they were left to their passions and everything was permitted.[13]

American Stories is a fulfilment of the wish that modernity and exile had not destroyed the small rituals of Jewish daily life that had been passed down through the generations, before, in other words, everything had come undone. As Akerman explained elsewhere, she wanted to make the past come alive: if these stories could be told, so could others.

Her relationship to her own Jewish heritage was complicated, she has explained. Her parents were displaced Polish Jews who settled in Belgium. They had experienced things that they needed to put behind them. Akerman repeated in many interviews that her mother was in a concentration camp – Auschwitz – and she never said a word about it. One explanation for this silence, Akerman explained, was that survivors wanted to spare their children. But their repressed histories returned to haunt the second generation:

When I look at my parents, I see that they are very well integrated here. They have strong ties to Belgium. For them, coming here represented an extraordinary opportunity. They don't have this feeling of exile. In a way, they have made a break with their past. They have found a place here. They have found something more easily than I have. I think that we represent the generation in which the repressed comes back. That's why we have problems. Instead of asking questions about the past, they had to rebuild their lives. And because they didn't tell us about that past, because they didn't pass it down to us, what they did pass down was precisely this sense of uprootedness.[14]

Both the jokes and the stories Akerman constructed based on the immigrants' letters served as a way into this unknown territory of memory, a way to replace the void of not knowing:

People of my parents' generation told themselves: we are going to spare them the story of what happened to us. Because they did not transmit their histories, I searched for a false memory, a kind of imaginary, reconstructed memory rather than the truth, as if I had no access to the things that were true...The jokes are part of the same thing, like a return of the repressed. The jokes were told because life was unbearable. It was a way of denying what happened through mockery, keeping it at a distance by making fun of it. When history becomes unbearable, you stage your own misery and laugh at it.[15]

Akerman created memories to mourn and to make up for the disruption of a continuous oral tradition passed down from one generation to the next, most importantly from mother to daughter. Almost all her films seem motivated by this need, but *American Stories* is the closest she has yet come to making her film of rememoration. Akerman explained when the film was released:

Instead of knowing my history by having it passed down directly from parents to child, I had to go through literature and read, for instance, Isaac Bashevis Singer. But that wasn't enough. His memories could never really be mine. So, from one kind of borrowing to another, I am constituted by imaginary memories. [*American Stories*] is a work of memory, but invented memories.[16]

II. Splitting

Akerman described her distinctive approach to the cinema at the time *Meetings with Anna* was released in 1978 by drawing an analogy with Kafka's "deterritorialization", his "minor literature", as it had been presented a few years earlier by Deleuze and Guattari.[17] Her references to their reading of Kafka, as well as her own observations about Kafka's diaries and letters, provide a way to understand better two unique aspects of Akerman's films: first, her "voice" or her position of enunciation, which is presented to the audience as if it were split; and second, her unusual way – partly conscious and partly unconscious, I believe – of focusing her films on her personal experiences. These two aspects are related, for personal experience is presented through Akerman's mode of enunciation as if an invisible wedge had been forced between the represented experience and the audience: we look onto a stylised world that would not be called autobiographical in the usual sense, as we have observed of *American Stories*. While Akerman uses some aspects of autobiography, she keeps her own life at a distance.

"Keeping a distance", in fact, is a key element of Akerman's cinema, more fundamental than a formal or a stylistic strategy. Rather, Akerman's distance can be understood as a manifestation of the unconscious process of splitting. Freud's theory of the splitting of the ego in defence, in self-protection, is central to French psychoanalyst André Green's discussion of the psychical phenomenon he calls "the dead mother".[18] Green's analysis, together with Deleuze and Guattari's perspective on Kafka, sheds a great deal of light on recurring "dominants" (to use Eisenstein's term) in Akerman's films – for instance, why and how they return so often to a mother/daughter relationship. What is striking about the many interviews Akerman has given over the past 30 years is not the autobiographical element *per se*, but rather how few of the events from her past she has spoken about repeatedly. It is that important nexus which we need to examine more closely.

Akerman has protested against almost every specialised category that critics, sympathetic to her work, have wanted to assign. On the other hand, she has described herself many times in a specific way that stresses her Jewish, non-French identity and her cinematic genealogy. For instance, in an interview with *Le Monde* in 1976, occasioned by the huge critical success of *Jeanne Dielman, 23 quai du Commerce, 1080 Bruxelles* (1975), she stated succinctly: "I am Belgian, a Polish Jew by origin. I was born in Brussels June 6, 1950 and I wanted to make films very young, after I saw *Pierrot le fou* [1965] by Godard".[19] Akerman has spoken freely about the decisive experience of living in New York in the early 1970s, the importance for her of the American feminist movement at that time, and the minimalist/structuralist films of Michael

Snow and Warhol. And she has repeated that her mother was in a concentration camp during the Second World War and that she would never talk about it.

Deterritorialisation is explained by Deleuze and Guattari in the process of describing Kafka's work as an example of a "minor literature":

The problem of expression is staked out by Kafka not in an abstract and universal fashion but in relation to those literatures that are considered minor, for example, the Jewish literature of Warsaw and Prague. *A minor literature doesn't come from a minor language*; it is rather that which a minority constructs within a major language. But the first characteristic of minor literature in any case is that in it language is affected with a high coefficient of deterritorialization.[20]

Later in their discussion, they summarise:

The three characteristics of minor literature are the deterritorialization of language, the connection of the individual to a political immediacy, and the collective assemblage of enunciation.[21]

Akerman spoke about her unusual form of cinematic expression, that is, her mode of enunciation – *how* she presents a fictional world – as well as what she chose to represent, in terms of this conception of minor literature – as if hers were a minor cinema inside the dominant cinema – precisely because minor literature was strongly marked by Deleuze and Guattari as Jewish and nomadic, and because they posed the problem in terms of expression and its process. An essential part of their definition had to do with a form of enunciation in which personal expression also represents a collective state. This is precisely how she saw herself with respect to a much larger familial and Jewish history. She spoke about the correspondence she saw between Kafka's solitude as discussed by Deleuze and Guattari, and her own sense that solitude was a necessity, even though she was still connected with others, as she put it, through "death, love, politics, sexuality, economics, the social".[22] Anyone who has seen Akerman's films will recognise solitude as one of their most haunting characteristics.

Akerman's films demonstrate aspects of splitting which one would not need to describe in psychoanalytic terms; usually they are noted as formal features. But I would argue that they have an underlying unconscious motive. The aspect of Akerman's visual style that has been most remarked on, and which is apparent in *Jeanne Dielman*, is the separation she maintains rigorously between two distinct visual fields:

the field occupied by the camera, which Akerman has often equated with her own view, and the field observed by the camera. There is an absence of the conventional shot/reverse-shot rhetoric of editing, and a skilled use of ellipsis which emphasises both the separation of these two spatial fields, which are also fields of meaning, and the observational quality of Akerman's films. A choice has been made, and is continually manifested as we watch her films, *not* to draw the viewer into the psychological depths of dramatic verisimilitude. Instead, there is a split between what is represented and who is doing the representing, and an emphasis on the fact that the *énoncé* (statement) and the *énonciation* (the act of making the statement) are not the same thing. This strategy may be borrowed from avant-garde structural film, yet Akerman inflects it in many different ways in her obsessive and unique presentation of people, "characters" who are sometimes fictionalised, sometimes not, with a dense, suggestive opacity that cannot be penetrated. The people she captures on film are very often in transition or waiting, which is why train stations, bus-stops, subways, hotels and elevators are so frequently seen, where people are observed staring into space, alone in their own world of thought: both in her films with a strong documentary component, where many people, who never become characters as such, are watched intently from the position of an outsider whom they do not know, such as *Hotel Monterey* (1972), *News from Home* (1976) and *D'Est* (*From the East*, 1993), as well as in her films with actors, such as *Meetings with Anna* or *Jeanne Dielman*, and *All Night Long*, which is a mixture of the two.

Transitional, "in between" or split characteristics are common denominators of Akerman's films, and take many forms. The title of *Histoires d'Amérique: Food, Family, Philosophy* is half-French, half-English. The film takes place in the United States, but the characters are Jewish immigrants who are portrayed non-naturalistically by actors. Their stories belong to the generation of their parents, but the actors are dressed in rather contemporary clothing (possibly "vintage"), so that temporality oscillates between past and present. The film takes place in New York, but not quite, since the familiar skyline of the city is seen in the distance. In many of Akerman's films there is a disjunctive use of language, usually "in between" English and French, as in *News from Home*, when the "daughter" (in voice-over) reads her mother's letters in English with a strong French accent while we watch a succession of images of New York. A back-and-forth movement between Europe and New York, the old world and the new, is a key structural and imaginary component of a number of her films, not only *News from Home* and *American Stories*: it is the premise of her most recent feature, *Un Divan à New York* (*A Couch in New York*, 1996), in which an American man, a psychoanalyst, exchanges apartments with a bohemian French woman. *Meetings with Anna* follows a young woman filmmaker as she travels from Germany to Belgium to France, with strong linguistic and territorial markings, for instance, when the two German men she encounters speak to her in French, a language foreign to them, as if Anna's impassive and non-German presence allowed them to give voice to personal thoughts welled up inside for which they had no outlet, which they recite as if they were confessions to themselves. Akerman's films also criss-cross a line between commercial and independent cinema, as we would describe the situation in the United States, and they mix fictional and documentary modes of presentation, as in *From the East* and the installation piece based on it, and most of her New York films, such as *News from Home*, *Hotel Monterey* and *La Chambre* (*The Room*, 1972).

Splitting, in its psychoanalytic sense, allows for incompatible realities to coexist in the subject's ego at the same time, unknown to each other. The "splitting of the ego", according to Laplanche and Pontalis, is a "[t]erm used by Freud to denote a very specific phenomenon which he deems to be at work above all in fetishism and in the psychoses: the coexistence at the heart of the ego of two psychical attitudes towards external reality in so far as this stands in the way of an instinctual demand. The first of these attitudes takes reality into consideration, while the second disavows it and replaces it by a product of desire. The two attitudes persist side by side without influencing each other."[23]

On the one hand, Akerman's films represent what Brenda Longfellow has beautifully called "love letters to the mother".[24] Because *Jeanne Dielman* is devoted to observing a mother in what Akerman has described as loving detail; because, in *News from Home*, we can hear Akerman's voice as she reads letters sent from Belgium that express a mother's love and worry for her daughter, far away in New York; because, in *Meetings with Anna*, the young filmmaker, Anna, makes her mother the centre of her journey and her sole confidant about an unexpected night of love with a woman, when she thought about her mother; and because, in *Golden Eighties/Window Shopping* (1986), we discover that Delphine Seyrig, named Jeanne (as in *Jeanne Dielman*), is a survivor from the camps, appearances to the contrary, whose past emerges like a flash when she happens to encounter the man who nursed her back to health 30 years earlier and, after first reacting by pretending that she does not know him and trying to keep the past in its place, she finally responds to the exquisitely tender way he describes what she was like when he met her, how she got better, his fear of telling her that he had fallen in love with her, her sudden disappearance because, as Jeanne can now explain, she did not know her benefactor loved her, that he never married and remained ever since that time devoted to her memory – because of all this, we can agree that Akerman is effectively representing the mother's story – her own mother's story – as a love story. It is also, we might hypothesise, a gift of reparation, as if the daughter's films are meant to give her mother a better past to make up for the terrible one she managed to endure.

Akerman's first film, *Saute ma ville* (*Blow up My Town*, 1968), on the other hand, could be seen as an expression of need – or a demand for attention – from the child. It is characteristic of children of survivors of the Holocaust that they understand from the earliest age that they must not express aggression against their parent (or parents) because the survivor has already suffered too much. The children are treated as if they are little adults who must protect their parents, who are often self-absorbed, for instance, in warding off possible dangers. The child's expressions of need must be suppressed and even punished, if not physically, then with blame and guilt. But because aggression is a basic component of any child's psychological makeup, it must surface somewhere, in some form. Often in children of survivors this aggression is directed against the self. But it can also be expressed in disguised acts of revenge against the parent, who has ignored or seemed to be indifferent to the child's need for the expression of parental love.[25]

Blow up My Town is a love letter of sorts, but it is also, I believe, a cry of despair and a claim for attention. Made when Akerman was eighteen, this short film was later described by her in the following way: "You saw an adolescent girl, 18 years old, go into a kitchen, do ordinary things but in a way that is off-kilter, and finally, commit suicide. The opposite of *Jeanne Dielman*: Jeanne, that is resignation. There, it was rage and death."[26] The adolescent is played by Akerman and she chooses gas to kill herself.

The film is structured around ordinary actions, like a series of gags with a rhythmic, Chaplinesque side bespeaking mimicry. The humour, or the horror, emerges from the way in which simple actions that take place in a kitchen, such as cooking and cleaning, veer out of control. Many reviewers described it as a comic film. In fact, after leaving the film in the lab for two years because she did not have any money and she had lost confidence in it, Akerman finally asked the director of the lab if he would watch it and tell her what he thought: "it made him laugh", she said, "he liked it a lot".[27] Yet, the girl "sings" (la-la-la-la) with the intrusiveness of a troubled child vying for attention, especially as she becomes louder and more persistent. The way the actions get off-track is also disturbing, because every action looks like the externalisation of psychic implosion.

If this film represented a cry of distress, a plea for attention and perhaps an unconscious expression of transgressive aggression, it was not the only one of Akerman's to do so. The project she proposed to the Ministère de la Culture Française de Belgique (Belgian Ministry of French Culture) for funding (which was denied) after *Blow up My Town* was, Akerman said, about "a little girl, eight years old, who poisons her parents and is happy about it".[28] She described a film she made later in

New York, called *New York, New York bis* (1984), a film she subsequently lost, as follows: "I made that film for myself. I arrive in New York, I go to see a friend, I arrive at her apartment, she says, 'Wait, I'm a bit busy,' then I kill myself".[29] Aggression directed outwards, aggression directed against the self. *Blow up My Town* ends with a romantic gesture that I do not believe has an equivalent in any of Akerman's later films. Holding a large bouquet of flowers down at her side, the girl sets fire to a letter she has propped on the stove (we never see what it says), turns on the gas and leans over the stove, awaiting the explosion that blows up not only "her city", but also, first of all, herself. A sound-image carried over from this scene opens *Jeanne Dielman*, although we can recognise it only if we see the film more than once: before the opening credits, we can hear the loud sound of a jet of gas, a sound we hear later every time Jeanne turns on the kitchen stove.

When Akerman talks about how *Pierrot le fou* made her want to make films, she says that it was because Godard's film made her feel, viscerally, that films could tell a story in a completely different way from anything she had seen before. When I asked her if she would comment more specifically about *Pierrot le fou*, she replied, "When I saw *Pierrot le fou*, I realised that [film] was a language as strong as literature can be. I have not seen *Pierrot le fou* since that time, so I cannot even say what it was that had such a big effect on me, but it was like talking to one person."[30] If one watches *Pierrot le fou* again, one notices that it is permeated with extreme romanticism which ends in suicide. Belmondo and Karina cannot communicate; she acts against him, although she appears to love him; she continually makes up stories to hide the fact that she lies to him and does not reveal to him the *framework* – the *meaning*, which is never clarified for the audience either – which compels them to be endlessly on the move, and for her to keep leaving him. When, finally, he kills her in a confused gunfight, he loses his reason for living. Alone, he brushes azure blue paint across his face, wraps a belt of dynamite around his head, and blows himself up.

Another way to approach Akerman's cinematic mode and her repeated representation of subjects such as the mother in *Jeanne Dielman*, and the child – whether the son in *Jeanne Dielman*, or, more explicitly, the daughter who appears in *Blow up My Town* and elsewhere – is by way of André Green's clinical description of "the dead mother". Green classifies "the dead mother" phenomenon among problems of mourning. Although he does not mention survivors from the camps or their children – the example he gives is a mother who has lost another child – his description fits this situation perfectly. Green's subject is not, he specifies, "the psychical consequences of the real death of the mother, but rather that of an imago which has been constituted in the child's mind, following maternal depression, brutally transforming a living object...into a distant figure, toneless, practically inanimate...Thus, the dead mother, contrary to what one might think, is a mother who remains alive but who is, so to speak, psychically dead in the eyes of the young child in her care".[31] The child feels not only the effects of the loss of its mother's love, but also "the loss of *meaning*, for the baby disposes of no explication to account for what has happened":[32]

> After the child has attempted in vain to repair the mother who is absorbed by her bereavement, which has made him feel the measure of his impotence, after having experienced the loss of his mother's love and the threat of the loss of the mother herself, and after he has fought against anxiety by various active methods, amongst which agitation, insomnia and nocturnal terrors are indications, the ego will deploy a series of defences of a different kind.
>
> The first and most important is a unique movement with two aspects: *the decathexis of the maternal object and the unconscious identification with the dead mother*. The decathexis, which is principally affective, but also representative, constitutes a psychical murder of the object, accomplished without hatred. One will understand that the mother's affliction excludes the emergence of any contingency of hatred susceptible of damaging her image even more.[33]

If, in *Jeanne Dielman*, Akerman is attempting to portray this dead mother, to identify with her and to reconstitute her by giving her a violent outlet, enabling her to externalise, to act, *Blow up My Town* shows the despair of a failed attempt to communicate: in Green's words, "failed complementarity".

> The other aspect of the decathexis is the primary mode of identification with the object. This mirror-identification is almost obligatory, after reactions of complementarity (artificial gaiety, agitation, etc.) have failed. This reactive symmetry is the only means by which to establish a reunion with the mother – perhaps by way of sympathy. In fact there is no real reparation, but a mimicry, with the aim of continuing to possess the object (who one can no longer have) by becoming, not like it but, the object itself.[34]

Flowers give way to manic activity. The girl's disturbing dance with her mirror image, with its weird enthusiasm, corresponds to Green's description of the child's "frantic need for play which does not come about as in the freedom for playing, but under the *compulsion to imagine*, just as intellectual development is inscribed in a *compulsion to think*".[35] Other actions tilt into manic activity without affect and without their expected practical objective, cascading out of control after beginning by mimicking a housewife's domestic routine: cooking, eating, washing dishes, cleaning the kitchen floor, polishing shoes. Many of these specific activities will be reworked in meticulous detail in *Jeanne Dielman*. The girl's frenetic activity is the despairing prelude to self-entombment (taping shut the door and windows), aggression against the self, suicide.

And now we find a new context for the theme of solitude, which we previously encountered in connection with Kafka:

> Arrested in their capacity to love, subjects who are under the empire of the dead mother can only aspire to autonomy...Thus, solitude, which was a situation creating anxiety and to be avoided, changes sign. From negative it becomes positive. Having previously been shunned, it is now sought after.[36]

The reason it is now desired is because at least the child is able to control itself in solitude, having failed to control the object of its desire. *Jeanne Dielman* is the flip side of *Blow up My Town*, all control. Green describes the unconscious motive for the overriding need to maintain order in such cases:

> One also always finds the use of reality as a defence, as though the subject feels the need to cling to the presence of what is perceived as real and untouched by any projection, because he is far from sure of the distinction between fantasy and reality, which he does his utmost to keep apart...When reality and fantasy are telescoped together, intense anxiety appears. Subjective and objective are confused, which gives the subject the impression of a threat of psychosis. *Order must be maintained at any price*, by a structuring anal reference which allows splitting to continue to function, and above all keeps the subject away from what he has learned of his unconscious.[37]

What better description could one find of the stakes of Jeanne Dielman's order, and the consequences of its breakdown, which is also her own? As Akerman described her film in 1976: "I decided to show that this order that seemed so 'natural' could disintegrate with one speck of dust...Jeanne Dielman's defences had snapped, and I wanted to show that in terms of the strongest sign of her oppression: prostitution, because things often explode through sexuality. Jeanne Dielman kills to recover her order, not because she has become conscious of something."[38] It is striking how much Green's description of the dead mother shares with one of the principle syndromes of survivors of the Holocaust and their children.

Akerman insists that she is not writing her own autobiography on the screen, yet in her interviews there is slippage between fiction and memory when it comes to her descriptions of the mother/daughter relationship. Here are a few examples referring to *Jeanne Dielman*, selected from so many others that span Akerman's entire body of work:

> I remembered, at first fleetingly but then very strongly, that I wanted to dedicate this film to my mother: that I wanted to say 'for my mother Natalia, called Nelly' and that I immediately repressed this idea out of modesty or censorship...and I also tell myself that if I had not known my mother, I would not have made this film, which is, however, absolutely not the portrait of my mother.[39]

> I began with several very precise images from my childhood: watching my mother at the stove; my mother carrying packages...Why did I chose a beautiful woman? Because men always think that women inside their homes are ugly. My mother is beautiful.[40]

> I think that Delphine [Seyrig] carried with her all the roles that she had played up to then, that is to say, the cinema...If I had used my mother, it would have only been my mother.[41]

> At the beginning, I thought I was simply telling the story of three days in the life of a woman, but later I realised that it was a film about occupying time to avoid anguish, to keep moving so as not to think about the fundamental thing, which is being. There is also the contradictory aspect of these movements; when you see that woman, you tell yourself that it isn't possible; at the same time, I am talking about a woman I love who is my mother. All that is very ambiguous; for a lot of people, Jeanne Dielman could represent the ideal woman, but when you look at the life of an ideal woman, it is unbearable. The camera is not positioned to say that, but it is so obvious. For me this is very old; it goes back to images of my mother when I was a child.[42]

In an interview with *Camera Obscura*, Akerman emphasised her love for the mother's gestures which she observed with so much care in *Jeanne Dielman*, and how her framing allowed her to express her love and respect for domestic movements that are normally elided in films. Moreover, she emphasised her position as passionate onlooker:

You *know* who is looking; you always know what the point of view is, all the time. It's always the same. But still, I was looking with a great deal of attention and the attention wasn't distanced. It was not a natural look – that doesn't exist anyhow. For me, the way I looked at what was going on was a look of love and respect. Maybe that's difficult to understand but I really think that's it. I *let* her live her life in the middle of the frame. I didn't go in too close, but I was not *very* far away. I let her be in her space. It's not uncontrolled. But the camera was not voyeuristic in the commercial way because you always knew where I was. You know, it wasn't shot through the keyhole.[43]

Perhaps we can agree with Akerman, and yet suggest another meaning as well.

Akerman's point of view and framing in *Jeanne Dielman* also represent her control over the mother's every movement. This is perhaps the will to omnipotence that motivates every child, but, in Akerman's case, given the history of her mother's refusal to speak about what must have seemed to be the most important thing in her past, the stakes were larger. Not only was the framing of the film precise, but also every movement was rehearsed meticulously and adjusted to fit Akerman's conceptions:

With *Jeanne Dielman*, [Delphine Seyrig and I] rehearsed everything in the morning with video. It was very precise: how much time it takes to do this or that...We would look at the tape together, and I would say, 'Don't come so close, do that faster, get closer when you do that, do this more smoothly, do that more forcefully'. Then it was ready. We shot from noon to seven.'[44]

Between *Blow up My Town* and *Jeanne Dielman*, ambivalence is expressed in a twisting form that follows Green's description: I love you. You don't show love (affect) for me. I will imitate you and repeat your suffering. Or else: I should have died, or I will die for you, to substitute for your unspeakable pain. Or, again: I cry for help, for recognition of my subjectivity and need in my own (the daughter's) right. What could be more like Green's description of the dead mother than Jeanne Dielman's zero-degree of affect for her son, who does not even seem to notice because of his own abjection, except that he observes every single change in his mother's demeanour and routine as soon as it begins to come apart? Jeanne's inability to cope with the baby whom her neighbour deposits with her, the baby that shrieks every time Jeanne picks it up, is yet another sign. (We never see this other mother; her voice belongs to Akerman.)

Here and there over the years, and often in connection with *News from Home* and *Meetings with Anna*, Akerman has talked about her identification with the wandering Jew. This is one of the places where she refers to Kafka. When asked in an interview with *Cahiers du Cinéma* in 1977 about nomadism in her films and their relationship to her life, Akerman's response brought out another aspect of her identification with Kafka, Jewish identity and deterritorialisation: the absence of a homeland, a consequent supervaluation of the family, the anguish that the child who does not have children to promise the continuation of the family causes the parents, and the guilt leading to neurosis that, in turn, is created in the child:

In fact, [nomadism is about] finding your place, and I don't know if you ever find your place...I think that goes back to my Jewish origin. As far as I'm concerned, I don't have a relationship with any place. I am no more Parisian than Belgian. If I have to feel that I'm from somewhere, it would undoubtedly be New York more than anywhere else. I don't have the idea of land. Just the opposite, I have the feeling that I am not attached to the land under my feet...Among Jews, precisely, the family replaces everything. It is an even greater source of neurosis than elsewhere, if that's possible. For example, the fact that I have not yet had any children terrifies my father. The fact of not perpetuating [the family] is very serious. When one has no land, one must have children, or something like that. You only have to read Kafka: the relationship he had with his father, the fact that he didn't have children and that he wasn't married was absolutely unbearable for him and for others (in any case, he believed that it was for his father).[45]

At the beginning of *American Stories*, as we watch New York from a ship approaching the city (the opposite of *News from Home*, which ends with New York receding in the distance, seen from a ship that is departing), we hear Akerman's voice reciting a traditional story:

A rabbi always passed through a village to get to the forest, and there, at the foot of a tree, and it was always the same one, he began to pray, and God heard him. His son too always passed through the same village to get to the forest, but he could not remember where the tree was, so he prayed at the foot of any old tree, and God heard him. His grandson did not know where the tree was, nor the forest, so he went to pray in the village, and God heard him. His great-grandson did not know where the tree was, nor the forest, not even the village, but he still knew the words of the prayer, so he prayed in his house, and God heard him. *His* great-grandson did not know where the tree, nor the forest nor the village were, not even the words of the prayer, but he still knew the story, so he told it to his children, and God heard him.

Then she adds: "My own story is full of missing links, full of blanks, and I do not even have a child".[46] Whence the anguish of knowing that she is not continuing her own family, except, as Frieda Grafe has suggested,[47] by way of her films, especially this film which is dedicated to preserving the memory of the experiences of Eastern European Jewish families such as her own. Akerman passes down whatever remains of the traditional prayer for help, which also reiterates that there is someone to hear, a listener who, perhaps by that fact alone, gives comfort.

Akerman's recent video installation, *Bordering on Fiction: Chantal Akerman's "D'Est"*,[48] responds to this earlier work on reconstituting memories, replacing pain and death with life, however uncertain. In the final section of this three-part installation – *From the East* (Akerman's documentary film) is projected continuously in the first; in the second, 24 eye-level television monitors are grouped in threes, each monitor repeating several shots from that film in a continuous loop – we find ourselves in a dark space with a single monitor on the floor showing the edge of a city at night, only the tops of buildings, street lights, with much of the frame black. Compared to the two previous sections, which had no commentary and no characters, but rather real spaces and people which the spectator could watch or not, as an outsider, here we seem to have part of an image accompanied by Akerman's voice and the slow strains of Sonia Wieder-Atherton's cello. In effect, here Akerman, some twenty years later, restates her reply to Godard about the relationship, for her, between filmmaking and writing, a sign of how profoundly these ideas have motivated her vocation. She begins by reading the Old Testament interdiction against making images by the jealous God who will pursue transgressors through the generations (Exodus 20: 4-5). Following her reading of the commandment in Hebrew and French, she begins her own text by invoking writing, not images: "To write a film before even knowing it. To write to make an ending."[49] But the reason she is writing is because she is making a film, *From the East*, that will take her through East Germany, Poland and Russia, places that recall her mother and father, and the generations before them, before the Jewish diaspora. Akerman's position of enunciation is in between the interdiction and the creation of images, unable to forget the one, unable to stop the other. Near the end of her recitation, she describes images that haunt her, despite her attempts to replace them:

[O]ld images of evacuation, of people with packages marching in the snow toward an unknown place, of faces and bodies placed side by side, faces that vacillate between a strong life and the possibility of a death that would come to strike them without their having asked for anything.
And it's always like that.
Yesterday, today, and tomorrow, there were, there will be, there are right now even, people that history (without a capital H) comes to strike. People who are there, rounded up in herds, waiting to be killed, hit, or starved; people who walk without knowing where they're going, in a group or all alone.
There's nothing to be done; it's obsessive and it obsesses me. Despite the cello, despite the cinema.
The film finished, I say to myself, *that's* what it was: once again, *that*.[50]

Part of the dilemma Akerman evokes is also explored by French historian Pierre Nora in his monumental work on history and memory, *Les Lieux de mémoire* (1984). This multivolume, multiauthored work, a testament to Nora's work on the history of the present, sets out places and shared traditions that contribute to a living sense of France as a nation, including its pluralities and regionalisms, from Joan of Arc to the monuments commemorating Verdun, to the Tour de France. In all this, Nora singles out the special problem that the Jewish tradition poses for the "art of memory", because according to that tradition, history is absolutely tied to memory in such a way that it represents an impossible psychological debt: "In [the Jewish] tradition, which has no other history than its own memory, to be Jewish is to remember that one is such; but once this incontestable memory has been interiorised, it eventually demands full recognition. What is being remembered? In a sense, it is memory itself. The psychologization of memory has thus given every individual the sense that his or her salvation ultimately depends on the repayment of an impossible debt."[51] Perhaps this is the nexus of Akerman's work that carries such a strong resonance, and not only for those in the Jewish tradition.

Notes

[1] Translated from the French: "Chantal Akerman: Mais il y a tout un problème par rapport à l'image chez les Juifs: on n'a pas le droit de faire des images, on est dans la transgression quand on en fait, parce qu'elles sont liées à l'idolâtrie. Jean-Luc Godard: Et ça vous intéresse d'être dans la transgression? Chantal Akerman: Oui, probablement. Mais c'est pour ça que j'essaie de faire un cinéma très essentialisé, où il n'y a pas, disons, d'image sensationnaliste. Par exemple, au lieu de montrer un événement 'public' parce

que sensationnel ou avec plein de choses, je raconterai juste la petite chose à côté." Jean-Luc Godard, "Entretien sur un projet: Chantal Akerman", *Ça Cinéma* 19 (1980): 12-13. The interview is dated 27 April 1979.

2   Translated from the French: "un autre film que je rêve de faire depuis longtemps, et qui est un film sur la diaspora". Ibid: 9.

3   Ibid: 10.

4   Translated from the French: "Tout le début du livre se passe à la campagne. Or je n'aime pas la campagne, je n'aime pas la filmer. Je me suis donc dit: 'Je vais mettre ça dans une ville puisque j'aime filmer les villes'. J'aime les filmer parce qu'il y a des lignes." Ibid: 15.

5   Chantal Akerman, in collaboration with Eric de Kuyper, "Le Manoir", *Cahiers du Cinéma*, supplement to issue 400 (October 1987): [8].

6   Translated from the French: "un monde perdu, un monde fantomatique d'une certaine manière". Jean-Luc Outers, "*Histoires d'Amérique*", *Cinérgie* February 1989: 6.

7   Ibid.

8   Translated from the French: "Dans le courrier des lecteurs, les gens racontent leur vie et leurs problèmes. Il y a aussi des informations, des blagues, ce qu'on appelle des 'histoires juives.' J'ai été bouleversée par toutes ces histoires et je les ai réécrites à ma manière, fictionalisées." Jacqueline Aubenas, "Histoires d'Amérique", *Art & Culture* January 1989: 56.

9   Translated from the French: "il m'a semblé évident qu'il n'était pas nécessaire de parler directement de lui ou de ses livres pour faire sentir ce sur quoi il a toujours écrit: la mémoire, l'identité, la force de la vie et la souffrance de l'exil". Ibid.

10   Translated from the French: "J'avais d'abord repéré plein d'endroits new-yorkais. Puis, je me suis rendu compte que tout était dans un terrain abandonné sous le pont de Williamsbourgh: les herbes qui sortaient des maisons à moitié détruites, comme si la nature reprenait le dessus, me donnaient une impression de science-fiction plantée dans le passé. Ensuite, le ciel de New York est derrière tout le temps, on y trouve des graffitis, des odeurs, des bruits, des bouts de couleur, l'essence même de la ville. J'étais en décor naturel mais en même temps dans une sorte de studio: la fiction naissait immédiatement de la réalité." L. H. [Luc Honorez], "L'oncle d'Amérique de Chantal Akerman", *Le Soir* 15 February 1989.

11   Asked about the hitchhiking sequence in *Je tu il elle* (*I...You...He...She,* 1974), Akerman insisted on the importance of the neutral listener: "I think it is much more important to talk about your life than to be driven somewhere. You have to realise what it can mean for someone to have the opportunity, all of a sudden, to have an apparently neutral listener, someone who enters your life for a brief moment and disappears afterwards." ("Je crois que c'est beaucoup plus important de raconter sa vie que d'être conduit quelque part. Il faut se rendre compte de ce que ça peut être comme chance pour quelqu'un d'avoir tout d'un coup la possibilité d'une écoute apparemment

neutre, qui interférera un petit moment dans ta vie et ensuite disparaîtra.")
Danièle Dubroux, Thérèse Giraud and Louis Skorecki, "Entretien avec Chantal
Akerman", *Cahiers du Cinéma* 278 (July 1977): 38.

[12] Unpublished interview with the author, 27 June 1989. English in original.

[13] Translated from the French: "Godard: Qu'est-ce que vous avez de
différent? Akerman: Je ne sais pas, mais par exemple, avec d'autres Juifs il y
a déjà tout un terrain qui est déblayé quand on parle: on se comprend...
Godard: Mais vous vivez dans des rites ou des traditions? Là, par exemple, les
chapeaux, les barbes et les papillotes, vous avez dit que vous sentez une
violence extrême. Est-ce que cette violence n'est pas aussi dans le fait de se
revendiquer fondamentalement différent de tous les autres? Akerman: Mais
pour les gens qui sont comme ça, ils ne se revendiquent pas, ils suivent des
rites qui leur sont chers et nécessaires, auxquels ils croient. Ce n'est pas une
revendication par rapport à l'extérieur, c'est par rapport à eux-mêmes.
Godard: Mais vous, vous ne suivez pas ces rites? Akerman: Non, je les ai
perdus. Godard: Ça vous inquiète de les avoir perdus? Akerman: Non. Ce qui
est bizarre, c'est que je les ai perdus sans les avoir tout à fait perdus quand
même. Il y a des tas de choses qui restent, par rapport justement au
quotidien, à la vie, à l'amour... Godard: C'est ce que vous allez essayer de
chercher de... Akerman: C'est ce que je vais essayer de chercher, oui. Ce qui
m'intéresse justement dans ce roman, c'est qu'il y avait une communauté qui
suivait ses rites, qui avait des doutes par rapport à un dieu, mais des doutes
à l'intérieur même d'une croyance: ils ne remettaient pas vraiment en cause
Dieu, et donc ils ne remettaient pas non plus en cause les rites. Mais à partir
du moment où ils ont lâché une toute petite chose, tout a lâché, et ils se sont
laissés aller à leurs passions et tout était permis." Godard: 11-12.

[14] Translated from the French: "Quand je vois mes parents, ils sont très bien
intégrés ici finalement, ils ont un rapport à la Belgique qui est très fort. Pour
eux, arriver ici, ça représentait une chance extraordinaire. Eux n'ont donc pas
ce sentiment d'exil. Ils ont d'une certaine manière rompu avec leur passé, ils
se sont accrochés ici, ils y ont trouvé quelque chose plus facilement que moi.
Je crois que nous représentons la génération où il y a un retour du refoulé:
c'est pour cela que l'on a du mal. Eux, ils avaient à refaire leur vie, ne pas se
poser de questions sur le passé et à force de ne pas nous le transmettre, ils
nous ont transmis plus précisément ce déracinement." Outers: 6.

[15] Translated from the French: "Ce qui s'est passé avec des gens de la
génération de mes parents, c'est qu'ils se sont dit: on va leur épargner le récit
de ce qu'il nous est arrivé. En ne nous transmettant pas leurs histoires, ils ont
suscité chez moi non pas la recherche de la vérité mais une fausse mémoire,
comme si on n'avait pas accès à des choses vraies, une sorte de mémoire
imaginaire, reconstruite. A partir de certaines choses vraies et à partir de
certaines choses plus traditionnelles qui sont les blagues. Mais ces blagues
aussi ça fait partie de la même chose, c'est comme si c'était un retour du
refoulé. Les blagues sont faites parce que la vie est insupportable. C'est une
manière par la dérision de nier ce qui arrive, de s'en moquer et c'est une
mise à distance. Quand l'histoire devient insupportable, on se met en scène
soi-même dans son propre malheur et on en rit." Ibid.

[16] Translated from the French: "Au lieu de connaître mon histoire par une

transmission directe de parents à enfant, il m'a fallu passer par la littérature et lire Isaac Bashevis Singer par exemple. Mais cela ne suffisait pas. Ses souvenirs à lui ne pouvaient pas être tout à fait les miens. Alors d'un emprunt à l'autre, je me suis constitué des souvenirs imaginaires. Et ce film [*Histoires d'Amérique*] est un travail sur le souvenir, mais des souvenirs inventés." Jacqueline Aubenas, "Souvenirs imaginaires", *Contreplongée* 15-16 (November 1989): 31.

[17] Gilles Deleuze and Félix Guattari, *Kafka: Toward a Minor Literature*, translated by Dana Polan (Minneapolis: University of Minnesota Press, 1986 [1975]). For Akerman's statements, see, for example, "Présentation", in Chantal Akerman, *Les Rendez-vous d'Anna* (Paris: Editions Albatros, 1978): 17-24; Michèle Levieux, "Du Côté de Chez Kafka", *Écran* 78: 75 (15 December 1978): 45-46; and Michèle Levieux, "Propos de Chantal Akerman", *Écran* 78: 75 (15 December 1978): 47-51.

[18] André Green, "The Dead Mother", in André Green, *On Private Madness* (London: The Hogarth Press and the Institute of Psycho-Analysis, 1986): 142-173. In establishing the background for his contribution, Green makes reference to "authors who have laid the foundations of what we know about the problems of mourning: Freud, Karl Abraham and Melanie Klein. But in particular the more recent studies of Winnicott (1971b), Kohut (1971), N. Abraham (1978), Torok (1978) and Rosolato (1975)" (143).

[19] Translated from the French: "Je suis belge, juive polonaise d'origine. Je suis née à Bruxelles, le 6 juin 1950, et j'ai eu envie de faire du cinéma, toute jeune, après avoir vu *Pierrot le fou*, de Godard." Louis Marcorelles, "Comment dire chef-d'œuvre au féminin?", *Le Monde* 22 January 1976.

[20] Deleuze and Guattari: 16. Emphasis added.

[21] Ibid: 18.

[22] Translated from the French: "la mort, l'amour, la politique, la sexualité, l'économie, le social". Levieux: 46.

[23] J Laplanche and J-B Pontalis, *The Language of Psycho-Analysis*, translated by Donald Nicholson-Smith (London: The Hogarth Press and the Institute of Psycho-Analysis, 1985 [1967]): 427.

[24] Brenda Longfellow, "Love Letters to the Mother: The Work of Chantal Akerman", *Canadian Journal of Political and Social Theory* 13: 1-2 (1989): 73-90.

[25] Martin S Bergmann and Milton E Jucovy (eds), *Generations of the Holocaust* (New York: Basic Books, 1982); Helen Epstein, *Children of the Holocaust* (New York: Putnam's Sons, 1979).

[26] Translated from the French: "On y voyait une adolescente de 18 ans entrer dans une cuisine, faire des gestes quotidiens, mais décalés, et finalement se suicider. Le contraire de *Jeanne Dielman*: Jeanne, c'est la résignation. Là, c'était la rage et la mort." Quoted in Claude-Marie Tremois, "Chantal Akerman: 'A partir de quelques images de mon enfance'", *Télérama* 14 January 1976: 66.

27 Translated from the French: "ça l'a fait rire, il a beaucoup aimé". Dubroux, Giraud and Skorecki: 40.

28 Translated from the French: "une petite fille de 8 ans, qui empoisonne ses parents et qui est contente". Jacques Siclier, "Un film hyperréaliste sur l'occupation du temps", *Le Monde* 22 January 1976: 15.

29 Unpublished interview with the author, 27 June 1989. English in original.

30 Ibid.

31 Green: 142.

32 Ibid: 150. Emphasis in original.

33 Ibid: 150-151. Emphasis in original.

34 Ibid: 151.

35 Ibid: 152.

36 Ibid: 156.

37 Ibid: 157-158. Emphasis added.

38 Translated from the French: "j'ai décidé de montrer que cet ordre qui semble si 'naturel' peut se dégrader avec un grain de poussière.... Les défenses de Jeanne Dielman ont sauté et j'ai trouvé intéressant de montrer cela au signe le plus fort de son oppression: la prostitution; parce qu'aussi les choses éclatent souvent par rapport à la sexualité. Jeanne Dielman tue pour rattraper son ordre, pas parce qu'elle a pris conscience de quelque chose." Interview with Blandine Jeanson and Martine Storti, "Dans le plan des pommes de terre, il y a tout", *Libération* 9 February 1976.

39 Translated from the French: "j'ai alors le souvenir d'abord très furtif et puis qui s'impose très fortement à moi que je voulais dédicacer ce film à ma mère: que je voulais dire 'pour ma mère Natalia dite Nelly' et que j'ai aussitôt repoussé cette idée par pudeur ou censure...et je me dis aussi que si je n'avais pas connu ma mère, je n'aurais pas fait ce film qui n'est pourtant absolument pas le portrait de ma mère." Gérard Courant, *"Jeanne Dielman"*, *Cinéma Différent* 1 [1976]: 1. Courant's essay is dated July 1975.

40 Translated from the French: "Je suis partie de quelques images très précises de mon enfance: ma mère que je voyais à l'évier; ma mère portant des paquets... Pourquoi j'ai choisi une femme belle? Parce que les hommes s'imaginent toujours que les femmes qui sont dans leur maison sont laides. Ma mère est belle." Tremois: 67.

41 Translated from the French: "je pense que Delphine transbahute avec elle tous les rôles qu'elle a tenus jusqu'à présent, c'est-à-dire le cinéma...Si j'avais pris ma mère, ce n'aurait été que ma mère". See Marie-Claude Treilhou, "Chantal Akerman: 'La vie, il faut la mettre en scène...'", *Cinéma* 76: 206 (February 1976): 90.

42 Translated from the French: "Au début, je pensais que je racontais

simplement trois journées de la vie d'une femme, je me suis rendu compte ensuite qu'en fait c'était un film sur l'occupation du temps, sur l'angoisse; faire des gestes pour ne pas penser à la chose fondamentale qui est d'être. Il y a aussi toute la contradiction de ces gestes; quand on voit cette femme, on se dit ce n'est pas possible; en même temps, je parle d'une femme que j'aime qui est ma mère. Tout cela est très ambigu; pour beaucoup de gens, Jeanne Dielman peut représenter la femme idéale et lorsqu'on regarde la vie d'une femme idéale, c'est insupportable; pourtant, il n'y a pas dans le film de prises de position de la caméra pour dire que c'est insupportable, mais c'est tellement évident. Pour moi cela est très ancien et renvoie à des images de ma mère quand j'étais petite." Jeanson and Storti.

43   "Chantal Akerman on *Jeanne Dielman*", *Camera Obscura* 2 (autumn 1977): 119. Emphases in original.

44   Unpublished interview with the author, 27 June 1989. English in original.

45   Translated from the French: "En fait c'est la question de trouver sa place, et je ne sais pas si on trouve jamais sa place...Ça je crois que c'est explicable par mon origine juive. Finalement, moi, je n'ai rien à voir avec rien. Je ne suis pas plus parisienne que belge. Si je devais me sentir de quelque part, ce serait sans doute plus de New-York que de n'importe où ailleurs. Je n'ai pas la notion de terre, j'ai au contraire la notion que je ne suis attachée à la terre que là où sont mes pieds...Et justement, chez les Juifs, la famille remplace tout. Elle est encore plus, si c'est possible, source de névrose qu'ailleurs. Par exemple, le fait que je n'ai pas encore d'enfants, c'est complètement effrayant pour mon père. Le fait de ne pas perpétuer, c'est très grave. Quand on n'a pas de terre, il faut avoir des enfants, c'est quelque chose comme ça. Il n'y a qu'à lire Kafka; la relation qu'il a à son père, le fait qu'il n'ait pas d'enfants et qu'il ne soit pas marié, c'est quelque chose qui est absolument insupportable pour lui et pour les autres (en tout cas il croit que ça l'est pour son père)." Dubroux, Giraud and Skorecki: 36-37.

46   English in original.

47   Frieda Grafe, "Die drei Fs der jüdischen Hausfrau: *Histoires d'Amérique*, ein neuer Film von Chantal Akerman", *Süddeutsche Zeitung* 2 February 1990.

48   See the fine exhibition catalogue, Kathy Halbreich and Bruce Jenkins (eds), *Bordering on Fiction: Chantal Akerman's* D'Est (Minneapolis: Walker Art Center, 1995).

49   Akerman's entire text in French, "La vingt-cinquième image", is reproduced in *Trafic* 17 (winter 1996): 57-58.

50   From the audio-text for the installation, cited in Catherine David, "*D'Est*: Akerman Variations", in Halbreich and Jenkins (eds): 63. Emphases in original.

51   Pierre Nora, "Between History and Memory: Les Lieux de mémoire", *Representations* 26 (spring 1989): 16. This essay was originally published as the introduction to the first volume of Nora's work, *Les Lieux de mémoire: La République* (1984).

Night and Day: **a Parisian fairy tale**

Ginette Vincendeau

In Akerman's slow trajectory from 1970s-style feminist filmmaking (*Jeanne Dielman, 23 quai du Commerce, 1080 Bruxelles* [1975]) to Euro-American art film (*Un Divan à New York* [*A Couch in New York*, 1996]), *Nuit et jour* (*Night and Day*, 1991) takes its place as her "French" auteur film. Shot for the locations in Paris with French actors and largely French subsidies, *Night and Day* was co-scripted by Pascal Bonitzer, a name emblematic of both an historical French critical context – *Cahiers du Cinéma* – and contemporary French auteur cinema: Bonitzer worked on the script of, among others, Jacques Rivette's *La Belle noiseuse* (1991).

The critical reception of *Night and Day* was muted, although in France Akerman found support, among others, in *Cahiers du Cinéma*;[1] in the English-language press, J Hoberman in *The Village Voice*[2] and Angela McRobbie in *Sight and Sound*[3] wrote sympathetic pieces. Otherwise, the film elicited the usual irritated or hostile response from the mainstream press, and, apart from McRobbie's article, relative indifference from feminists, in common with much of Akerman's recent features. As Akerman's work has become less avant-garde and less overtly concerned with women's issues, both theoretical and feminist interest have waned.[4] As McRobbie puts it, "it is more difficult now to place her concerns within broader [feminist] debates". In the absence of a clear gender-based agenda, the distinctiveness of *Night and Day* in the Akerman œuvre has been sought along national lines: McRobbie's assertion that it is "a profoundly French film", and Hoberman's that it is "steeped in French movies...the sort of conceit that might only work in French" were widely echoed in the mainstream press: "One of those French films about a triangular tale of love and obsession";[5] "latest in the long line of French film love triangles";[6] "The theme of *ménage à trois* is, of course, a staple of French cinema";[7] · "Only in France could people endlessly discuss their feelings";[8] many more could be quoted. While a certain amount of national stereotyping informs these views, the issue of how *Night and Day* inserts itself in the context of French cinema is relevant to an understanding not only of its aesthetic features, but also of its engagement with gender.

The name of scriptwriter Bonitzer alerts us to a dual filiation between *Night and Day* and French cinema: an historical link, through *Cahiers du Cinéma*, to the New Wave, and a contemporaneous link to the French auteur cinema of today. Akerman's "debt" to the New Wave and, in particular, to Godard is already well-documented; it is playfully acknowledged in *Night and Day*. The plot explicitly recalls that of François Truffaut's *Jules et Jim* (1961): a young woman, Julie (Guillaine Londez) is in love with two men, Jack (Thomas Langmann) and Joseph (François Négret), with whom she conducts simultaneous affairs. Jack is a taxi-driver at night, and spends his days with Julie in their apartment, while Joseph, who drives the same taxi during the day, spends his nights with Julie. Jack's insistence on the anglophone pronunciation of his name (as opposed to the soft French "Jacques") is a quote from Truffaut's film, in which "Jim" must be pronounced in the English way. The voice-over used throughout *Night and Day* recalls many Truffaut films – including *Jules et Jim* – and Julie reads straight out of the book of another Truffaut film, *Baisers volés* (*Stolen Kisses*, 1968): "And then, I am not an apparition, I am a woman, which is just the opposite". More generally, Julie and Joseph's wanderings through the streets of night-time Paris draw on the romantic image of the city, and, in particular, the trope of Paris as playground for young lovers, which was so central to the New Wave; comparisons could also be made with Godard's *Une femme est une femme* (*A Woman Is a Woman*, 1961), in which one woman (Anna Karina) oscillates between two men (Jean-Claude Brialy and Jean-Paul Belmondo). But, whereas the heroes of *Jules et Jim* lived their amorous liaisons against the background of epic social and historical change, and those of Godard's 1960s films interacted with the busy, lively city, those of Akerman are confined – literally and metaphorically – to their apartment, and to empty Parisian squares and hotel bedrooms at night. In this respect, Akerman's film is closer to what Olivier De Bruyn has termed "an *un*certain tendency of the young French cinema".[9] De Bruyn's contention is that new auteur films in France, while showing strong authorial marks, and therefore a degree of individuality, all share certain tendencies: a Parisian setting; "small topics" (for example, young lovers' relationships); forms of intimate realism; and, most strikingly, a lack of opening onto the social world. Indeed, Jean-Pierre Jeancolas' review of *Night and Day* in an earlier issue of *Positif* adopts a similar perspective, especially elaborating on the film's lack of social anchorage: "Everything takes place a little detached from messy reality: Akerman's cinema levitates...on a small cloud. A blue cloud, of course."[10]

The noted lack of opening onto the social world of much contemporary French cinema corresponds, in Akerman's cinema, to a lack of interest – at least of *overt* interest – in the gender issues which had informed her feminist "classics", in particular *Je tu il elle* (*I...You...*

He...She, 1974; a lesbian relationship), *Jeanne Dielman* (the construction of traditional femininity and motherhood), *News from Home* (1976; the mother-daughter relationship) and *Toute une nuit* (*All Night Long*, 1982; gender and melodrama). With *Golden Eighties/ Window Shopping* (1986), Akerman moved into musical territory, but used generic features as a framework for an analysis of gender relations, femininity and consumption. By contrast, *Night and Day* celebrates heterosexual love and shows its female heroine, Julie, in complete isolation from other women. I will argue, however, that *Night and Day* embraces heterosexual romance as an expression of a woman's desire, while simultaneously outlining the limits of such romance. I will examine this question through the representation of lovers as "children", the significance of casting, the use of the female voice, and through a comparison with *Jules et Jim*. Finally, I will examine Akerman's use of the city of Paris.

Lovers as "children"

The evocation of New Wave cinema by *Night and Day* is evident firstly in the film's use of the motif of *young* lovers. The New Wave's taste for the amorous tribulations of young lovers has been considered one of its most charming traits, although it has also been criticised in some cases for removing the films from the realm of social relations.[11] But, whereas the New Wave heroes' detachment from social relations was jarring because the films encouraged us to view them as "authentic" (through *mise en scène* strategies such as location-shooting, black-and-white film stock and a handheld camera, as well as performance styles), *Night and Day*, in the tradition of Akerman's previous work, self-consciously acknowledges and celebrates its artifice. The first images of the film are two overhead medium shots of first Jack and then Julie, whose faces and naked arms can be seen covered with, and on a background of, brilliant, deep blue sheets, and who both directly address the camera.

Jack and Julie are introduced to us as young adults deliriously happy in their physical intimacy, frequently naked and about to make love, or having just made love – a point singled out by all reviewers, including Angela McRobbie: "Much of the film's imagery is given over to sex scenes".[12] But, in fact, we do not – with one exception – see either of the two couples (Julie and Jack, and later Julie and Joseph) making love, even though they frequently talk about it. Julie and Jack's bodies are shown wandering through their apartment partly shrouded in vividly coloured sheets, while Julie and Joseph are concealed by dim lighting in their hotel bedrooms. Akerman's *mise en scène* highlights the reflection of light on their moist skin (it is a hot summer), horizontal pans espouse the curves of Julie's hips, and the smooth torsos of Jack and Joseph are frequently on display, but the characters' nudity is a chaste and *painterly* one, aesthetically pleasing, rather than erotic. This paradox is reinforced by other representational strategies which show Julie, Jack and Joseph as symbolic children. Julie and Jack "play house", walking barefoot in a virtually empty, furniture-less apartment with a sparse but intense, "hyperreal" colour scheme which recalls that of *All Night Long*, but also illustrations from children's books, or even a doll's house. The apartment's walls are dark red, except for one room covered in wallpaper with giant red poppies, and the kitchen which is lime green. When Jack's parents visit the apartment, two chairs from the kitchen form a vivid colour composition of lime green against the dark red, and when Julie goes out at night, her vivid blue or red tops "float" into the dark nightscape, taking the apartment's colour scheme into the street. Towards the end of the film, the imminent departure of Julie and Jack from their haven is signalled by the painting of the walls by neighbours in a more "sensible" colour (pale blue). The apartment also proclaims itself as a set in its configuration. Its disposition around a courtyard allows vision of the space from separate planes, as in some Jean Renoir films of the 1930s – such as *Le Crime de Monsieur Lange* (*The Crime of Monsieur Lange*, 1935) and *Boudu sauvé des eaux* (*Boudu Saved From Drowning*, 1932). But, whereas, in Renoir, the device was adduced to producing greater *depth* and promoting a sense of community, here, added to the framing of the action as tableaux, through doorways or sets of doorways, it emphasises the theatricality of the space – as Godard does in *Le Mépris* (*Contempt*, 1963), in the long sequence in Brigitte Bardot and Michel Piccoli's apartment. The performance of everyday domesticity – making coffee, having showers, shaving, opening windows, ironing, reading – is thus depicted as child's play, as a perpetual game punctuated by virtually identical shots of Julie and Jack leaving the apartment (going down the stairs and stepping out onto the street) and by the comic intrusions of Jack's parents and the neighbour from downstairs, all preoccupied with the possibility of Julie hurting her feet with splinters.

Julie and Jack are not simply detached from social realities, they deliberately postpone "the real", refusing job, child, friends and the telephone until a mythical "next year", feared but recognised as inevitable. As Julie deplores towards the end of the film, "if we go on like this, it's going to be next year straight away". We are at that point shocked to see that Julie and Jack have now acquired a television, and as Jack switches it on, the sound of news that emanates from the set (which we do not see) feels like an invasion of their space. Julie and Jack's perpetual "childhood" is also signified by the shutting out of daylight – blinds half-down filtering red light, shutters letting through a blue light – as they spend most of their time in bed, re-creating an artificial space where time stands still. When Julie steps out of the apartment with Jack, both are bathed in a strange yellow glow, but immediately as Julie meets Joseph, it is night-time again, establishing further the dreamlike nature of both relationships. Julie's ambiguous statement to Jack, "on a une histoire sans histoire", translates as both "our story is trouble-free" and "our story is without a plot", an accurate description of the circular structure of her double life, based on the alternation of "night and day", yet a night and a day that are strangely identical, a suspended time in which she never sleeps while the city itself does. Julie and Joseph's existence outside the apartment is paradoxically self-enclosed; they have no contact with the city's inhabitants, and spend most of their time in hotel bedrooms. In an ironic comment on the film's title, both couples inhabit a fairy tale twilight universe, which, as the voice-over warns, will come to an end if Julie fails to come back home before dawn. As she runs, Cinderella-like, in order to get back home before Jack, after she has indeed overslept with Joseph for the first time, a sense of doom and foreboding is established, which will not be dispelled, except temporarily when Jack makes her laugh by clowning around. Perfect romance, in which desire is forever satisfied, is only sustainable in this ideal, fairy tale world, in which the three "children" (whose names all begin with "J") can play, free of guilt and negative feelings or desires. But Akerman shows this idyllic world to be ultimately as suffocating as it is comforting, a dilemma echoed by the lyrics of the song heard at the end of the film: "If you must chose a cage, I will share it with you".[13]

Night and Day's depiction of young lovers as symbolic lost children caught "playing" by their parents inserts itself – albeit in an extreme form – as a strong thematic strand in French cinema, exemplified by the New Wave (for example, *A Woman Is a Woman*, Truffaut's *Stolen Kisses* and *Domicile conjugal* [*Bed and Board*, 1970]). But it is a tradition whose antecedents can be traced back to the early films of René Clair in the 1930s, such as *Le Million* (1931) and *Quatorze juillet* (*The Fourteenth of July*, 1932), and those of Marcel Carné, such as *Hôtel du Nord* (1938), and others scripted by Jacques Prévert (for example, *Le Quai des brumes* [1938]). In Clair's and Carné's films, the innocence and romanticism of the young lovers were established by contrast with older and more cynical (although more interesting) characters. In the New Wave cinema, the rhetoric of youth eliminated the older generation, and promoted youthful irresponsibility as a mode of life. In the late-1980s and 1990s, a "neo-romantic" streak has brought back the New Wave lovers who had disappeared with the realist cinema of the 1970s and early 1980s. It is worth pausing on this phenomenon, as it informs *Night and Day* and is sufficiently widespread to characterise a whole generation of filmmakers, as De

Bruyn points out. Several strands are manifest in this overall tendency. I would single out three. Firstly, there are films which place the young lovers (despite De Bruyn's argument) in a socially marked or "difficult" context (*Les Nuits fauves* [*Savage Nights*, 1992], *Paris s'éveille* [*Paris Awakens*, 1991], *Mina Tannenbaum* [1993]). Secondly, some films offer a deliberately theatrical or extravagant context (especially the work of Léos Carax: *Mauvais sang* [*The Night Is Young*, 1986], *Les Amants du Pont-Neuf* [1991], or Jean-Jacques Beineix: *37°2 le matin* [*Betty Blue*, 1986]). Finally, some films rework the motif of young lovers through an acknowledgment of changing gender relations; for instance: Eric Rochant's *Un Monde sans pitié* (*A World Without Pity*, 1989) and Laetitia Masson's *En avoir ou pas* (*To Have [Or Not]*, 1995). *Night and Day* could be seen as combining the latter two tendencies, sharing with Carax a deliberately stylised, theatrical *mise en scène*, foregrounding the theatrical in recognition of the impossibility of a realistic depiction of idealistic young love in the 1990s. At the same time, like *A World Without Pity* and *To Have (Or Not)*, Akerman's tale also subtly challenges the neo-romantic model through its concern with gender. The fact that feminism in the French context seeks to accommodate the romantic framework, rather than challenge or reject it[14] – as in the work of a number of contemporary French women directors (Marion Vernoux, Masson, Tonie Marshall, Claire Denis) – is one reason for the difficulty in mapping out a film such as *Night and Day* onto Anglo-American feminist concerns. In *Night and Day*, the desire to give the female protagonist more room to manœuvre within a romantic heterosexual framework is reflected in the portrayal of masculinity, as well as femininity, and informs questions of casting, as well as the use of the female body and voice.

The body and the voice

Akerman's casting for her three protagonists relates her central plot of young heterosexual romance to concerns not only of gender, but also of female authorship. No star with an established persona, as in *Jeanne Dielman* (Delphine Seyrig) or in *A Couch in New York* (Juliette Binoche, William Hurt), appears in *Night and Day*. However, the film's casting reflects another pattern. Firstly, Akerman's choice of male actors for the parts of Jack and Joseph conforms to the tendency, identified by Giorgiana Colville, of French women directors to "favour a less muscular type of actor [as opposed to Gérard Depardieu and Alain Delon] such as Michel Lonsdale, Jean-Michel Folon, Peter Coyote or Sami Frey among others" who "please women according to their own criteria".[15] Thomas Langmann and François Négret, following Akerman's wish,[16] look remarkably similar. They are both handsome but slim men with the "dark, soft and feminised look that French women filmmakers

122

are fond of",[17] both indeed recalling the young Sami Frey. They can also be seen as modernised and unthreatening versions of the "dark" heroes of heterosexual romance literature, who, in mainstream cinema, have tended to appear in romantic costume films (Gérard Philipe, Louis Jourdan, Vincent Pérez, Olivier Martinez), a genre also popular with female spectators.

While Akerman's choice of male actors fits in a pattern of both French women filmmakers and romance films, her choice of Guillaine Londez for Julie moves the film further along considerations of female authorship. Londez does not share the evanescent features of romantic French actresses such as Annabella, Micheline Presle and Juliette Binoche, nor of the more "ethereal" New Wave actresses such as Emmanuele Riva and Delphine Seyrig. Indeed, unlike the way Seyrig appears to Antoine Doinel (Jean-Pierre Léaud) in *Stolen Kisses*, Londez is "not an apparition, but a woman". She is of solid build, generous "Renoiresque"[18] body and abundant hair, features emphasised by Akerman's camera. There is, in fact, an interesting tension between the recitative type of elocution Londez is made to adopt (like the two men) throughout the film, which has prompted comparisons with the work of Robert Bresson,[19] and her presence on the screen, clearly also a decision on the part of Akerman, who chose her "because she came from a small village in the south of France, and you could believe in her sincerity".[20]

The foregrounding of Julie's body, highlighting the dominance of the feminine principle, is reinforced by a female voice-over. Mary Ann Doane and Kaja Silverman[21] have argued that men's voices are frequently allowed the privilege of being present at the level of cinematic apparatus through authorial (third-person) voice-over, a "disembodied voice" not anchored to a body. On the contrary, they argue, women's voices are seldom, if ever, allowed such authorial position, and instead remain contained within the diegetic world of the film, always brought back to a body, thereby undermining their authority. *Night and Day*, however, makes a different and powerful use of the female voice in two ways. The film uses a classic, "disembodied" voice-over, but that of a woman, expressing female authorial control: the voice speaks in the first person, commenting on the action throughout the film. The power of female speech is also inscribed in Julie's aural presence: she is a character who addresses the camera directly, and boldly verbalises her own desires. Female voice and body, with the backing of the female voice-over, organise a visual and aural female space where symmetry of desire is possible. Indeed, the moment which signals the beginning of the end of the three characters' idyll is that of Joseph's assertion of his sexual desire while Julie is *asleep*.

Through casting and use of the female voice and body, Akerman's film recasts neo-romantic celebrations of young heterosexual love into a female-centred film, foregrounding the materiality of a woman's body and voice. It is useful to examine her inflection of the film's "model" plot, that of *Jules et Jim*, to see how far she pushes the film further in the direction of a female-authored and female-centred text. *Jules et Jim* has long been celebrated for its portrayal of a joyful, "free" heroine, including by Akerman who said, at the time of the release of *Night and Day*: "[W]hen *Jules et Jim* was done it was very provocative, with Jeanne Moreau's Catherine doing exactly what she felt".[22] On close inspection, this reading is largely a tribute to Moreau's star persona and charisma. In the first half of the film, which portrays the forming of the three-way relationship between Jules, Jim and Catherine, culminating in an idyllic stay in the South of France, the two men's attraction to Catherine is clearly described as a desire for an ideal image of femininity, a distant figure mediated through art forms. Before the "real" Catherine appears in the film, she has been figured as a Greek statue, a drawing and a photographic slide, not to mention a succession of other women whom the two men have desired and exchanged. The second half of the film, while pointing to the continued fascination of the men with Catherine, also charts her increasing despair and lack of direction, and her dependency on men's desires. It culminates in her suicide and, simultaneously, her killing of Jim and abandonment of her daughter. As mentioned earlier, Akerman's choice of actress for Julie in *Night and Day* emphasises the *solidity* of her presence and the importance of the female voice, as opposed to the male voice-over of *Jules et Jim*. In this sense, too, compared to Catherine, Julie is not an "apparition" conjured up by the two men. She is not an art object admired from afar by Jack and Joseph. *Night and Day*, on the contrary, emphasises the *closeness* between Julie and each of the two men. Julie, unlike Catherine, remains the emotional and geographical centre of the film, from whom neither the camera nor the men ever stray. Her increasing difficulties with controlling her double relationship are not, as in *Jules et Jim*, a reflection of her insecurity, but the result of the men's increasing demands on her, as well as the inevitable encroachment of "the real" into their charmed lives. It is clear, too, that Julie is the author of her own narrative. Her calm postponing of a child until the mythical "next year" contrasts with the frantic desire for affirmation Catherine seeks by trying to get pregnant with Jim. Even in her increasingly distracted state, when she knocks off the coffee pot (like Jeanne Dielman burning the potatoes), she does not forget to take her pill.

The greatest difference between *Night and Day* and *Jules et Jim* resides in the ending, which crystallises major issues in the representation of femininity and female desire in a classic male-authored text – and doubly so, as Truffaut's film is based on Henri-Pierre Roché's novel – as opposed to a female-authored and female-centred text. Truffaut's Catherine is a classic blank page for the projection of male desire; as Sandy Flitterman-Lewis puts it, she crystallises the "fascinating lure of the cinema".[23] She is also, on a more immediate narrative level, the doomed representative of the end of an era and the object of exchange between two men whose strong homosocial bond preceded her entry into the fiction.[24] By contrast, Akerman's Julie is a woman whose materiality is foregrounded (through voice and body), a character in charge of her own story and desire. The fact that this desire is strictly heterosexual – a somewhat taboo subject in feminist filmmaking since the 1970s, as Colville observes[25] – should not obscure the progressive nature of this resolution. The end of Julie's fairy tale double romance is not death and destruction, as for Catherine, but growth and rebirth. Julie has lived one scenario of desire to the full, and, in a singularly affirmative ending, moves on to another life. A long tracking shot shows her walking ahead in a purposeful manner, very much awake after her "long night". She has severed both men's dependency on her, symbolised by her throwing away of two pairs of shoes. Akerman proclaims the Cinderella tale over and returns her heroine to the "real" of a contemporary Parisian street, with its familiar looks and noises, a Paris we see for the first time in daylight.

* * *

Revisiting Paris

Like so many French films, *Night and Day* uses the city of Paris as more than mere décor. Akerman's treatment of the city displays in equal measure her awareness of French film history and her own inflection of that history, to produce a representation of the city which recalls her use of Brussels in *All Night Long*, and of New York in *News from Home*.

Akerman acknowledges classic monumental Paris only in the most allusive way. While she remains within historic Paris *intra-muros*, her chosen locations are devoid of the iconic status of, for example, the Eiffel Tower or the Sacré-Cœur (whereas the New Wave films always included some traditional Parisian icons). The action of the film takes place in the busy central areas between Place du Châtelet and Place de la République, old *quartiers* with historic buildings (although not particularly touristy) which combine residential with business and artisan locations; their population is a mixture of working class and petit-bourgeois, including, because of the rag trade and for other historic reasons, a significant Jewish element. As a result of this choice, the film affords a recognition of "Paris" as a generic category – we are told by the voice-over that Julie and Jack's apartment is off Boulevard de Sébastopol, and that they come "probably from the provinces" – but also elicits a sense of ordinariness: you would have to be familiar with Paris to recognise the locations. The story can unfold within the myth of "lovers in Paris", thereby acquiring an additional aura of romance thanks to the city's cultural capital accumulated through a rich tradition in French literature, painting, songs, and now tourism material. Within this myth, Paris itself functions as an eroticised object of desire, traditionally perceived as feminine.[26] Hence Joseph came to Paris "to be happy", a goal he realises in his twin meeting of the city and of Julie, and which is encapsulated in their having their first kiss on the banks of the Seine, a romantic spot celebrated by so many French and American films (archetypally Vincente Minnelli's *An American In Paris* [1951]). At the same time, the refusal of more iconic locations (such as the Eiffel Tower in *A World Without Pity*) or, on the other hand, of more naturalistic representations, such as the portrayal of the 11th *arrondissement* in *Chacun cherche son chat* (*When the Cat's Away*, 1996), means that the film can transcend its Parisian location and function as a "global" tale of young lovers in a hot summertime European city, recalling the Brussels of *All Night Long*. We have seen how the lovers were presented as symbolic children, living a fairy-tale existence. Akerman's treatment of the city outside them confirms this, making it both distanced and magic.

Whereas many contemporary French films, such as *A World Without Pity*, *Les Amants du Pont-Neuf*, Rohmer's *Les Rendez-vous de Paris* (*Rendez-vous in Paris*, 1995) and *When the Cat's Away*, have tried, within the constraints of shooting in today's Paris, to make the living city a "real" character, *Night and Day* proposes a self-consciously distanced city, one that is turned into a set. This is symbolised by the view outside Julie and Jack's apartment's window, evocative of the 1930s Poetic Realist films. But Akerman also turns the "real" city into a set. The long back-tracking shot of Julie and Joseph standing in front of the statue at the centre of the Place de la République is emblematic of this: it starts off on a real exhibit of Paris history (as well as on the two characters), only to detach itself from this referent, the circular movement of the cars around the square increasingly filling the frame, a series of blurred movements and lights. Joseph's recitation over the two-minute-long shot is a poetic discourse on the everyday, in the tradition of poet and scriptwriter, Jacques Prévert. Joseph's text tells us what he likes about Paris. It evokes the quotidian pleasures the cosmopolitan city offers its inhabitants, such as eating couscous in Belleville; drinking café-crème; shopping for toothbrushes, cigarettes or pistachio nuts; going to the cinema; reading the newspaper at café

126

terraces; taking the métro. These are activities which the film will deliberately *not* show us, but which Akerman acknowledges as part of the cinematic heritage of the city, a heritage so culturally familiar that it can be reduced to this verbal rendering.

Julie and then Julie and Joseph walk Parisian streets as if on an empty set, the outdoor equivalent of Julie and Jack's apartment. While being undoubtedly the real city, Paris in *Night and Day* is offered as a disembodied, self-conscious representation, illustrated by Julie's singing "Moi, la nuit j'erre dans Paris" ("At night I wander around Paris"), as she is walking the streets, a reference to Jacques Demy's musicals. As in the Demy films, this also signals another dimension conferred onto the city by Akerman's film, and that is its "magic".

Early French cinema widely used the streets and buildings of Paris for naturalistic purposes, but the city also inspired directors who endowed it with a surreal, magic dimension. This is evident in Louis Feuillade's serial fantastic thriller, *Les Vampires* (1915-16), and in avant-garde fantasies such as René Clair's *Paris qui dort* (*The Crazy Ray*, 1924). The 1930s, especially in the early films of Clair (*Sous les toits de Paris* [*Under the Roofs of Paris*, 1929]; *The Fourteenth of July*) and the tradition of Poetic Realism, produced a stylised view, literally reconstructing the city with sets, which derived poetry from the minute observation of the everyday. Akerman acknowledges this tradition by placing Julie and Jack's apartment in a popular *quartier*, on the 5th floor "without a lift", under the roofs of Paris. Poetic Realism also retained a dimension of magic, illustrated by the presence (sometimes literally as a character) of "fate" in the films. The New Wave introduced a more "authentic" city, based on the practice of location-shooting. Paris, not yet utterly dominated by traffic, allowed actors and filmmakers the exhilaration of exploring the city as a playground – literally in Truffaut's *Les Quatre cents coups* (*The 400 Blows*, 1959) – or metaphorically in so many others: *A bout de souffle* (*Breathless*, 1960), *Les Cousins* (*The Cousins*, 1959), *Paris vu par...* (*Six in Paris*, 1964), as well as as the locus of self-discovery and danger – Varda's *Cléo de 5 à 7* (*Cléo from 5 to 7*, 1961), Godard's *Vivre sa vie* (*It's My Life*, 1962) and others.[27] But, even then, the magic dimension of the city was retained: Truffaut wondered at the function of the *pneumatique* as a device to connect lovers in *Stolen Kisses*; Rivette staged elaborate plots across the city in, among others, *Céline et Julie vont en bateau* (*Céline and Julie Go Boating*, 1974) and *Le Pont du Nord* (1984); and Rohmer's *Conte d'hiver* (*A Winter's Tale*, 1992) makes long-estranged lovers meet again by divine chance on a bus. French auteur films in the 1980s and 1990s continue this trend – notably Olivier Assayax's *Irma Vep* (1996) and Rochant's *A World Without Pity*. The former, the story of a failed attempt at filming a remake of *Les Vampires*, features a scene in which "Irma Vep" (Maggie Cheung) steals jewels from a hotel room and throws them down in an eerily poetic – yet location-shot – rooftop scene. *A World Without Pity* puns on the idea of magic with a scene in which the hero "switches off" the Eiffel Tower for the woman he loves by clicking his fingers at the exact moment (midnight) when the lights go off.

The Paris of Julie and Joseph, like the fairy-tale apartment of Julie and Jack, is a magic city, with an endless supply of hotel rooms, squares and fountains, in which nothing unpleasant can happen, especially to Julie as she wanders the streets at night on her own ("nothing happened to her", confirms the voice-over) with her "magic shoes" which she throws away at the end. It is a city which exists for the lovers and in relation to them, and in which golden coaches are replaced by taxis. It is noticeably a city free of inhabitants. When other characters might have been present – for instance, when Julie buys shirts, or when either Julie or Joseph sits in a café waiting for each other – they are cut off, metonymically replaced by fleetingly-seen hands or the anonymous backs of their heads. The only encounters the lovers make in *Night and Day* are with cars, but these too are, as in the Place de la République sequence, mostly blurred movements and lights, brushing past the lovers as they stand on the edge of the pavement, or seen from Jack's moving taxi on the night he takes Julie with him. As in *Savage Nights*, *Boy Meets Girl* (1984), *Les Amants du Pont-Neuf* and many others, a new motif – strings of light filing past as a car is riding in a tunnel – has been added to the visual repertoire of the modern city. Jack and Joseph as taxi-drivers are no longer the friendly, comic taxi-drivers of classical French cinema (as played by Michel Simon or Louis de Funès), but part of a new breed of shadowy characters prowling the city – as in Jacques Braal's *Extérieur, nuit* (*Exterior, Night*, 1979) – part of it, yet distanced and stripped of the social identity that such an occupation would normally suggest, emblematic of the stylisation of the whole city.

From Paris to New York, and back to Paris

Throughout her career, Chantal Akerman has produced a truly international body of work, whose aesthetics stretched from both sides of the Atlantic, from Michael Snow to Jean-Luc Godard. Within Europe, she has also acknowledged her cultural roots in Belgian as well as French cinema, and, more recently, her work has brought to the fore her Jewish identity. This international identity has been unified, however, by a deliberate positioning of herself as an auteur, in contradistinction to both national and gender identities, as illustrated by many of her declarations.[28] Such a passionate allegiance to the identity of the art film auteur, itself an international construct, but one with a central place in the national identity of French cinema, has won her the support of French cinéphile journals, and especially *Cahiers du Cinéma*. In her usual allusive way, as we have seen, Akerman has inscribed over the text of *Night and Day* both her presence as an auteur – through her minimalist *mise en scène* and use of colour, and through the female voice-over – and her multiple cultural identity, through an acknowledgment of the cultural heritage of Paris, through verbal references to its changing multi-ethnicity (Joseph's recitation), and through the dual identity of the male characters themselves. As Amina Danton aptly puts it: "Jack is the American pole and Joseph the biblical pole between which Chantal Akerman's identity and culture exist";[29] I would add that Julie, the girl from the South of France, represents the French/francophone pole in this complex identity map.

A Couch in New York, starring Juliette Binoche and William Hurt, and with a soundtrack predominantly in English, materialises Akerman's Franco-American polarity. Binoche plays an artist who swaps her picturesque but chaotic apartment under the roofs of Paris for William Hurt's luxury apartment in New York, through a newspaper advertisement. She is an artist who leaves behind a trail of unhappy lovers; he is a psychoanalyst who leaves behind a trail of unsatisfied patients. But, while she comically – and without the slightest qualification – takes his place in New York (his patients are much keener on her as a psychoanalyst than on him), the best he can do is to mend her plumbing. In the tradition of Hollywood romantic comedies and musicals of the 1930s and 1940s, *A Couch in New York* mixes misunderstandings and near-misses with a romantic plot, in which hero and heroine are comically kept apart but eventually united or reunited, and fall in love. It is tempting to see the Binoche character as Julie post-*Night and Day*, and the male voices lamenting her absence on her answering machine as Jack and Joseph still pining for her. Compared to any previous Akerman film, *A Couch in New York* is more seductive, more glamorous and more accessible; as Akerman put it regarding *Night and Day*: "nobody wants to see anything any more if it's not accessible".[30] Yet, it still retains obvious marks of the "Akermanesque" – for instance, in her use of colour and the minimal, yet detailed observation of characters' quotidian gestures. This time, however, she has lost even the support of *Cahiers du Cinéma* which reviewed the film rather negatively. This could be because of its stereotypical representation of Paris, a apartment under the roofs, Binoche and Hurt at the end not a little like Humphrey Bogart and Ingrid Bergman in *Casablanca*. But there could be another reason. The vital part of the film is set in New York, Paris is reduced to a picture postcard, and, more fundamentally, the film dispenses with the irreducible sign of French/francophone identity: language. The question arises, for us as for *Cahiers du Cinéma*, as to what Akerman's next move will be.

Notes

¹ See Amina Danton, "Tout ou rien", *Cahiers du Cinéma* 447 (September 1991): 62-63. Another supportive French review is Raphaël Bassan, "*Nuit et jour*: Nomadisme des passions", *La Revue du Cinéma* 474 (September 1991): 26-27. Interestingly, this support was no longer available for *A Couch in New York*.

² J Hoberman, "A story of all-consuming love", *The Village Voice* 15 December 1992.

³ Angela McRobbie, "Passionate uncertainty", *Sight and Sound* 2: 5 (September 1992): 28-29; Angela McRobbie, "Nuit et jour (Night and Day)", *Sight and Sound* 2: 5 (September 1992): 54-55.

⁴ See Catherine Fowler, "Chantal Akerman: A cinema in-between", unpublished PhD thesis, University of Warwick, 1995.

⁵ Chris Peachment, "Days When Nothing Happens", *The Daily Telegraph* 6 August 1993.

⁶ Angie Errigo, "Night and Day", *Today* 6 August 1993.

⁷ Jeff Dawson, "Night and Day", *Empire* 51 (September 1993): 40.

⁸ Geoff Brown, "Th-th-that's all too cute for words, folks!", *The Times* 5 August 1993: 29.

⁹ Olivier De Bruyn, "Une incertaine tendance du jeune cinéma français", *Positif* 399 (May 1994): 48-50. Emphasis added. The title is a pun on François Truffaut's famous article, "A Certain Tendency of the French Cinema", reprinted in Bill Nichols (ed), *Movies and Methods: An Anthology* (Berkeley; Los Angeles; London: University of California Press, 1976): 224-237. The article was originally published as "Une certaine tendance du cinéma français", *Cahiers du Cinéma* 6: 31 (January 1954): 15-29.

¹⁰ Translated from the French: "Tout se passe un peu au-dessus du réel salissant: le cinéma d'Akerman est en état de lévitation...sur un petit nuage. Bleu, évidemment, le nuage." J.-P.J., "Nuit et jour", *Positif* 368 (October 1991): 62.

¹¹ Terry Lovell, "Sociology of Aesthetic Structures and Contextualism", in Denis McQuail (ed), *Sociology of Mass Communications: Selected Readings* (Harmondsworth: Penguin Books, 1972): 329-349.

¹² McRobbie, "Nuit et jour (Night and Day)": 55.

¹³ Translated from the French: "S'il te faut choisir une cage, avec toi je la partage".

¹⁴ As shown by the feminist work on the concept of seduction and the interest in men.

¹⁵ Giorgiana Colville, "Mais qu'est-ce qu'elles voient Regards de Françaises

à la caméra?", unpublished paper, University of Colorado, BO: 1-2.

[16] "I wanted the two men to be a bit alike". "Big Time", interview with Mansel Stimpson, *What's On In London* 4 August 1993: 22.

[17] Colville: 14.

[18] Lisa Nesselson, "Nuit et jour (Night and Day)", *Variety* 9 September 1991.

[19] Danton: 63.

[20] Stimpson: 22.

[21] Mary Ann Doane, "The Voice in the Cinema: The Articulation of Body and Space", in Elisabeth Weis and John Belton (eds), *Film Sound: Theory and Practice* (New York: Columbia University Press, 1985): 162-176. Kaja Silverman, *The Acoustic Mirror: The Female Voice in Psychoanalysis and Cinema* (Bloomington; Indianapolis: Indiana University Press, 1988).

[22] Stimpson: 22.

[23] Sandy Flitterman-Lewis, "Fascination, Friendship and the 'Eternal Feminine'", unpublished paper, Rutgers University: 9.

[24] See "Anxious Affinities: Text as Screen in Truffaut's *Jules et Jim*", in T Jefferson Kline, *Screening the Text: Intertextuality in New Wave French Cinema* (Baltimore; London: The Johns Hopkins University Press, 1992): 7-23.

[25] Colville: 15.

[26] Elizabeth Wilson, "The City of the Floating World: Paris", in *The Sphinx in the City: Urban Life, the Control of Disaster, and Women* (Berkeley; Los Angeles; Oxford: University of California Press, 1991): 47-64.

[27] That Akerman herself contributed explicitly to this dominant tradition had already been signalled in her episode for *Paris vu par...20 ans après* (*Paris Seen By, 20 Years Later*, 1984) – *J'ai faim, j'ai froid* (*I'm Hungry, I'm Cold*) – a film which itself was a reference to the New Wave film, *Six in Paris*.

[28] Ginette Vincendeau, "Women's Cinema, Film Theory and Feminism in France", *Screen* 28: 4 (autumn 1987): 4.

[29] Translated from the French: "c'est Jack le pôle américain et Joseph, le pôle biblique entre lesquels se tendent l'identité et la culture de Chantal Akerman". Danton: 62.

[30] Stimpson: 22.

The mechanics of the performative body in *The Eighties*

Gwendolyn Audrey Foster

In *Les Années 80* (*The Eighties*, 1983), Chantal Akerman playfully deconstructs the making of her later film, *Golden Eighties/Window Shopping* (1986). *The Eighties* consists of out-takes and raw footage of auditions and rehearsals for *Golden Eighties/Window Shopping*. *The Eighties* can loosely be described as an experimental film that toys with repetition, serial variation and the mechanics of performance. As Ivone Margulies has written: "*The Eighties*, about people who work in neighboring shops in a fashion mall, parades a dizzying number of disjunctive strategies under the guise of transferring a casting rehearsal from video to film".[1]

The film is a meditation as camp, and a contemplation of the mechanics of the performative body as it is constructed in the heterotopic musical comedy. Songs, lines of dialogue, and fragments of choreography are repeatedly rehearsed and reframed, in a demystification of the filmic construction of the musical and a meditation on the nature of filmic spectacle as simulacrum. The simulacrum, the copy without an original, is the centrepiece of the film. The multiple readings of dialogue lines, for example, mark a playful deconstructive heterosexual performativity and an embrace of serial repetition that is not unlike a filmic version of serial repetition in two-dimensional artwork such as the *Marilyn* or *Elvis* series by Andy Warhol. Clichéd dialogue such as "I know, but I hoped. I love him. I love him so. Now it's all over, all is over, no one will love me", appears and reappears in a dizzying myriad of forms, often from the mouths of various different players, sometimes sung, sometimes spoken, and often sung or spoken by the director herself. Like Warhol, Akerman uses serial repetition to investigate and to queer this overdetermined, highly emotional subject-matter. These serial variations of music, dialogue and performances are removed from the formal rules of the musical comedy, in which people erupt into spontaneous song and dance numbers, only to return to equally absurd narratives that usually centre around predictable, heterosexually-centred romantic plots in traditional musical comedies. I suggest that Akerman, as a lesbian auteur, is commenting on the constructed nature of gendered performance through the use of repetitive acts. Judith Butler writes gendered identity as "an identity instituted through a stylized repetition of acts".[2] *The Eighties* thus barrages the viewer with a highly stylised, rapidly edited, manipulation of gests, or repeated acts, especially those acts associated with heterotopic musicals and melodramas: the sigh, the song, the dance sequence, the musical number. The film culminates in a fifteen-minute musical sequence which is a sort of trailer for *Golden Eighties/ Window Shopping*, itself a feminist camp send-up of the musical form.

In some ways, Akerman's obvious fondness for syrupy musical comedy seems completely at odds with her penchant for cinematic formalism. But in the context of her entire body of work, one can find numerous displays of a fascination with camp and with the performative nature of song and dance. However, as Margulies observes, "Akerman's brush with the musical runs deeper than a momentary reach for a different, lighter mode: paradigmatically abstracted in *The Eighties* or frozen in a caricature of spontaneity in *Golden Eighties/Window Shopping*, the musical is for Akerman the cheerful form of a basic perversion, an overflowing of affect present in all of the filmmaker's work".[3] Even in Akerman's first short film, *Saute ma ville* (*Blow up My Town*, 1968), the central character, played by Akerman herself, sings and dances in her kitchen as she destroys everything around her. There is a medusan feminist humour to be found in much of Akerman's work, often displayed in song and dance and other gestures of performance. Indeed, it seems to me that many critics have approached her work with such a moribund seriousness that they have often overlooked the embrace of camp humour implicit in many of her films. Critics have also tended to denarrate Akerman's sexuality, in the same manner that many critics ignored the queer alterity implicit in Andy Warhol's films (instead concentrating on "straight" formalist readings), at least until the publication of the recent anthology, *Pop Out: Queer Warhol*.[4] It should come as no surprise, therefore, that Akerman and Warhol embrace camp in both its formalist and its humorous strategies. As transgendered performance artist Kate Bornstein writes, "[c]amp can be a leading edge in the deconstruction of gender...Camp in fact reclaims gender and re-shapes it as a game".[5] In addition, the formalism of the mechanics of queer performativity in Akerman's films invigorates the possibility for agency, as well as the feminist possibilities for a queer reclaiming of subjective positionality through a manipulation of tropes of gendered identity. Margulies' writing on *The Eighties* gestures towards this very issue. Margulies places the film within the context of a discussion of soap opera, melodrama and performance, associating the film with hyperrealist layering. Although deeming the sequences in the film centreless, Margulies notes that "[t]he film's fragmentary structure keeps its pop elements – the musical's song, soap opera's dialogue – intact".[6] In other words, the serial performances both invite and disinvite the spectator into a contemplation of gendered performativity. As Lili Berko notes:

> Offering oneself as image, facing the live camera or simply turning a camera onto oneself, the postmodern subject confronts herself finally as object – becoming the object of her own desire, caught in between subjectivity and objectivity, between seeing and being seen. She not only consumes the object of her desire, but can only recognize this act of consumption through the process of objectification offered by the apparatus of surveillance.[7]

It is this question of gendered or genderless performativity coupled with the act of surveillance which Akerman addresses here, as she invites the performers within her film, as well as the audience of the completed work, to contemplate the production of spectacle implicit in the staging of *The Eighties*, which is all the more hyperreal and steeped in artifice because of the film's embrace of/distancing from the format of the classical Hollywood heterotopia of the musical.

Furthermore, as Margulies writes, "*The Eighties* thus poses a question at the core of postmodernist aesthetics: Is the film stating the impossibility of difference or, cumulatively, through a putative emerging *différance* [sic], stating the force of the cliché?".[8] In performing difference through the self-reflexive medium of the experimental film, Akerman makes a political statement about the nature of performance in the musical and melodrama film, for, as Georges Vigarello observes, "playing a role involves putting it at a distance in order to dominate it better".[9] *The Eighties* embraces difference through the display of serial repetitions of gendered performances across the limitations of the cinematic apparatus, thus rearticulating the bodies and gestures of Akerman's performers into a confrontational displacement of our expectations of traditional musical and narrative film.

The Eighties insists on an examination of acting, performance, rehearsal and, perhaps most importantly, simulation. Akerman interrogates the simulacrum, the copy lacking an original, as it is described by Jean Baudrillard in *Simulacra and Simulation*. In Baudrillard's work, the author repeatedly returns to the copy or simulacrum, finding that representation itself "attempts to absorb simulation by interpreting it as a false representation, [while] simulation envelops the whole edifice of representation itself as simulacrum".[10] With *The Eighties* and *Golden Eighties/Window Shopping*, Akerman inverts the stages of the usual practice of releasing a film and then later releasing a documentary on the making of that film. Instead, *The Eighties* is a simulacrum at its purest form. It is not only a duplicate of an original that does not yet exist, but also, paradoxically, an original

134

in the sense that it contemplates the concept of mass production, and simulated reproduction of performed sexualities. It is not only *The Eighties* itself that displays the simulacrum, but also the performances themselves which embody simulacra; as copies without originals, each performance, gesture and musical number is serially performed and reperformed.

The simulation of production in both *The Eighties* and *Golden Eighties/Window Shopping* marks a reworking of film as spectacle and the place of the performing body in the musical genre. *The Eighties* deconstructs the alignment of images into a whole spectacle, demonstrating Guy Debord's thesis that "the spectacle is not a collection of images; rather it is a social relationship between people that is mediated by images".[11] At several points in *The Eighties*, Akerman highlights the social relationships between the simulators, the actors and the director. Indeed, the most pleasurable "scenes" or constructions in the film usually centre around playful movements between "natural" and "artificial" performances. In one case, for example, an actress and the director (heard offscreen) discuss the manner in which to convey emotion in a particular scene. The actress returns to the scene (actually the rehearsal of a scene) and emotes in an overly melodramatic fashion. Next, the camera pauses on the face of the actor while the director explains how she would like her to play the scene. As Akerman speaks, the actress drops the simulation of artificial emotion, looks almost directly into the camera, and, for a second, displays a hint of "natural performance" in a display of slightly guarded annoyance and boredom: a direct hint of *anti-sprezzatura*. It is evocative and unexpected moments such as these that punctuate the text of *The Eighties*. Even while savouring the critique of simulated emotion, we are drawn to the "real". But it is, in fact, the copy itself that defines and exposes the "real".

The Eighties and *Golden Eighties/Window Shopping* are therefore spectacles of antinaturalism, as are all musicals, but they are occasionally punctured by moments of naturalistic gesture. Akerman plays with gesture as it is represented across the spectrum of natural and antinatural performance. In *The Eighties*, there is often a blurring of these categories. If an actor is simulating a real emotion, is not she, to some extent, performing the real? In fact, *The Eighties* deconstructs norms of behaviour that are designed to obscure the constructedness of emotion. Those norms dictate that we smile, for example, even when we might be experiencing anger, hostility or boredom. Furthermore, these norms require that we hide our ability to perform this behaviour; that we make an art of artifice. These 20th-century conceptions of the body are informed by the Renaissance embrace of *sprezzatura*. Bizzell and Herzberg define *sprezzatura* as a process whereby "the talented and humanistically learned person should make his or her accomplishments appear to be the outcome of unstudied nature, not art".[12] The concept of *sprezzatura*, a kind of feigned natural performance, is consistently used as a trope in performance, whether in the social arena of everyday life, or in the spectacle of the most insipid melodramatic musical. The musical is a form of spectacle that depends upon excessive display of artifice. The performed bodies in the musical and performed *sprezzatura* thus combine to celebrate the spectacle of artifice and the possibilities of cross-dressing around the spectrum of gender, sexuality and identity.

It has become popular to accept a universalising approach to the modern body as a mechanised being, to evoke a "problem of the body in machine culture",[13] for example. Looking back at earlier, culturally defined notions of the gendered performing body problematises a postmodern inquiry into the mechanics of gesture. Classical rhetoricians, for example, worked from a culturally defined body which does not easily fit into our 20th-century notions of rhetoric and gesture. While it may seem obvious that regulation of the body is a prerequisite for female-gendered performance, a rereading of the history of gesture in rhetorical literature provides a glimpse into the phenomenological corseting of the gendered body in Eurocentric discourse. I am interested in the binary splits between "natural" and "artificial" stances, particularly as they can be applied to performances of gender and sexuality in *The Eighties*. I would like to explore the relationship of gesture to the performance of gender and *sprezzatura* in *The Eighties*.

Feminist performance artists such as Karen Finley and Annie Sprinkle work to reject classical rhetorical definitions of gesture. This involves the whole speaking public-private body. 20th-century conceptions of the body are informed not only by a religious dogma of distrust for the body, but also by the Renaissance embrace of *sprezzatura*. As a woman, I am quite familiar with the art of *sprezzatura*, having been acculturated to value feigned naturalness. A handbook on beauty from 1955 reads: "the more natural you look after making up, the better job you've done".[14] European women are quite accustomed to the ideology of *sprezzatura* as it applies to the production of an artificial "natural" self. The effortlessness of *sprezzatura* comes into play in every bodily performance. The classical rhetoric of gesture which embraced all excess and the passions of the body was largely lost with the rise of a culturally accepted dominance of *sprezzatura* in the Renaissance period. The rhetoric of gesture has therefore had a profound effect on female body experience. The dominance of *sprezzatura* as a behavioural model for women in conduct literature, the strict enforcement of modesty upon the female body, and the many ideologies designed to silence women have had an immeasurable effect on women's ability to become "rhetors" or performers. It has become commonplace to regard rhetoric as an empty gesture, and even the word "gesture" conjures a notion of emptiness, quite possibly informed by the rise of *sprezzatura*. But the history of gesture is ideologically important in a feminist examination of the performing female body. In a sense, gesture itself has been colonised – shorn of its original meaning and displaced from the offices of classical rhetoric in which it was indelibly inscribed. The classical rhetors could not actively conceive a model in which the speaker is disconnected from her own gesturing body, much less her audience. Plato, for example, distrusted *sprezzatura* for its cookery and flattery.[15]

Akerman's *The Eighties* reclaims the margin between these falsely contrived definitions of modality. The overripe performances of banal, commercialised love ballads, melodramatic speech-acts, and the gestures of highly romanticised dance sequences in *The Eighties* suggest a playful camp embrace of excess of simulation of gendered and sexed tropes of emotion characteristic of heterotopic romance and ballad. *The Eighties*, like the feminist performance art of Karen Finley, refashions the performing body around a reclamation of space and an embrace of excess. Iris Marion Young, a Socialist feminist and philosopher, has examined the connection between the cultural disciple of the female body and the objectification of the women:

> The young girl acquires many subtle habits of feminine body comportment – walking like a girl, tilting her head like a girl, standing and sitting like a girl, gesturing like a girl, and so on. The girl learns actively to hamper her movements...The source of this objectified bodily existence is in the attitude of others regarding her, but the woman herself often actively takes up her body as a mere thing. She gazes at it in the mirror, worries about how it looks to others, prunes it, shapes it, molds and decorates it...This objectified bodily existence accounts for the self-consciousness of the feminine relation to her body and resulting distance she takes from her body.[16]

The regulation of the female body becomes an history of restraint. Furthermore, as Judith Butler explains, we are culturally trained to avoid "incorrect" performance of gender:

> Performing one's gender wrong initiates a set of punishments both obvious and indirect, and performing it well provides the reassurance that there is an essentialism of gender identity after all. That this reassurance is so easily displaced by anxiety, that culture so readily punishes or marginalizes those who fail to perform the illusion of gender essentialism should be sufficient sign that on some level there is social knowledge that the truth or falsity of gender is only socially compelled and in no sense ontologically necessitated.[17]

One of the reasons for the popularity of the musical and the melodrama, for women and gay men, is that these filmic genres provide a stage on which we have been allowed to perform gender in ways that are forbidden in everyday life. More importantly, these genres have allowed and encouraged audience-members to identify with the gendered performers in these films, whose acts mimic *sprezzatura*, problematise gender, and revel in excess. Using parody, mimicry and repetition, the performances of gender identity in *The Eighties* question the notion of a body constituted by *sprezzatura*. It is this wide spectrum of artifice that Akerman exposes through a number of postmodern strategies in *The Eighties*. As Lucy Fischer points out, Akerman's use of serial repetition, her use of multiple actors to play a single role, her ephemeral presence throughout the text of the film both as a participant, and in her insistent use of voice-overs, coupled with her choice of sets (a clothes shop and a hair salon), "reduce melodrama to a series of gestural poses".[18] Surprisingly, in *The Eighties*, the fragmentation of the musical as spectacle does not at all do away with pleasure. In this assertion I agree with Margulies, who finds pleasure in the manner in which *The Eighties* self-reflexively works "to intensify the melodramatic affect of the love song or soap-opera dialogue".[19] After viewing the "final product" invoked and introduced by Akerman's film, *Golden Eighties/Window Shopping*, *The Eighties* is even more pleasurable because it exposes the ludic playfulness of the director and the joy of discovering the transgressions across boundaries of "real" and "artificial" simulacra.

Akerman mines the implicit humour in the recognition of artifice, in the repetition of melodramatic displays of simulated excessive emotion. One of the funniest sequences in the film occurs as an actress records a doomed heterodystopic ballad. Firstly, we hear Akerman offscreen, commenting on the performance; then another shot reveals the back of Akerman's head and body as she directs the actress. At the end of the song, Akerman and the actress both dissolve into "authentic" laughter. Akerman displays excessive pleasure as she turns to the camera, smiling. Later, Akerman herself is seen and heard overdubbing the same song with an overwrought excess of artificial emotion. The excess of simulated emotion is seemingly inexhaustible in *The Eighties*. There is a considerable degree of feminist/queer pleasure to be derived from the spectatorial act of viewing Akerman and her other female performers assume the masquerade of excess emotion. Following this sequence, we see the actress Delphine Seyrig performing a scene, while Seyrig's "voice" is dubbed by Akerman. Throughout this simulated/removed/mimetic performance we are treated to lines such as "He's handsome, but dumb", and other trite, yet innately hilarious comments that gain value as tropes of feminine excess and feminist camp.

Akerman locates pleasure in the spectacle of the performing body by returning to the simulated performance, thus calling into question the viability of uniform subjectivity as she refashions the performing body as a floating identity, a signifier of mimetic performance. As performance critic Ellen Brinks notes, "mimetic performance makes its commodified subjects and objects interchangeable".[20] Like Warhol's famous three-minute static screen tests, Akerman's series of implacable tableaux encourages an interchangeable unfixed subjectivity, with one difference: Akerman's interventionist presence as director, which is notably absent in most of Warhol's films. In *The Eighties*, Akerman directly displays her interventions, both onscreen during the shooting of *The Eighties*, and also as an authorial presence during the post-production of the film. Onscreen, for one example, Akerman prods an actor with offscreen (voice-over) directorial instructions such as "That's too emphatic". In post-production, Akerman further emphasises her directorial presence within the work by hyper-manipulation of the film's soundtrack, including the asynchronous placement of "Foley" sounds (artificial footsteps, door slams, and so on) to heighten the constructedness of the completed work.

Akerman thus includes the sounds of doors slamming and heels clicking where there is no corresponding image to go with these sounds, effectively undermining the supposed "veracity" of the film spectacle. These aural interventions displace ocularcentrism as it has been identified by Martin Jay. Jay notes that the invention of visual apparatus from the microscope to the camera has encouraged us to assume the fidelity of any image as true, and, paradoxically, encouraged an ocularcentric "scopic regime",[21] one in which the spectator no longer seems to be able to discriminate between a "real" image and a copy or reproduction.

The Eighties therefore displaces ocularcentrism in order to unveil in the act of simulation, and remind us of the manner in which film tends to rely upon sound and music seamlessly to draw together disparate images in a performance which amounts to filmic *sprezzatura*. Indeed, Akerman's aural and visual interventions remind the viewer that she/he must actively look, rather than passively listen and gaze, at the spectacle she/he is witnessing. One of the most resonant instances of this contemplation of spectacle occurs in those sequences in *The Eighties* that are reminiscent of early Muybridge studies of body movement. In these sequences, both male and female actors repetitively perform acts and gestures such as walking, dancing, singing and vogueing. Akerman draws together these (de)gendered performances and gestures by scoring them to an uncut song on the soundtrack. Because the song is whole and uncut, however, Akerman uses jump cuts in the visuals to expose her attempt to capture the performative body outside the limits of essentialised notions of gender and sexual identity.

This reconception of the musical sequence lays bare the tendency of film directors to depend upon what dance theorist Judith Lynne Hanna terms "managing bodies".[22] In *The Eighties*, the audience is called upon to do the work of managing bodies and managing gender. As a viewer, one is confronted with a lack of context, but, at the same time, one is treated to an excess of emotion and gesture within the space of the musical sequence. In the absence of seamlessness of sound and image embraced by the dominant Hollywood musical, one has little idea what is being simulated in the hyper-deconstructed cinematic world of *The Eighties*; it is a spectacle without precedent. In Akerman's film, the viewer is forced out of a traditionally passive ocularcentric position into the role of active observer-participant, and must pay keen attention to the performative gestures presented within the work. Gilles Deleuze accurately describes the performing body of *The Eighties*: "Chantal Akerman's novelty lies in showing in this way bodily attitudes as the sign of states of body particular to the female character...[b]ut the chain of states of female body is *not* closed...the states of body have become burlesque, sources of a ballad".[23]

Although simulated performances in *The Eighties* examine the burlesque nature of gendered performance, the film cannot simply be described as a camp parody of the musical. Because of its exposure of *sprezzatura* and ocularcentrism, perhaps it could be more accurately described as a series of poetic celebrations of camp and translations of burlesque: a ballad of the performing body. By foregrounding the body, Akerman engages in what feminist anthropologist Allison Jablonko terms "'haptic' learning, learning by bodily identification".[24] Moving across the boundaries of visual pleasure, both scopic and haptic, Akerman carves out a performative space for the skin, the body, the uncontainable vessel of subjectivity. The body as haptic and scopic is thus irreducible and yet embodied. As Jennifer M Barker explains, "the body as excess presents such a problem for current theories...that posit narration as a cohesive, unambiguous *containment* of different and contradicting voices within the text".[25] In this sense, Akerman is similar to other filmmakers who address assumptions behind narrative theory and ethnographic theory, as well as the larger issues around the representation of subjectivity. *The Eighties* is a film of excess; it explores space and subjectivity in ways not usually seen in narrative film. Akerman confronts the viewer of *The Eighties* with an excess of subjectivity, pain, pleasure, work and daily routine. *The Eighties* is, above all other considerations, a film of the body, and it demands that we rethink the way in which we experience the body in the spectacle of film, the apparatus of film, and the implied objective-subjective power relationship of film spectatorship. It subtly reworks the boundaries of cinematic pleasure to reveal another fold: a queer space where gender, sexuality and identity are mobile.

Kristin Thompson reminds us that "[e]ach film dictates the way it wants to be viewed",[26] and that responding to a film's excesses can renew "its ability to intrigue us by its strangeness".[27] Thompson adds that "it also can help us to be aware of how the whole film – not just its narrative – works upon our perception".[28] Traditional film methodologies thus ignore facets of queer performative experiential perception in film, both through and with the body. Borrowing, therefore, from ethnography and phenomenology, I would like to push the envelope of filmic reception towards another possible reading of subjectivity and alterity. It is often assumed in film theory, for example, that the introduction of the film apparatus necessitates the obliteration of subjectivity, that the film "captures", and therefore objectifies and negates, the subject. This is one way of looking at film, and many narrative films conform to this paradigm; but perhaps we have missed opportunities for intervention in formulating such a universalising concept. Jean-Louis Baudry proposes that film theorists have been so intent on the characteristics of film image that they have not noticed that the apparatus "in its totality includes the subject":

> Almost exclusively, it is the technique and content of film which have retained attention: characteristics of the image, depth of field, offscreen space, shot, single-shot sequence, montage, etc.; the key to the impression of reality has been sought in the structuring of image and movement, in complete ignorance of the fact that the impression of reality is dependent first of all on a subject effect and that it might be necessary to examine the position of the subject facing the image in order to determine the raison d'être for the cinema effect.[29]

The Eighties provides a case in point when the apparatus of the cinematograph indeed positions the subject somewhere, as Henri Bergson writes, "halfway between the 'thing' and the representation".[30] Moving through the body, *The Eighties* problematises most film theoretical models, because experiencing the film moves us into a negotiation across our own haptic zones, our own experience of the body.

Traditionally, the centre of gravity is located in the ontological space occupied by the critic and/or theoretician, discounting any performative rupture across the filmic apparatus. What is at stake here, therefore, is the underlying facticity of the phenomenon of filmic/ audience perception. Perhaps this is what Christian Metz was hinting at when he wrote that "*[t]he fact that must be understood is that films are understood*".[31] "Understanding" would therefore necessitate facilitating perception of the body by the external senses of the human corpus. Or, as Michael Taussig suggests: "Might not the mimetic faculty and the sensuous knowledge it embodies be precisely this hard-to-imagine state wherein the senses therefore become directly in their practise theoreticians?".[32] Taussig, rereading Walter Benjamin's famous and often-quoted work on subject-object relations in spectatorship, thus suggests that the camera can "create a new sensorium involving a new subject-object relation and therefore a new person".[33]

The replication of performative acts and sequences in *The Eighties* brings to mind the discussion of the inherently mimetic function of the photographic process. In particular, the emphasis on the replication of various acts, songs and performative gestures in *The Eighties* suggests a replication of the function of the "aura" at work. This notion of the "aura" is particularly applicable to both *The Eighties* and *Golden Eighties/Window Shopping*. Far from destroying the original, or decaying the aura of subjectivity of *The Eighties*, Akerman's film can be seen, in Benjamin's phrase, as "meet[ing] the beholder halfway"[34] between subjectivities. Benjamin continues:

> The definition of the aura as a 'unique phenomenon of a distance however close it may be' represents nothing but the formulation of the cult value of the work of art in categories of space and time perception. Distance is the opposite of closeness. The essentially distant object is the unapproachable one. Unapproachability is indeed a major quality of the cult image. True to its nature, it remains 'distant, however close it may be.' The closeness which one may gain from its subject matter does not impair the distance which it retains in its appearance.[35]

I would suggest that, in its multiplicity of reproduction(s), the metapoetic refraction of repetitive performative acts in *The Eighties* serves to break down the distance of the aura, in which distance is automatically presumed between spectator and spectacle. Susan Buck-Morss suggests that it is only when "the gaze is returned"[36] that we can break down the aura. Yet, the gaze is only one of the senses that moves the body of *The Eighties* across the spectacle of filmic apparatus, and suggests the possibility for a shared sense of embodied subjectivity.

Performances comprised of fragments of female gesture move through the body in the cinematic world of Akerman's film. Every gesture is indicative of the gendered performative zones of the haptic and scopic, the skin, the ineluctable experience of alterity. Deleuze underscores the political implications of the female gesture or "gest", in his discussion of Akerman's films when he notes that "[t]he states of the body secrete the slow ceremony which joins together the corresponding attitudes, and develop a female gest which overcomes the history of men and the crisis of the world".[37]

The characters of the ballad that is the text of *The Eighties* are as much the roles that are repeatedly taken off and reassumed as they are the personalities and simulated gestures that are asserted, copied, simulated and rejected. In *The Eighties*, the repetition of lines, performances and musical sequences become examinations of performative/cinematic excess. Signalling this, the film opens and closes with the repetition of the line, "At your age, grief soon wears off", which becomes absurd through multiple repetitions. *The Eighties* thus emerges as a study of repetitions, in which actions are broken down into their component parts and then reconstructed in new and restructured moving-image glyphs. Akerman deconstructs and calls into question the notion of meaning through repetition, much in the manner of the work of Trinh T Minh-Ha, who notes that:

> As viewers, we often fix a meaning or metaphor by identifying or associating the image with the commentary that accompanies it. Repetitions of the same sentence in slightly different forms and in ever-changing contexts help to unsettle such a fixity, and to perceive the plural, sliding relationship between ear and eye, image and word.[38]

As one example of this revisualising function, the ballad used in *The Eighties* is suggestive of a Wittgensteinian sense of de-worlding, where, according to Karl-Otto Apel, "the connection of the 'significative references' inherent in the life-world, in the sense of the relatedness or meaningfulness of entities is dissolved".[39] De-worlded, the performing body is free yet captured. It is signifying, yet devoid of the corporeal sense of representational signification. Perhaps, in a sense, the performing body of *The Eighties* may be dependent upon an artificial and simulated apprehension of time, which is dependent upon the liminal fabric of the cinematic "real time"/"reel time" trope which informs the basic essence of cinematographic representationalism. It is in the ballad which Akerman constructs in *The Eighties* that we contemplate this time differential. *The Eighties* synthesises time in circuitous expressions of excess desire, punctuated by moments of an absence of pleasure. Between contemplation and action, the film redefines time through the act of simulation. Gesturing towards this haptic trope, Éric Alliez suggests a notion of time that moves primarily in the symbolic:

> It is not two 'varieties' of the Image that are to be understood by contemplation-image and action-image, but rather two tendencies, two movements of opposite orientation that constitute the double regime of referral for images. A pure

image, and a truthless image: a trace, a shadow, a reflection with no consistency and no longer a hypostasis, a centrifugal scattering that no longer knows any folding back toward 'what is up ahead': the simulacrum-image.[40]

The simulacrum-image of Akerman, Warhol, Trinh T Minh-Ha and other postmodernists is built upon the simulacrum of bodies and time in and outside hypostasis. Emotion in *The Eighties* is thus overwrought and compressed, performed at high-speed in contrast to the vicissitudes of actual existence, as experienced by the simulated, lived body in everyday existence. The act of performance does mimetic violence to real time, life and experience, and to lived bodies, individualities and communities. Can the postmodern hyperreality of experience exhibited in *The Eighties* transform identity? What is at stake in the manufacture and observation of the manufacture of performing bodies? Perhaps it is manifestly true, as Herbert Blau insists, that performance "may transform the one performing...[yet in the act of performance, one is nevertheless reminded that] at the level of community, whatever the powers of performance once were, they no longer are".[41]

Yet, I think that what is most at stake in this series of moving-image transformations is the representation of performed bodies and the simulation of cinematic and actual time, which moves towards what Nell Tenhaff terms "the unbounded body".[42] The unbounded body is, however, not easily rendered across cinematic or televisual subjectivities. In the ballad of *The Eighties* and *Golden Eighties/Window Shopping*, a ballad that highlights the routine commodification of the body and its excess pleasures, we find the representation of what is most at odds with commodification, the pure "becoming body" as described by Deleuze:

It is not the distinction between the Model and the copy, but rather between copies and simulacra. Pure becoming, the unlimited, is the matter of the simulacrum insofar as it eludes the action of the Idea and insofar as it contests both model and copy at once...the paradox of pure becoming, with its capacity to elude the present, is the paradox of infinite identity.[43]

Gendered identity is unbound in *The Eighties*, and found to be endlessly multiple, endlessly signifying, an enabler of feminist and queer alterity that manifests itself in moments of intense, shared feminist camp pleasure. *The Eighties* provides a sharp contrast to traditional musicals of the dominant heterotopic Hollywood cinema, which, when deconstructed, are no longer vehicles of captive bodies, captured performances, time held in bondage. To borrow a phrase from both *The Eighties* and *Golden Eighties/Window Shopping*, "that's no life...cooped up in the shop with the customers", and it is precisely cinematic and alteric imprisonment which Akerman both abrogates and interrogates in her works.

However, in the case of *The Eighties*, this zone of performative existence constitutes a simulacrum of tourism. As televisual tourists, we are invited "to go and see what has become trite".[44] What has become trite is not just human emotion, performed heterosexualities, romance or spectacle, but identity itself. In exposing the vehicle that commodifies individuals and makes them interchangeable and insipid, Akerman draws us towards a reclamation of identity as daily lived performance. Gendered identity and heterosexual romance are thus both problematised and celebrated in the film. Identification with the postmodern spectacle, the hyperreal performing bodies of *The Eighties*, reminds us that the average Hollywood spectacle works to "keep identity at a distance...even as it makes possible the illusion of identity as immediate, secure, and totalizable".[45]

Identity as a salesperson, "cooped up in the shop with customers", is the main challenge to the subject of *The Eighties*. It is romance, spectacle, the community of performing bodies and the vehicle of excess romantic melodrama in song that provide Akerman's audience with an effective and liberating (although possibly illusory) catharsis. But identity as the passive spectator of the simulacrum, where "this is not life", can paradoxically be perceived as a liberating position. As spectators, we are invited into the spectacle Akerman creates by the repeated performances of excess she provides for us, coupled with the commentary and self-reflexivity of the performances, dance sequences, and her resolutely self-reflexive direction of the actors. We, working as spectators/directors in concert with Akerman, are as much choreographers of the onscreen identities presented to us in *The Eighties* as the choreographers of our own shifting, endlessly performed and transmuted personal identities.

The Eighties is probably one of Akerman's least well-known and least celebrated feature films, yet I think it is one of her best. In some ways, it is the most difficult; it works in parodic fragments, and moves spectatorial pleasure outside the boundaries of traditional film form. Unlike some of the director's earlier films, particularly *Je tu il elle* (*I... You...He...She*, 1974) and *Les Rendez-vous d'Anna* (*Meetings with Anna*, 1978), *The Eighties* has never reached a particularly wide international audience, and it remains at the margins of the discussion in most examinations of Akerman's work. This is unfortunate for a number of reasons, most markedly because *The Eighties* questions the rites of performance, of even non-performance (and perhaps existence itself), in a manner which takes precedence from both the realities of our corporeal existence, and the shared commonality of the cinematic experience that we have constructed through decades of viewing as the "movie musical". As such, it inevitably queers Astaire, Rogers and other earlier practitioners of the cinematic musical spectacle, even as it also gestures towards *Un Divan à New York* (*A Couch in New York*, 1996), a film in which a man and woman virtually swap identities in yet another celebration of simulation. *The Eighties* is a remarkable study of simulation in film form, revealing the space between documentary and fiction, excess and lack of emotion, and, in the process, exposing the identity politics of the musical film. As Akerman states, "between a script and a movie, one must go through a whole landscape. *Les Années 80* [*The Eighties*] covers the time spent in this landscape".[46]

Akerman mines this landscape, not only to theorise the performative, but also to perform the theoretical. Akerman locates performative spaces and opportunities for intervention. In the process, she opens up new modes of experiencing alterity, subjectivity and gender. As B. Ruby Rich remarks, "[i]n Chantal Akerman's work, what is most valuable for us is her decoding of oppressive cinematic conventions and her invention of new codes".[47] These codes disrupt the boundaries between film, performance art and theory, dragging us kicking and screaming into an engagement with our performative bodies, our lived bodies, and our identity constructs.

Notes

1   Ivone Margulies, *Nothing Happens: Chantal Akerman's Hyperrealist Everyday* (Durham, NC; London: Duke University Press, 1996): 185.

2   Judith Butler, "Performative Acts and Gender Constitution: An Essay in Phenomenology and Feminist Theory", in Sue-Ellen Case (ed), *Performing Feminisms: Feminist Critical Theory and Theatre* (Baltimore: The Johns Hopkins University Press, 1990): 270.

3   Margulies: 191.

4   Jennifer Doyle, Jonathan Flatley and José Esteban Muñoz (eds), *Pop Out: Queer Warhol* (Durham, NC: Duke University Press, 1996).

5   Kate Bornstein, *Gender Outlaw* (New York: Vintage Books, 1995): 138.

6   Margulies: 189.

7   Lili Berko, "Surveying the Surveilled: Video, Space and Subjectivity", *Quarterly Review of Film and Video* 14: 1-2 (1992): 76.

8   Margulies: 189.

9   Georges Vigarello, "The Upward Training of the Body from the Age of Chivalry to Courtly Civility", in Michel Fehrer (ed), *Fragments for a History of the Human Body* (New York: Zone Books, 1989): 188.

[10] Jean Baudrillard, *Simulacra and Simulation*, translated by Sheila Faria Glaser (Ann Arbor, MI: The University of Michigan Press, 1994): 6.

[11] Guy Debord, *The Society of Spectacle*, translated by Donald Nicholson-Smith (New York: Zone Books, 1995): 120.

[12] Patricia Bizzell and Bruce Herzberg (eds), *The Rhetorical Tradition: Readings from Classical Times to the Present* (Boston: Bedford, 1990): 468.

[13] Mark Seltzer, *Bodies and Machines* (New York: Routledge, 1992): 21.

[14] Constance Hart, *The Handbook of Beauty* (New York: Dell, 1955): 212.

[15] Plato's attitude towards *sprezzatura* is discussed in Bizzell and Herzberg.

[16] Iris Marion Young (ed), *Throwing Like a Girl and Other Essays in Feminist Philosophy and Social Theory* (Bloomington: Indiana University Press, 1990): 154-155.

[17] Butler: 279.

[18] Lucy Fischer, *Shot/Countershot: Film Tradition and Women's Cinema* (Princeton, NJ: Princeton University Press, 1989): 164.

[19] Margulies: 188.

[20] Ellen Brinks, "Who's Been in My Closet?", in Sue-Ellen Case, Philip Brett and Susan Leigh Foster (eds), *Cruising the Performative* (Bloomington: Indiana University Press, 1995): 9.

[21] Martin Jay, "Photo-unrealism: The Contribution of the Camera to the Crisis of Ocularcentrism", in Stephen Melville and Bill Readings (eds), *Vision and Textuality* (Durham, NC: Duke University Press, 1995): 346.

[22] Judith Lynne Hanna, *The Performer-Audience Connection: Emotion to Metaphor in Dance and Society* (Austin, TX: University of Texas Press, 1983): 25.

[23] Gilles Deleuze, *Cinema 2: The Time-Image*, translated by Hugh Tomlinson and Robert Galeta (London: The Athlone Press, 1989): 196. Emphasis in original.

[24] Allison Jablonko, "New Guinea In Italy: An Analysis Of The Making Of An Italian Television Series From Research Footage Of The Maring People Of Papua New Guinea", in Jack R Rollwagon (ed), *Anthropological Filmmaking: Anthropological Perspectives on the Production of Film and Video for General Public Access* (Chur; London; Paris; New York; Melbourne: Harwood Academic Publishers, 1988): 182.

[25] Jennifer M Barker, "Bodily Irruptions: The Corporeal Assault on Ethnographic Narration", *Cinema Journal* 34: 3 (spring 1995): 68. Emphasis in original.

[26] Kristin Thompson, "The Concept of Cinematic Excess", in Philip Rosen

(ed), *Narrative, Apparatus, Ideology: A Film Theory Reader* (New York: Columbia University Press, 1986): 141.

[27] Ibid.

[28] Ibid.

[29] Jean-Louis Baudry, "The Apparatus: Metapsychological Approaches to the Impression of Reality in the Cinema", in Rosen (ed): 312.

[30] Henri Bergson, *Matter and Memory* (New York: Zone Books, 1988): 9.

[31] Christian Metz, "Problems of Denotation in the Fiction Film", in Rosen (ed): 59. Emphasis in original.

[32] Michael Taussig, *Mimesis and Alterity: A Particular History of the Senses* (New York: Routledge, 1993): 98. Emphasis in original.

[33] Ibid: 24.

[34] Walter Benjamin, *Illuminations*, edited with an introduction by Hannah Arendt, translated by Harry Zohn (London: Fontana, 1973): 214.

[35] Ibid: 236-237.

[36] Susan Buck-Morss, *The Dialectics of Seeing: Walter Benjamin and the Arcades Project* (Cambridge: MIT Press, 1989): 194.

[37] Deleuze: 196.

[38] Trinh T Minh-Ha, *Framer Framed* (New York; London: Routledge, 1992): 228.

[39] Karl-Otto Apel, "Wittgenstein and Heidegger: Language Games and Life Forms", in Christopher Macann (ed), *Critical Heidegger* (London: Routledge, 1996): 250.

[40] Éric Alliez, *Capital Times*, translated by Georges Van Den Abbeele (Minneapolis: University of Minnesota Press, 1996): 64.

[41] Herbert Blau, "Universals of performance; or amortizing play", in Richard Schechner and Willa Appel (eds), *By Means of Performance: Intercultural studies of theatre and ritual* (Cambridge: Cambridge University Press, 1990): 270.

[42] Nell Tenhaff, "Mysteries of the Bioapparatus", in Mary Anne Moser (ed), *Immersed in Technology: Art and Virtual environments* (Cambridge: MIT Press, 1996): 53. The unbounded body is not unlike the "body without organs" defined and described by Gilles Deleuze in, for example, "Delirium: World Historical, Not Familial", in Constantin V Boundas (ed), *The Deleuze Reader* (New York: Columbia University Press, 1993): 115-122.

[43] Deleuze (1993): 40.

[44] Debord: 120.

[45] Diana Fuss, *Identification Papers* (New York: Routledge, 1995): 2.

[46] Chantal Akerman, *Press Packet: Walker Art Center* (Minneapolis: Walker Art Center, 1995: 6.

[47] B. Ruby Rich, "In the Name of Feminist Film Criticism", in Diane Carson, Linda Dittmar and Janice R Welsch (eds), *Multiple Voices in Feminist Film Criticism* (Minneapolis; London: University of Minnesota Press, 1994): 33.

Girl talk: *Portrait of a Young Girl at the End of the 1960s in Brussels*

Judith Mayne

Chantal Akerman's 1993 film, *Portrait d'une jeune fille de la fin des années 60 à Bruxelles (Portrait of a Young Girl at the End of the 1960s in Brussels)*, is a beautiful and haunting evocation of female adolescence and its discontents – desire, loss and the complicated, ambiguous relationship to the transitions between girlhood and womanhood. Central to the film are the dynamics of a love that does not exactly *dare* not speak its name (according to Oscar Wilde's famous definition of homosexuality),[1] but rather does not quite know *how* to speak its name. *Portrait of a Young Girl* is in many ways a coming out story, for the love of one girl for another moves the film forward and structures its narrative development.[2] But it will come as no surprise to those familiar with Akerman's work that this is no transparent coming out tale, and that the film resists any of the simple oppositions between inside and outside, past and present, before and after, which are suggested by the very term "coming out".[3]

Rather, this film explores how lesbian desire is both shaped and repressed by the codes and conventions of heterosexual romance. On the surface, the film could be described as a somewhat conventional girl-meets-boy tale. But what shapes the girl-meets-boy story is the simultaneous desire, for the girl, to connect to another girl and to tell stories. In other words, this is a lesbian narrative with a difference; girl still meets boy, but that classical and timeworn plot is the pretext for the connection between two girls.

Portrait of a Young Girl was commissioned by the French television station ARTE for a series entitled *Tous les garçons et les filles de leur âge (All the Boys and Girls of Their Age)*. Nine filmmakers participated in the series, and the films (most of them, like Akerman's, an hour long or less) tell varied stories of adolescence, often focusing (unsurprisingly) on love and sexuality. In addition to the focus on adolescence, filmmakers were required to include a party scene in their films, as well as songs of the era. The series was designed to reflect, particularly through music, the feel and sensibility of an era, and to offer filmmakers the opportunity to create unique portraits of the past. Other films in the series included *U.S. Go Home* (1994), by Claire Denis (best-known in the United States for her autobiographical film,

Chocolat [1988]), and *Travolta et moi* (*Travolta and Me*, 1993) by Patricia Mazuy.

The opening titles of Akerman's film inform us that the film takes place in April 1968, just a month before the famous worker-student demonstrations and strikes that immobilised France and Western Europe, and that have provided a mythical point of reference for virtually every political movement in Europe in the last three decades. Akerman's film follows Michèle, portrayed with luminous intensity by the marvellous actress, Circé, on the day that she has decided not to return to school. The film begins with the sounds of a ticking clock, and then shows us Michèle, at home, going through a wallet, presumably her father's, for cash. It is early in the morning, and Michèle's father drops her off at the station where she is to catch her bus for school. The first words spoken in the film are Michèle's words of departure to her father, "au revoir Papa". These words prove to be prophetic in more ways than one in the course of the film.

Michèle's new-found liberty takes expression in a variety of forms. She goes to a café where she writes out a variety of excuses for school, beginning with "please excuse Michèle, she had the flu", passing through a series of imaginary funerals she had to attend (her grandmother's, her uncle's, her aunt's – who died after the uncle died – her father's) – and concluding with her own death, announced with flat finality: "She died".[4] The fantasy of her own death is also a fantasy of rebirth, of shedding the various institutional identities she possesses, those associated with the family and school. As if to celebrate this rebirth, Michèle leaves the café, tears up a school folder and exuberantly throws the pieces in the air.

Michèle goes to her school, but lurks outside, next to the bars that surround the grounds. First she encounters one friend Mireille, and announces that she will not return to school. Michèle then meets her best friend Danielle, and they go to a café where they sit with two young men and proceed to kiss them. At one point, Michèle pauses, turns away from the young man she is kissing, and observes Danielle as she continues to kiss the other boy. At this early point in the film, it is impossible to read Michèle's act of observation with any certainty. She looks at her friend, but also looks at her friend as she is kissing another boy. In other words, the look could well be one of longing directed at Danielle, or it could be a look seeking encouragement and approval. It soon becomes clear that Michèle takes as much, if not more, pleasure in talking with Danielle about the boys they encounter as in actually experiencing those encounters in the first place. Indeed, when Danielle and Michèle leave the café, they talk about how disappointing the kissing was, and their conversation occupies more screen time than the actual kissing did.

After Danielle returns to school, Michèle goes to the cinema, where she sits next to a young man. He begins to touch her knee, and Michèle tells him that he can kiss her. This encounter begins an apparently conventional girl/boy romance, but it is a romance from which Danielle is never absent. Indeed, Michèle immediately informs Paul that he cannot go any further than a kiss because she has to meet her friend at school. Michèle describes Danielle and says that he would probably like her. When they leave the cinema, she tells Paul that she let him kiss her not just because she wanted to, but "also to make someone else suffer...and it was to be able to talk about it, too".[5] Paul and Michèle discuss how Michèle will tell the story of her encounter at the cinema. This boy meets girl story, therefore, is from the outset a girl/girl-meets-boy story.

At one point in their wanderings Michèle leaves Paul abruptly, announcing that it is 4 o'clock. She runs to meet Danielle, and proceeds to tell her, in terms that she had "rehearsed" earlier with Paul, about going to the movies. Paul seems to be hovering offscreen; as Michèle performs for Danielle her version of going to the movies, Paul is located, figuratively and literally, in the reverse field of Michèle's sightline. Whether the story provokes any suffering on Danielle's part is debatable; she asks Michèle what is wrong with her and tells her that she appears to be in a rather odd mood. Michèle and Danielle confirm their plans to attend a party that evening.

Danielle goes home, while Michèle and Paul continue to wander around the city together, and it is revealed that Paul has deserted the Army. He and Michèle thus share a common, if tentative, status as drop-outs and wanderers with no particular place to go. Since Paul has no place to stay, Michèle takes him to her cousin's apartment, and we see the two in bed together and we are led to assume (although this is never explicitly shown) that they make love. On the soundtrack during their encounter in the apartment, we hear Leonard Cohen's song "Suzanne" (Michèle shoplifted the album from a music shop earlier during her and Paul's wanderings), the lyrics of which ("Suzanne takes you down/to a place by the river/you can see the boats go by/you could spend the night forever...") form a poignant counterpoint to the encounter shown and implied onscreen. This is Michèle's first sexual encounter, but given the importance accorded to Danielle and Michèle's connection, it is tempting to "hear" Cohen's song as the reminder of the presence of yet another woman in the room.

Michèle invites Paul to the party, but he says he does not like parties; he plans instead to meet Michèle afterwards. Michèle and Danielle meet and wait for the bus together; as in their previous encounter, Danielle tells Michèle that she seems to be "in an odd mood" ("t'as un drôle d'air"). Soon, the girls begin to laugh as they observe others in the bus who are going to the party, and in particular a young man with dark hair.

At the party, the young people dance in a circle, their arms around each other's shoulders. At the centre of the circle is a constantly changing couple, as one person chooses another, who then chooses another, and so on. We see the young man with dark hair dance with Danielle, and then Danielle chooses Michèle. They dance, giggling, and then when it is Michèle's turn to choose a partner, she looks around the circle and again chooses Danielle. During this part of the dance, Trini Lopez's version of the song "La Bamba" is playing. An abrupt change of mood occurs when James Brown's "It's a Man's, Man's, Man's World" begins to play, signalling a shift from group dancing to close, couples dancing.

Danielle again dances with the young man from the bus, and Michèle stands alone in the middle of the group of dancing couples. In the earlier scene at the café, we saw Michèle watch Danielle as she kissed a boy, but that look was brief, and Michèle too was a participant in the kissing. Here, however, something has changed. Michèle is alone; her gaze lingers, as does the camera's gaze on her. This extended shot of Michèle conveys passionate observation and sadness simultaneously. If "Suzanne" provided a poignant counterpoint in the earlier scene with Michèle and Paul in the apartment, here the James Brown song marks the obvious exclusion of Michèle.

Michèle leaves the party, and Danielle catches up with her. Danielle proceeds to tell her friend that she does not like the boy she was dancing with, and they discuss the possibility of another boy, a blond. But again, it is clear that something has changed, for Michèle acknowledges that hearing about the boys Danielle flirts with and dances with makes her suffer. Paradoxically, what sustains their friendship is also what separates them. The film ends as the two young women walk, hand-in-hand, through a field, where Paul awaits. Michèle is crying. The setting of the film changes abruptly in these final moments, for the field through which they walk seems rural and almost idyllic. Virtually everything else in the film has taken place in a decidedly urban setting. But here, the isolated field and the sudden vast expanse of nature make the words and movements of the two girls seem even more removed from the world of the city, the dance and the heterosexual couple.

At the conclusion of the film, Michèle tells Danielle that Paul is waiting for her, and Michèle walks away as Danielle exits from the frame, presumably to be with Paul. The last shot of the film shows Michèle alone, as she walks through the field, away from the camera. Throughout the final images of the film, Paul is there but not there – visually absent, yet present as the object given, as it were, by Michèle to Danielle. But, as Michèle turns her back and walks away, the possibility of storytelling among the two girls appears to be lost forever.

Portrait of a Young Girl thus remembers the late-1960s as both opening up and closing down possibilities of connection. True to the spirit of the series for which it was commissioned, Akerman's portrait of a young girl captures the era of the late-1960s through music, words, and the interactions of its characters. Michèle discusses Sartre and Kierkegaard, and she describes participating in a demonstration against the war in Vietnam. She and Paul share utopian dreams of a future in which there is no poverty, no war. But the film is also wilfully anachronistic; there is no attempt to re-create a Brussels of 1968, no period costumes. Paul and Michèle even browse in a shop that sells compact discs! The remembrance of the 1960s is one filtered through the present.

One sees in *Portrait of a Young Girl* many quintessential preoccupations of Akerman's work, from the patient observation of the passage of time and the everyday to the centrality of female subjectivity. Much of Akerman's work has demonstrated a preoccupation with the difference that lesbianism makes *vis-à-vis* notions of cinematic pleasure and desire, but *Portrait of a Young Girl* is perhaps Akerman's most sustained and provocative work on the topic to date. Several of Akerman's films have suggested how lesbianism upsets any fixed notions of subject/object relationships, while simultaneously suggesting that lesbianism is both inside and outside dominant practices of sexuality. *Portrait of a Young Girl* continues in these directions as well, but does something more at the same time; it evokes with great beauty and sadness the complex ways in which a girl's love for another girl inspires narrative and visual form.

Portrait of a Young Girl bears particularly obvious connections with two of Akerman's earlier works, *Je tu il elle* (*I...You...He...She*, 1974) and *Les Rendez-vous d'Anna* (*Meetings with Anna* [1978]). In *I...You... He...She*, lesbian desire problematises any neat symmetry of the pronouns of the film's title. The protagonist of the film, Julie, is portrayed by Akerman herself, and she engages in a series of self-representing acts, including making love with another woman. But lesbian authorship in the film is no simple "alternative" to heterosexuality, but rather a complex configuration of desire.[6] In *Meetings with Anna*, the series of heterosexual encounters undertaken by the title character of the film are undercut by the shadowy presence of the woman in Italy, who is marked only by a voice in the film. As a voice, as a figure who is both present and absent, the woman in Italy is a force of desire that keeps the film moving. Lesbian representation in both these films concerns cinematic address and the undoing of dualistic structures of communication. In both films, lesbian desire is not only present and absent at the same time (as is the case with *Portrait of a Young Girl*), but also seen as central to the very acts of self-representation. For *I...You...She* and *Meetings with Anna* are both portraits of the artist, and so, in a different but related way, is

Portrait of a Young Girl (as, of course, its title suggests). Michèle expresses a desire to write in the film, and the entire movement of the narrative follows the very process of learning how to see one's own desires.

In addition to its connections with these two other films, *Portrait of a Young Girl* builds upon many of the themes present in *J'ai faim, j'ai froid* (*I'm Hungry, I'm Cold* [1984]), Akerman's contribution to the omnibus film, *Paris vu par, 20 ans après* (*Paris Seen By, 20 Years Later*), a "remake" of the 1964 film in which six filmmakers contributed short films that depict different aspects of life in the city. The remake was marketed as a showcase for the contemporary filmmakers who are heirs to the directors included in the earlier film, including Jean-Luc Godard, Eric Rohmer and Claude Chabrol. Akerman's contribution is a 12-minute, black-and-white film about two teenage girls who have just run away from Brussels to Paris. While their movements are frenzied and always on the verge of the comic, they are nevertheless quite evocative of Michèle.

Like her, they wander the city and occupy a transitional place. And, like her, they have a complex relationship to heterosexuality. They say they want to fall in love, but they slap the faces of the first men who appear. The film offers another version of their budding desire; the two girls kiss each other in order to demonstrate their previous experiences with young men. In the conclusion of the film, the two girls go to the apartment of a man they met in a restaurant and go to bed. One of the girls – who is perpetually hungry – gets up to make something to eat, while the man comes to bed with the other. The camera shows us the girl in the kitchen as the other girl has sex for the first time – punctuated by her scream. The two girls leave and walk away from the camera.

I'm Hungry, I'm Cold might be described, like *Portrait of a Young Girl*, as a coming-of-age film. The process of coming of age involves a complicated relationship to heterosexual initiation, where the rituals shared by the two girls are as important as anything that occurs between a man and a woman. The very process of maturation has a homoerotic component, where the demonstration of how a boy kisses becomes the pretext for a shared kiss. The point here is less whether the girls "are" or "are not" heterosexual than that desire is mediated in a variety of ways – through each other as much as through men. In the process, the kisses are shown onscreen, and the sexual initiation is not – or rather, is shown only through the displaced view of the girl eating in the kitchen.

Like the two girls in *I'm Hungry, I'm Cold*, Michèle participates in a heterosexual world, but she does so obliquely. Michèle narrates that world, while Danielle, at least from Michèle's point of view, becomes increasingly a part of that world. In order to narrate that world, some

155

kind of distance is required. In *Portrait of a Young Girl*, both Danielle and Michèle take pleasure in dissecting romance, in talking after the fact, in connecting with each other. They both delight in girl talk, but Michèle's stakes in that talk are ultimately quite different from those of her friend. For Michèle, virtually every scene of apparent heterosexual desire is presented as quite literally that – a scene to be memorised, embellished perhaps, practised and then retold to Danielle.

The relationship between Danielle and Michèle is sustained and nurtured, at the same time that it is compromised and fractured, by its triangular quality. If Danielle and Michèle are adolescent girls who are being acculturated into the conventions and codes of heterosexuality, the very process of acculturation provides the ironic basis for their own connection, their own erotic bond, their own possibilities for detachment from the presumed expectations of the world around them. Lesbian culture and literature are full of testimonies to and anecdotes about how the conventions of heterosexuality and femininity misfire in one way or another, and an important direction in lesbian filmmaking has explored how the most heterosexual conventions of film can be quite readily inverted to lesbian ends. But Akerman's film is less preoccupied with how such "inversions" occur, and more preoccupied with the very dynamics of triangular desire.

In this context it is useful to examine the issues and debates that have surrounded the discussion of how heterosexual bonds are crossed, compromised, and often superseded by homosocial bonds. Eve Kosofsky Sedgwick's study of male homosociality in English literature, *Between Men*, has been enormously influential in defining the broad and far-ranging scope of homosocial desire. But Sedgwick's analysis is built upon what many have criticised as a most problematic assumption about women and homosociality.

In order to define the range of male homosocial desire, Sedgwick makes what has become a controversial distinction between women and men. For women, according to her, the connection between homosociality and homosexuality is largely unproblematic, while, for men, it is conflicted in such ways that promote and provoke intense narrative conflict and desires for resolution. Sedgwick writes that "the diacritical opposition between the 'homosocial' and the 'homosexual' seems to be much less thorough and dichotomous for women, in our society, than for men. At this particular historical moment, an intelligible continuum of aims, emotions, and valuations links lesbianism with the other forms of women's attention to women: the bond of mother and daughter, for instance, the bond of sister and sister, women's friendship, 'networking,' and the active struggles of feminism".[7] It is not only that the "lesbian continuum" (to use Adrienne Rich's term) differentiates women and men in Sedgwick's analysis, but also that the very nature of patriarchal power requires simultaneously the defence against male homosexuality and the maintenance of homosociality as the premier form of patriarchal relationship.[8]

Terry Castle proposes the obvious female counterpart to Sedgwick's erotic triangle – two women and a man, the woman's romantic connection to the man displaced by the relationship between the woman and the "other" woman. Castle notes that this triangle does not work in the body of literature to which Sedgwick's analysis is devoted (canonical British and American literature of the 18th and 19th centuries), but suggests that in 20th-century lesbian writing, a pattern exists that both confirms and challenges Sedgwick's account of the male erotic triangle. Using Sylvia Townsend Warner's 1936 novel, *Summer Will Show*, as her example, Castle sets out to demonstrate not only that the novel interferes with the male-female-male erotic triangle, but also that "this kind of subverted triangulation, or erotic 'counterplotting,'...is in fact characteristic of lesbian novels in general".[9]

Blakey Vermeule offers another reading of Sedgwick's analysis *vis-à-vis* lesbians, one that focuses on the problematic status of the lesbian continuum. Noting the difficulty of any simple inversion of the erotic triangle – a man in a patriarchal society cannot simply be assigned the place of a woman – Vermeule stresses a kind of symptomatic reading of the lesbian continuum: "The lesbian continuum goes deep – it goes, in fact, to the heart of what makes lesbian representation problematic. Far from erasing lesbians, the female homosocial-homosexual continuum puts us at the very center of female affective bonds."[10] Vermeule's test case, as it were, is a classical Hollywood film in which the boundary lines between rivalry and erotic connection are indeed blurred – *All About Eve* (1950). The film stages, as Vermeule demonstrates, "the displacement of lesbian desire as a function of growing up straight".[11]

Akerman's film does not make for a neat fit with either of the examples cited here – a 20th-century lesbian novel or a classical Hollywood film. But both Castle's and Vermeule's rereadings of Sedgwick's definition of the erotic triangle are relevant to Akerman's film. There may be no easy way to substitute a female-male-female erotic triangle for the male-female-male one which Sedgwick describes. But it is precisely the desire for such an alternative form of triangulation that sustains Akerman's film. Akerman's portrait of Michèle thus offers a significant twist on the desire to desire that characterises, in Mary Ann Doane's important contribution to feminist film theory, the woman's simultaneous exclusion from, yet desire to participate in, the narrative and scopic regimes of the classical Hollywood cinema.[12]

It is important in this context to remember the specific frame of the film – a reflection on adolescence. There may be much to criticise about the model of the lesbian continuum for any understanding of the specificity of lesbianism. But insofar as female adolescence is concerned, the lesbian continuum, proposing a fluid movement between friendship and erotic connection, has historical resonance. This is not to say that the lesbian continuum can be read as relevant to any time or to any place, but rather that it provides the possibility to understand how, in a period such as the late-1960s, female homosociality both facilitated and impeded a young girl's entry into the realm of heterosexual adulthood.

Why a particular relevance to the late-1960s? The film's signalling of the events of May 68 indicates that new forms of political revolt and representation were on the horizon, and the film juxtaposes the promise of freedom with Michèle's disgust at school, conformity and the routines of everyday life. Interestingly, the school in question is represented in a very displaced way. The girls' school is a classic site for representations of the lesbian continuum (a site where, according to Castle, "plots of lesbian desire are most likely to flourish").[13] The film takes place on the day Michèle has decided to leave school, and she is portrayed as an outsider when she approaches the school grounds. When we see Danielle and Michèle together, it is always in public spaces, whether outside the school, in a café, at a bus-stop or at a party. Certainly the two girls are portrayed so as to suggest their closeness and the special quality of their bond, but this bond exists fully in the same public sphere as Michèle's encounter with Paul. But that continuum cannot be maintained, and Michèle's position as confidant to Danielle and as mediator between Danielle and Paul is precarious. The continuous exchange of dancing partners does not last, and Michèle's position becomes, finally, that of a spectator.

The particular relevance of the late-1960s for the lesbian continuum is also shaped by the cinematic history to which *Portrait of a Young Girl* alludes. I would like to suggest that there is, in Akerman's film, a kind of "subverted triangulation" similar, although not identical, to what Castle describes. Situated in April 1968, *Portrait of a Young Girl* takes place in an imaginary landscape of the New Wave of French cinema, a cinemascape revisioned, adapted and paid homage to throughout the film.

At various times during her journey, Michèle embodies a range of figures from French films of the 1960s. Michèle wanders through Brussels, not Paris, but her journey evokes nevertheless that of many New Wave films of the 1960s. Indeed, one of the privileged narrative forms of French films of the period was that of wandering through the city, with the attendant preoccupation with the everyday, the commercial, and the patterns of both boredom and interruption. To be sure, Brussels has none of the mythic proportions of Paris, but it is an urban space that becomes both invisible backdrop and spectacle in its own right for Michèle. Like Nana in Jean-Luc Godard's *Vivre sa vie* (*It's My Life*, 1962) or Juliet in his *Deux ou trois choses que je sais d'elle*

(*Two or Three Things I Know About Her*, 1966), Michèle's itinerary follows the rhythms of city life.

And just as many films of the 1960s staged self-reflexive scenes at the movies, so too does *Portrait of a Young Girl* initiate the encounter between Michèle and Paul in a cinema, thus echoing scenes in a wide range of films, particularly those by Godard, such as *Masculin-Féminin* (*Masculine-Feminine*, 1966), in which film spectatorship provides both the acting out of fantasy and a moment of quiet contemplation for character and viewer alike. Finally, while most of the directors associated with the development of New Wave cinema were men, their films showcased – problematically perhaps, but showcased nevertheless – the journeys of female characters as embodiments of the desires of the directors. Godard once again serves as a primary example here, and while Akerman's character of Michèle is surely different to Nana in *It's My Life* (played by Anna Karina, Godard's wife at the time), or Juliet in *Two or Three Things I Know About Her*, the journey of this female protagonist is nevertheless quite evocative of the filmmaker's own.

Each time I have watched *Portrait of a Young Girl*, I have been struck by several moments where the piano music that accompanies the wanderings of Michèle through the city sounds much like one of the musical themes of Agnès Varda's *Cléo de 5 à 7* (*Cléo from 5 to 7*, 1961). For an equally brief moment, Michèle seems to retrace Cléo's steps – now in Brussels, not in Paris, and in a time several years later than the setting of Varda's film. As I have suggested, *Portrait of a Young Girl* can be read as an extended meditation on many themes associated with French cinema of the 1960s. But the brief echo of Varda's film seems particularly noteworthy in a film so preoccupied not only with an era that was so shaped by new directions in French filmmaking, but also with how, in a film directed by a woman, another young woman learns about love, desire and longing.

For the heroine of Varda's film sees the city of Paris anew as she wanders, awaiting the results of a medical examination to see if she has cancer. The waiting provides the occasion for a stripping down of the spoiled, childish Cléo, first literally – she removes her wig and her jewelry – and then more profoundly. Within this extended moment of transition in her life, she has a series of encounters that prove to be catalysts of change, most notably with a soldier on brief leave from the war in Algeria. While their encounter is not exactly the stuff of traditional Hollywood romance, it provides the resolution to the film.

There are aesthetic parallels between *Cléo from 5 to 7* and Akerman's film, particularly insofar as the passage of time is concerned. For *Cléo from 5 to 7* is perhaps best-known as an experiment in real time – while there are indeed ellipses in the film, there is nevertheless an attempt to preserve the sense of the passage of time. But the more haunting parallel between the two films concerns the narrative infrastructure. However dissimilar they might be in other ways, Akerman's Michèle, like Cléo, occupies a kind of transitional space as she wanders through the city of Brussels, and she, too, has a decisive encounter with a soldier – in this case (the difference between 1962 and 1968 is strikingly embodied here) a young French soldier who has deserted the Army. The budding relationship between Cléo and Antoine is meant to be seen as something of an alternative, if not to the heterosexual make-up of classical cinematic resolutions, then at least to the notion of "happy ever after". For Cléo does indeed have cancer, and Antoine still must leave to return to Algeria, but they still walk away together at the film's conclusion.

In order to get to Antoine, Cléo must leave her old self behind, and that old self is most definitely shaped by a female world of superstition (the first encounter staged in the film is with a female fortune teller who functions as a narrator; she summarises the entire film), exaggerated domesticity and companionship with Angèle, Cléo's assistant. Cléo's apartment, over which Angèle presides, is a self-contained fantasy world, an idealised private space that provides shelter from the city. Virtually everything associated with commodified femininity is dispensed with in the film, except, of course, the relationship with the man.

Some of the parallels between Akerman's film and Varda's are obvious – a journey, an encounter with a man who in both cases is a soldier, and a movement into some kind of self-awareness. How, therefore, does Castle's notion of "subverted triangulation" come into play? If, indeed, *Cléo from 5 to 7* provides a point of reference for Akerman's film, there is an obvious revision one would expect, particularly given my focus on lesbian narrative: get rid of the man, and substitute a woman. That, of course, is not what happens in Akerman's film. The man is still there. But what is subverted is the need, in Varda's film, to get rid of the world of women. *Portrait of a Young Girl* imagines and revisions an historical and cinematic past in which the desire of one girl for another can sustain an entire narrative, even if that narrative is one that, in the end, traces its own dissolution.

Notes

[1]   The phrase has always been attached to Wilde, but it originates in Lord Alfred Douglas' poem "Two Boys". See H Montgomery Hyde, *The Trials of Oscar Wilde* (New York: Dover, 1962): 200.

[2]   Amy Taubin describes the film as a "lesbian coming-of-age story, probably the most evocative ever made". Amy Taubin, "The Nouvelle Femmes", *The Village Voice* 7 March 1995: 65.

[3]   Bonnie Zimmerman defines the coming-out story as "a process that

includes an awareness of sexual feelings for another woman, a realization that society condemns lesbian love, and an acceptance of lesbian identity through either sexual initiation or self-naming". Zimmerman also notes that in feminist coming out novels, there is in addition "an affirmation of one's lesbianism to the outside world and a journey toward freedom". See *The Safe Sea of Women: Lesbian Fiction 1969-1989* (Boston: Beacon Press, 1990): 35.

[4]   Translated from the French: "Veuillez excuser ma fille Michèle, elle a eu la grippe. Veuillez excuser ma fille Michèle, elle a dû se rendre à un enterrement, sa grand-mère est morte...son oncle est mort...sa tante est morte à la suite de la mort de son oncle. Son père est mort. Elle est morte."

[5]   Translated from the French: "c'était aussi pour faire souffrir quelqu'un. C'est pour le raconter aussi."

[6]   For an extended discussion of *I...You...He...She* and lesbian authorship, see Judith Mayne, *The Woman at the Keyhole: Feminism and Women's Cinema* (Bloomington, Indianapolis: Indiana University Press, 1990): 127-135.

[7]   Eve Kosofsky Sedgwick, *Between Men: English Literature and Male Homosocial Desire* (New York: Columbia University Press, 1985): 2.

[8]   Adrienne Rich, "Compulsory Heterosexuality and Lesbian Existence", *Signs* 5: 4 (summer 1980): 631-660.

[9]   Terry Castle, *The Apparitional Lesbian: Female Homosexuality and Modern Culture* (New York: Columbia University Press, 1993): 74.

[10]   Blakey Vermeule, "Is There a Sedgwick School for Girls?", *Qui Parle* 5: 1 (autumn-winter 1991): 57.

[11]   Ibid: 57.

[12]   Mary Ann Doane, *The Desire to Desire: The Woman's Film of the 1940s* (Bloomington; Indianapolis: Indiana University Press, 1987).

[13]   Castle: 85.

Bordering on fiction: Chantal Akerman's *From the East*

Kristine Butler

In discussing the work of Chantal Akerman, one often speaks of the importance of the formal elements of her films: the systematic oppositions between light and dark, exteriors and interiors, silence and noise; the rhythmic use of tracking vs. fixed shots, and rhythmic juxtapositions of crowds vs. individuals; her affinity for real-time photography and preference for non-naturalistic extended monologues (what Ivone Margulies calls "talk-blocks")[1] over dialogue sequences. Regarding this attention to form, one critic writes: "Whether in her fictional or essayist works, conventional sources of meaning are displaced as character and plot development, location, and even language, are eschewed in favor of images and rhythms that allow meanings to surface organically. Hers is a cinema of waiting, of passages, of resolutions deferred."[2] The implication of this supposed "organicism" is that meaning in Akerman's films grows (naturally) from an aesthetic that uses the formal to complicate the discursive, in order for some other, "deeper" meaning to emerge. This, of course, is one of the particular powers of the camera and the sound-recording apparatus as Dziga Vertov understood it: "[t]he Camera Eye must be understood as 'that which cannot be seen by the human eye, as the microscope and telescope of time'...The Camera Eye is the possibility of making visible the invisible, of bringing light into darkness, of revealing what is hidden...of turning the lie into truth."[3] Vertov's theory of avant-garde film practice is ultimately a means by which to "reveal" a previously obscured truth; such was the aim of the anti-illusionism of the Camera Eye. Of course, that the quasi-magical powers of the camera as Vertov saw them are just as easily appropriable to the service of creating meaning as to that of revealing meaning was at the heart of postwar cinematic modernism. In the case of a formalist aesthetic such as Akerman's, the meanings "allowed to surface" are supposed to have been obscured less by the limits of human perception than by the conventions of dominant cinematic practices grown so familiar to spectators of this century.

B. Ruby Rich has reified the importance of Akerman's formalist aesthetic from a feminist perspective. Discussing *Jeanne Dielman, 23 quai du Commerce, 1080 Bruxelles* (1975), she states that:

The aesthetic repercussions of such a [feminist] sensibility are evident throughout the film. For example, the choice of camera angle is unusually low. In interviews, Akerman explained that the camera was positioned at her own height; since she is quite short, the entire perspective of the film is different from what we are used to seeing, as shot by male cinematographers. The perspective of every frame thus reveals a female ordering of that space.[4]

While one might well take issue with the easy elision of Akerman's height with feminism, and the underlying notion that low-angle filming is evidence of a feminist perspective (rather than, for example, a short person's perspective) which subverts ideological systems of the (tall) patriarchy, Rich's intended point is clear: Akerman's decision to use such an angle, reflective of her own height, rather than of an industrial standard, is seen as part of a larger project, a feminist critique of "the tradition of cinematic realism [which] has never included women in its alleged veracity".[5]

That these formal elements should be so consistently cited as somehow at the base of Akerman's avant-garde aesthetic reveals the continued perception of a need to develop formal textual operations that will disarticulate the ideological affiliations of a dominant cinema whose operations are interested to preserve the illusion of unity of the subject and spectator, as well as the continuity of onscreen and offscreen space. Akerman's cinema is widely held as one which works to disarticulate this unity formally, to subvert the norms of representation and subjectivity, and thus to reveal ideological ambitions of mainstream film in the service of dominant ideologies. The duration of this avant-garde aesthetic in the cinematic medium can be seen by going back to Eisenstein, whose theories of montage stem from an approach to film language that owes much to synchronic linguistics. Eisenstein privileges montage as an artistic practice that effectively foregrounds the image as sign, the symbolic content obtained by the placing side-by-side of two signs whose values stem from their interrelation. Eisenstein is primarily concerned, therefore, with cinematic language as revolutionary art, the very importance of which being its capacity as an instrument of communication with the masses.

Akerman's recent museum installation, entitled *Bordering on Fiction: Chantal Akerman's "D'Est"*, is uniquely positioned to question the film as an ideologically motivated artistic construction. Akerman explores the complexity of her relationship to the Eastern bloc in a museum installation made up of an interweaving of discourses around the film, *D'Est (From the East,* 1993) – a 107-minute feature film shot in Germany, Poland and Russia in three trips during 1992 and 1993.

Bordering on Fiction debuted at the San Francisco Museum of Modern Art in January 1995 before moving on to the Walker Art Center in Minneapolis, and from there to an international tour which included the Galerie Nationale du Jeu de Paume in Paris, the Société des Expositions du Palais des Beaux-Arts in Brussels, the Kunstmuseum Wolfsburg in Wolfsburg, Germany, and the IVAM Centre del Carme in Valencia, Spain. Funded in part by the Bohen Foundation and Etant Donnés, the French-American Endowment for Contemporary Art, and conceived by Akerman, Kathy Halbreich (then Beal Curator of Contemporary Art at the Museum of Fine Arts, Boston, and currently the director of the Walker Art Center), Susan Dowling (producer for WGBH Television), Michael Tarantino (an independent curator and critic), and later joined by Bruce Jenkins (film and video curator for the Walker Art Center) and Catherine David (then curator at the Galerie Nationale du Jeu de Paume in Paris), "Bordering on Fiction" represents a multinational collaboration on the coming together of the European community, and on the relation of the media of global communication and global politics to the poverty and socio-economic upheaval of that part of the world. At the same time, it is an exploration of Akerman's own artistic and personal preoccupations with the Eastern bloc.

A distinction must be made at the outset between the film, *From the East*, and the museum installation that surrounds and incorporates it. The installation itself consists of three integrated "movements" corresponding to the three galleries in which the exhibit is contained. Upon entering the first gallery, visitors are confronted with a darkened room where the finished version of *From the East* runs continuously. A second room holds 24 video monitors arranged into eight triptychs, all simultaneously playing different looping fragments of the film. The third gallery contains a single video monitor and a pair of small speakers placed on the floor, through which one hears Akerman's voice, reciting passages from the Hebrew Bible, as well as selections from the journal she kept while working on the film. Visitors are free to move about through the three spaces; moving forward through the installation, one moves conceptually backward ideationally and technologically through a deconstruction of the filmmaking process, both from the final product to the artist's vision of the work, and from the technologically "finished" film to a breakdown of the different pieces of its sound and image tracks.

The thesis that drives this essay has different and related strands. I will focus first on *From the East* itself, and then on the exhibit; although, in fact, the two are not so easily distinguished, their interrelationship as two separate works is of primary importance for the purposes of this discussion. I will argue that the exhibit implicitly raises questions about the too-easy appropriation of her films in the service of any particular oppositional theory, against a particular vision of a "dominant" cinema. Akerman conceived the project that ultimately produced *From the East*, a film free of dialogue, as an opportunity to make a film "in many languages".[6] Exploding the work itself as a unified whole, and presenting it as a museum exhibit containing the completed film as one of its parts, *Bordering on Fiction* inquires into oppositional filmmaking by suggesting the complexity of the web of discourses within the finished film. By disengaging Akerman's film from the enclosed space of the theatre, the museum installation resituates questions regarding the cinematic apparatus and the construction of a filmic document through a different physical and ideational space. In addition, Akerman's piece repositions questions of spectatorship, as its engagement of a critical relationship with its spectator exists at the level of the gendered, classed, cultured body in its varying degrees of attention or inattention to these discourses. By forcing the spectator to engage physically in an act of attention or distraction – by moving towards or away from the film itself – the film's critical discourses of the apparatus are complicated, and the spectator's own interest in continuing or discontinuing participation is actively engaged.

Finally, *Bordering on Fiction: Chantal Akerman's "D'Est"*, an exhibit that includes the director's name as a fiction within it, represents a collaboration of institutions, artists and administrators on the coming together of the European Community. Akerman's own participation in this project lends it a personal unity at the same time that it addresses questions of disunity and fragmentation, taking as her contribution to its subject "what was left out of this union as well, and...the concomitant rise of nationalism and anti-Semitism".[7] The piece explicitly engages the director's own voice for autobiographical purposes: as the site of multiple and intersecting ancestries, the directorial voice-off of *Bordering on Fiction* is a complex mode of address to a panoply of discourses surrounding the Eastern bloc: Judaism, nationalism, film genres (documentary and fiction), postwar avant-garde movements, East/West communications and feminisms.

Ça va sauter: Akerman and the avant-garde

Akerman began making films in 1968 with the thirteen-minute *Saute ma ville* (*Blow up My Town*), at a moment in which "the place of cinema in sociocultural formations, and particularly in the advanced capitalist formations, was of special interest to major film-theoretical impulses".[8] Her earliest explorations of cinematic form can thus be read in dialogue, with many of the questions being raised by filmmakers and theorists of that period. Accordingly, Akerman's films have most often been placed by critics in one of three distinct but related traditions of postwar cinematic practice. Within a European context, her work has regularly been discussed in the light of a francophone tradition, in which she is articulated as a sort of descendent of the likes of Jean-Luc Godard, Alain Resnais, Marguerite Duras and Agnès Varda. The aesthetic sensibilities of these directors are seen as arising out of the intellectual and artistic activity of the late-1950s and 1960s, a moment which in France saw the flowering of the New Wave, the *nouveau roman* and structuralism. The critical move of foregrounding the disparate and dispersive elements of the cinematic medium in film theory and practice has aimed to question the discourses of realism, documentary and fiction present within the cinematic and other communicative and/or artistic media. Much of this critical work has been essentially formalist in nature, and has grown out of 1960s leftist politics and Marxist conceptions of dominant ideology and false consciousness associated with what Godard called "bourgeois" cinema, implicitly in the service of maintaining the status quo – accompanied by the perception of the need for a revolutionary film practice which would subvert the normalising effects of genre. Thus, Brian Henderson, after Godard, can delineate the formal qualities of an anti-realist, anti-illusionist "non-bourgeois" camera style:

> Not only composition-in-depth but the *values* which Bazin found in composition-in-depth[9] are missing in Godard's version of the long take (and in late Godard generally): greater realism, greater participation on the part of the viewer, and a reintroduction of ambiguity into the structure of the film image... Godard of the later films is not interested in ambiguity – through flatness of frame and transparency of action, he seeks to eliminate ambiguity. Thus Godard uses the long take for none of the traditional reasons; in fact he reinvents the long take, and the tracking shot, for his own purposes.[10]

Godard's purposes, for Henderson, include critical distance, caused by the flatness of the image, the elimination of perspective to the extent possible by avoidance of in-depth composition and camera movements motivated by the tracking of a particular image. The line of Godard's tracking shots creates a mural or scroll that moves the spectator to read it – to be attentive to its surface in order not to be distracted by the chimera of its depth. This technique is a form of visual "description" aimed at a critique of cinematic realism, in much the same way in which Robbe-Grillet's obsessive description of surfaces was an oppositional strategy against what he considered illusionary depth in the novel.[11] The importance of dehumanising the text was not only to decontaminate it from the illness of anthropomorphism, but also to foreground the distance between objects obscured by the ideological effects of sociocultural structures. The existential undertones of this move are clear: it is the dismantling of these systems of representation which might open up a space for a new humanism based on informed choice. The militant bent of Godard's cinema presupposes that the spectator be attentive to the borders of ideology. Akerman's use of tracking shots in rhythmic composition with conspicuously lengthy static shots is often likened to Godard's, and is thus presented as taking part in a post-New Wave avant-garde legacy interested in foregrounding film as text for the purposes of demystifying bourgeois representation.

Related to but distinct from this European tradition is a North American contingent of structuralist filmmakers – including Michael Snow, Jonas Mekas and Andy Warhol – whose concerns for abstracting film form stem from a perceived need to question critically both an illusionist classical cinematic practice and an ethnographically influenced counter-practice that posits the "everyday" as its subject. In films by Michael Snow, with whose work Akerman became familiar on a first trip to New York in 1971, the pre-programmed "scanning" movement of the camera, indifferent to the objects it catches on films or to the spectator who watches, traces out a trajectory that unfurls behind it like so many feet of celluloid; it is the movement of the celluloid itself, therefore, that becomes the object of a film such as *La Région centrale* (*The Central Region,* 1971), rather than the images on the screen. Warhol's real-time minimalism shares with Akerman's extended duration shots that their approaches undo "any idea of symbolic transcendence. Besides injecting representation with the effect of a surplus of reality, literal time robs it of the possibility of standing for something other than that concrete instance".[12] This in an attempt to avoid the tendency towards an effect of "representativeness" in photographing the daily in documentary or ethnographic films.

Finally, Akerman is frequently seen to participate in a legacy of feminist film production: *Jeanne Dielman* – in which a Brussels housewife (Delphine Seyrig) turns tricks to support herself and her son, cooks and cleans, and eventually murders one of her clients – has become a canonical feminist text, provoking much discussion over the links between its politicised enquiries into the domestic sphere of the feminine, and its formalist questioning of conventional editing practices. The movement from the struggle to articulate the mundane in a non-hierarchical relationship with the dramatic often takes the form of extended duration of the quotidian existing alongside the unique: a singularly anti-climactic murder scene takes place quite undramatically alongside the other household chores. As Akerman herself states, the decision to film in this way has decidedly feminist implications:

I *do* think it's a feminist film because I give space to things which were never, almost never, shown in that way, like the daily gestures of a woman. They are the lowest in the hierarchy of film images. A kiss or a car crash come higher, and I don't think that's an accident.[13]

B. Ruby Rich points to the continuing problem of naming what, within a particular cinematic text, is specifically "feminist". She argues that one commonality of all feminist theory and practice is the insistence on "making the statements, in unsullied terms, in forms not already associated with the media's oppressiveness toward women".[14] She thus positions feminist film practice in opposition to both the dominant cinema ("Hollywood and all its corresponding manifestations in other cultures") and the avant-garde ("the experimental/personal cinema, which is positioned, by self-inclusion, within the art world") in the early 1970s – what she labels, respectively, as the "Cinema of the Fathers" and the "Cinema of the Sons".[15] That Akerman's work, as has been noted above, actually *shares* many of the formal qualities and ancestry of the "Cinema of the Sons", that she might have as much in common with Mekas, Snow or Godard as with Yvonne Rainer or Laura Mulvey, suggests that we are, in fact, witness to a legacy much more complicated than Rich allows for in her reading. It is obvious that one thing Akerman shares with all these filmmakers is an attention to film form as an effective means of enquiring into discourse and the relation of film to spectator. Perhaps her inclusion within all three of these groups/categories shows her as an important figure in understanding the limited nature of these borders – or at least the fact that the borders between all these different areas of critical thought arise from the different experiences of a similar cultural moment.

At home and away

If all three of the groupings referred to above indicate a particular context of social and political activity, Akerman's inclusion in each of them is problematic at best. Few, if any, critiques have adequately dealt with the importance of her own social and cultural position: the fact that she is not only a woman and a European, but also a Belgian and a Jew of Polish ancestry.[16] Her work on and around *Bordering on Fiction: Chantal Akerman's "D'Est"* reveals the importance of this ancestry in her interrogation of discourses of home, borders and zones:

My parents are from Poland. Since the thirties they've been living in Belgium, where they feel very much at home.
For a long time – my whole childhood – I believed that their way of life, the way they ate, talked, and thought, was the way all Belgians lived. It was only much later, as an adolescent, that I understood the differences: between them and other parents and even between me and the other young girls in my class.[17]

The differences between Akerman's parents and the other Belgians, or between Akerman and her schoolmates, are not articulated beyond this vague suggestion of their existence. The above citation comes from a personal journal Akerman kept while at work on *From the East*. In the journal, she writes of her own complex relationship to the Eastern bloc, first as a young girl, then later as a documentary filmmaker:

> Last year, I took a trip to the Soviet Union to prepare for a film on the poet Anna Akhmatova.
>
> It was winter, and I was far from home in a strange land where I didn't speak the language. I felt at once a little lost, without really being so, troubled without knowing why, and in a foreign country that was not altogether foreign. It was a strange language, to be sure, but one whose musicality and resonance were so familiar that words and even whole sentences came back to me in the midst of my incomprehension as if I were an amnesiac suddenly remembering. And the way people lived, their way of thinking, was all too familiar to me. I would find the same food on the table that my mother always made, even after fifty years of living in Belgium.[18]

This quasi-amnesiac state, of a life not lived, not remembered, yet echoed in her own complex, as yet unarticulated sensations of "the foreign that is not altogether foreign", is indicative of Akerman's own awareness of the complex relationship of her identity with the identity of the East. As independent filmmaker Trinh T Minh-Ha has succinctly pointed out:

> To raise the question of identity is to reopen again the discussion on the self/other relationship in its enactment of power relations...The search for an identity is, therefore, usually a search for that lost, pure, true, real, genuine, original, authentic self, often situated within a process of elimination of all that is considered other, superfluous, fake, corrupted or Westernized.[19]

It is noteworthy that the idea of the "West" – itself a hegemonising concept which tends to obliterate any particularity of experience within it – not only has been considered the vantage point of objectivity, but also, within the question of "authentic" ethnic identity, has come to signify "corrupted". The seemingly stultifying paradox of this double identity of the West becomes apparent when Minh-Ha discusses its consequences in ethnographic (film) practice: "The place of the native is always well-delimited. 'Correct' cultural filmmaking, for example, usually implies that Africans show Africa; Asians, Asia: and Euro-

169

Americans, the world".[20] This implies that the West does not perceive a need to worry about the integrity of its own identity, either because Western identity is homogenous and sufficiently stable to withstand outside influence, or because, as the objective standard, its claim to truth is somehow unshakeable. The ethnographic outsider's view posits itself as an objective, objectifying view: it can be supplemented by the insider's view, but not supplanted. At the same time, this privileged position of the West puts it in a unique position regarding cultural others, allowing the quasi-scientific camera of the ethnographer to speak, and/or film objectively what supposedly is outside itself. The borders of the West are therefore permeable in only one direction: the West itself can corrupt the authenticity of other cultures, and, at the same time, can use the similarities it finds between those cultures and itself as "proof" of its own authentic status as the representative of a more universal, "human" standard.

Akerman is in a unique position from which to repose these questions of identity and authenticity in *Bordering on Fiction* and *From the East*. Not a uniquely authentic position, but one unique in the sense that her experience is unique to her, although sharing characteristics of the experiences of others. Unique, too, in that she has created a work at a temporal moment in which so many discourses seem to be in a heightened state of flux and conflict with one another. The discourses of unification and solidarity surrounding the European Community, those of independence and nationalism in the former Soviet bloc, are dissolving and reshaping themselves. The need to find new ways to discuss the changes occurring is evident in Akerman's cautionary note to herself, in the journal she kept while working on the film:

> While there's still time, I would like to make a grand journey across Eastern Europe. To Russia, Poland, Hungary, Czechoslovakia, the former East Germany, and back to Belgium. I'd like to film there, in my own style of documentary bordering on fiction. I'd like to shoot everything. Everything that moves me...
> I was saying: 'while there's still time.'
> Time for what, and why? Time before the Western 'invasion' becomes too blatant?
> As if there had been a before and after, before and after the Ice Age or the cold war. The time of a realized utopia and the time of a fallen utopia, or the time of yet another utopia?
> There has always been a sort of love/hate relationship with the West, perhaps even stronger before – especially with America, that object of troubled desire. And for some time now, not in spite but I would say *because* of the system, certain

iconic objects of American culture have been infiltrating these
countries – from blue jeans to the jazz played by the seven
Simeon brothers in the depths of Siberia, where they died. Now
the signs are just more visible (some would say more arrogant)
like the McDonald's in Moscow's Pushkin Square.
But, of course, there is no pure 'before' that would now be
perverted or contaminated.[21]

Akerman's recognises that the discourses of purity, authenticity and
corruption surrounding the West-East divide are inappropriate and
ultimately destructive, rather than constructive. The need to explore
productively the permeability of the borders of these discourses is
inseparable from the need to incorporate her own position as not quite
an insider and not quite an outsider. Moreover, these questions are
implicitly linked to critical examination of the zones separating subject,
filmmaker and audience articulated through the interrelated film and
museum installation, *Bordering on Fiction: Chantal Akerman's "D'Est"*.

Where are we (going)? *D'Est*i-nation

In *From the East*, one is confronted with two sets of questions, both
organised around the ambiguity of the name and the ability to speak
and/or write that name. The spoken word "D'Est" suggests ambiguous
beginnings, possible endings: what follows could be *dest-ruction*,
dest-in (fate or destiny), *destiner* (a verb, to intend or aim at), *destination*; words which, like their prefix, all resonate with expectation
and possibilities of meaning. A second level of suggestiveness in the
film's title is organised not around aiming at, but coming from: *D'Est*,
literally "from/of/about East", refers to origins, East as a place
historically and culturally in dynamic opposition to West. At the same
time, the title includes another word, which it resembles not
homonymically but graphically: "Est" (is), from *être*, "to be". The film
is "from/of/about *being*", and *specifically* about being *written*. Written
into an history, that between West and East, between Communism and
capitalism.

The Eastern bloc is undergoing a moment in which its identity can
be described precisely as differing from its identity. The different
countries and zones are in a place of neither/nor, a position indicated
in some of the names of transition: the former Soviet Union. A place
which, to be sure, is in actuality much more the norm than an
exception globally speaking, despite the unflinching edifices of country
and state names. How to represent such a state of flux in *Bordering on
Fiction* indicates an awareness of changes in frontiers, boundaries, and
thus of definitions. At the same time, as it examines this moment in the
sociopolitical world, *Bordering on Fiction* is also about a filmic identity

171

crisis, occurring around the limiting, rigid borders of the mainstream and the avant-garde, and of genre. To read *From the East* as an example of Akerman's avant-garde formalism is certainly valid; however, it is an attempt not at destruction of meaning, but at the suggestion of future meaning. The formal rhythms of images and sounds in *From the East* succeed in disarticulating them from the narratives recalled by past memory-images, in which the future unity must occur at the expense of a search into the past.

> [The United States and Russia] are two worlds whose images have been ingrained in us through cinema. Dovzhenko and Ford. The American landscape and Russian wheat fields. Ideal images contradicted by those of grayness and Stalinist architecture, of waiting in lines and gulags. Contradicted by literature also – the infinite landscapes and birch trees of Pasternak, the tears and tea of Chekhov, the good in the evil of Dostoyevski.[22]

The memory-images that exist in the minds of generations of film-goers suggest the emergence of memory-cities. The odd sense of belonging and not belonging in a place is not simply an experience particular to Akerman; it is also part of the experience of being cinema-goers, consumers of culture.

In Godard's *Alphaville* (1965), the hero, Lemmy Caution (Eddie Constantine), in order to awaken the brainwashed Natasha Von Braun (Anna Karina) and escape with her to the Pays Extérieurs, must engage her in an exercise of memory-recall. The way in which Lemmy does this is by forcing her to call up a verbal cliché of her native city. The monikers for the different cities, half-real and half-fantasy, call up memory-image effects in the spectator that have the strange Technicolor tint of so many travel-brochure photos. The question of belonging or not belonging is mediated through a discourse reminiscent at once of poetic language and of the capitalistic interests of tourism:

> Lemmy:... where were you born? ...
> Natasha: Here, in *Alphaville*.
> Lemmy: No, you were born in Tokyrama, the Land of the Rising Sun. Go on ... say it after me.
> Natasha: At Tokyrama, the Land of the Rising Sun.
> Lemmy: Or perhaps in Florence ... or... or... try and discover it for yourself, Natasha... *Where?*
> Natasha: Where? ... I don't know!
> Lemmy: Where the sky is the blue of Southern Seas ... Natasha:
> Florence ... where the sky ... seas ...

Lemmy: Or else in Nueva York!
Natasha: Nueva York! ... Where the winter ... Broadway ...
sparkles under the snow, as soft and gentle as mink ... .
Lemmy: You see! You know the Outerlands extremely well!
Your father was banished from Nueva York in 1964 ... he
brought you here ... which means you don't belong here.[23]

In Godard's film, the mainstream cinema's emphasis on narrative
continuity and the established techniques of realism are exposed in
their connection to "bourgeois" values and corporate interests.
Authenticity is revealed as a lie, and the question of identity and
difference is relevant only in relation to the trope of genre as illusion.
Lemmy does not belong in Alphaville because he is from a different
film genre: not that of the futuristic science-fiction film, but rather that
of the B-movie detective genre. Natasha does not belong in Alphaville
either, because of the fact of her birth in the Outerlands, but also
because she is Lemmy's love interest, and therefore must be taken to
the film-city where he lives, to play out the end of the story. The law
of genre thus overcomes even the law of the father, and the end of the
film has them driving off together towards the lights of intergalactic
space: the classic Hollywood ending.

Of course, Godard's Alphaville is also blatantly Paris, and the Alpha
60 computer a backlit fan and the mechanised burping voice of a
tracheotomy patient. Thus, the film is involved not à la *The Wizard of
Oz*, with answering the question "Who's behind the curtain?", but rather
with filming *The Wizard of Oz* with the curtain pushed back, a corner
of it still visible in the frame: in other words, the film aims at revealing
the constructedness of all text.

Reading the East

As the long, slow, steady tracking shots of *From the East*, from left to
right and right to left, echo horizontal movements of writing, both
Western and Eastern, the camera is working specifically not to engage
in an ethnography; it seems indifferent to "event", often moving away
just as something seems to be beginning: an exchange between two
individuals, the movement of a person (towards something?). Or else
the camera remains at rest, and people walk into and out of the frame,
or do nothing. *From the East* is engaging in a critique of ethnographic
film as an objective and objectifying view that links place
unproblematically to identity. The difficulty of avoiding the discursive
transformation of what appears on the screen into naturalised images
"representativeness of Eastness" in such a film is clear. Akerman seeks
to undermine this tendency towards the representative, elliptical image
by operating an "aesthetics of homogeneity":[24] her minutes-long takes,

whether static or tracking, foreground the self-consciously non-elliptical duration of the images; moreover, the obsessive seriality of her style refuses a too-easy interpretation of the image as an exemplar. Instead of organising a sense-making search for authenticity around and through the metaphor of vision, the film's stubborn gaze complicates "attentive" vision by forcing distraction.

The exhibit around *From the East* is a spatial continuation of Akerman's interrogation of film representation. It mobilises different zones – that of the offscreen and the onscreen, East and West, fiction and the real, art and life, film vs. video, urban and rural, centre and margin, actor and spectator – and blurs them in order to interrogate the act of viewing. The mobility of the spectator follows but one trajectory among an infinite number of possible trajectories. As certain shots will inevitably remind one of other cinematic experiences – foregrounding our investment in cinematic tradition, as minds wander to invent stories – the camera, in refusing to develop the echoes of narrative, gives rise to new relationships between the image and its spectators in the space of each encounter.

(Not) paying attention

As Jonathan Crary has pointed out, the concept of attention is a crucial one for understanding the place of cinema in discourses of modern vision. The Western crisis of vision occurring in the mid- to late-19th century involved a shift from a classical regime of visuality to one grounded in the density and materiality of the body. Crary points to many of the developments of the late-19th century as being inflected by the unreliability and faultiness of this vision, among them the development of cinema as one of the "various techniques for imposing specific kinds of perceptual synthesis", and institutional psychology's definition of psychic normality as having "the ability to synthetically bind perceptions into a functional whole, thereby warding off the threat of dissociation".[25] The problem of attention is thus related to this crisis in vision, and the notion of normal concentration develops alongside that of a pathologised inattention, one of the first articulations of which was Théodule Ribot's *Psychologie de l'attention* (1889). In this work, "determinations of race, gender, nationality, and class are central to his evaluations. For Ribot, those characterised by deficient capacity for attention included children, prostitutes, savages, vagabonds, and South Americans".[26]

What made the 19th century's investment in the study of perception so great was the disturbing idea that attention carries within it always the threat of inattention, the constant haunt of its disintegration: "Attention and distraction were not two essentially different states but existed on a single continuum, and thus attention was, as most increasingly agreed, a dynamic process, intensifying and diminishing, rising and falling, ebbing and flowing according to an indeterminate set of variables". Paradoxically, although attention was supposed to be about perceptual fixity and the apprehension of presence, it was in actuality about flux, "within which objects and sensation had a mutating provisional existence, and it was ultimately that which obliterated its objects".[27]

This "threat" of inattention which exists alongside a concept of normalised attention became part of the core of possibility of a certain theory of the avant-garde, as Surrealist experiments such as automatic writing grew in part from psychological discourses that bespoke a seemingly paradoxical proximity of dreaming, sleep and attention. The idea of an "other" consciousness that could surface held a hint of the radical and the revolutionary. Automatic writing in its essence was pure "distraction" – that is, it was conceived as a means of tapping into the unconscious that effectively bypassed a conscious fettered by an attentiveness, the origins of which were in scientific and analytical Western society. It thus afforded access to the realm of a pure perception, unmediated by discourses of representation. Interestingly, Vertov also sought to define his hyper-perceptual Camera Eye through recourse to a discourse of attention and distraction:

> What am I to do with my camera? What is its role in the offensive I am launching against the visible world?
> I think of the Camera Eye...I abolish the customary sixteen frames-per-second...high speed cinematography...frame-by-frame animation and many other techniques...become commonplace.
> The Camera Eye must be understood as 'that which cannot be seen by the human eye, as the microscope and telescope of time...'
> The Camera Eye is the possibility of making visible the invisible, of bringing light into darkness, of revealing what is hidden...of turning the lie into truth.[28]

The apparatus of the camera, with its ultra-attentive gaze, would be the privileged instrument to do the hard work of bridging the gap between the viewer's faulty vision and the reality to be perceived. It is a cognitive aid, a microscope or a telescope, capable of giving an exaggerated attention to the truth. The ambivalence of the camera's place within Vertov's model is clear: in launching an "offensive" against the visible world, he also seeks to distinguish his camera from that of the common discursive practices of cinema. His is a revolution, unleashed by an augmented attention span.

Both the film, *From the East*, and the exhibit, *Bordering on Fiction*, speak to many senses of attention. Perhaps most interestingly, the coexistence of the two within the space of the museum points to a "tension" between the types of *attend*ance (in both the French and the English senses: of waiting – *attendre* – and of presence at an event) that is expected of the film spectator and the museum-goer. Catherine David has linked Akerman's non-individualising, non-hierarchical treatment of Soviet crowds to Lacoue-Labarthe's notion of the "communauté désœuvrée", or idle community:[29]

> Rarely (and not since the beginning of cinema and the early Soviet depiction of the heroic masses of the revolution) have the modern crowd and individual, the 'idle community' of post-Communism, been filmed with such startling intimacy, in their abandon and dispossession.[30]

In David's confusing and anachronistic equivalence of the early Soviet cinematic representations of the revolution, the post-Communist moment, the phenomenon of the modern crowd, and the idle community of Lacoue-Labarthe, it is possible to see the presumption that *From the East* is somehow "representative" of a concept. She effectively fails to perceive precisely the antinaturalist tensions between structure and event, between surface and depth, which exist not only in *From the East*, but also in Akerman's other films. In speaking of her own debt to structural filmmaking, she states: "When you look at a picture, if you look just one second you get the information, 'that's a corridor.' But after a while you forget it's a corridor, you just see that it's yellow, red, lines: and then it comes back as a corridor."[31] This principle of optical illusion is mobilised in *Bordering on Fiction*: by breaking down the work into different parts, the exhibit examines the film itself both as a theoretical possibility and as a finished product, as well as the conditions that make up its creation and reception. At the same time, it demonstrates the rhythms of attention and distraction at the level of human physicality, marking its difference from modernist film. This tension between attention and distraction, therefore, is played out at the level of the body of the spectator, whose movements echo in many respects those of the bodies on the screens: people waiting in train stations and on snowy streets at dawn, people walking, sitting in their kitchens, standing, waiting in long lines, quietly conversing. Privileged places of passage and transit, of the kind of waiting that provokes fluctuation of attention and distraction. The very personal movement of each museum-goer, who walks, sits, looks or does not look, listens to out-of-sync noises and dialogue, leaves or does not leave, creates the movement of the installation itself; we as an audience are caught up in the waiting, the absence of knowing when, or if, something will "happen". Blurring the borders between the event and its reception, between spectator and participant, *Bordering on Fiction* is a contemplation of meaning in suspense.

176

Notes

[1] Ivone Margulies, *Nothing Happens: Chantal Akerman's Hyperrealist Everyday* (Durham, NC; London: Duke University Press, 1996): 154.

[2] Kathy Halbreich and Bruce Jenkins (eds), *Bordering on Fiction: Chantal Akerman's D'Est* (Minneapolis: Walker Art Center, 1995): 7.

[3] Cited in Noël Burch, "Primitivism and the Avant-Gardes: A Dialectical Approach", in Philip Rosen (ed), *Narrative, Apparatus, Ideology: A Film Theory Reader* (New York: Columbia University Press, 1986): 483.

[4] B. Ruby Rich, "In the Name of Feminist Film Criticism", in Diane Carson, Linda Dittmar and Janice R Welsch (eds), *Multiple Voices in Feminist Film Criticism* (Minneapolis; London: University of Minnesota Press, 1994): 30.

[5] Ibid: 31.

[6] Cited in Halbreich and Jenkins (eds): 8.

[7] Ibid.

[8] Rosen (ed): 375.

[9] Bazin's privileging of realist techniques such as deep-focus photography and the long take stems from his belief that such elements, as opposed to the "tricks" of montage, "[bring] the spectator into a relation with the image closer to that which he enjoys with reality", introduce the ambiguity of reality into the structure of the image, and therefore demand "a more active mental attitude on the part of the spectator and a more positive contribution on his part to the action in progress". See André Bazin, "The Evolution of the Language of Cinema", in Gerald Mast, Marshall Cohen and Leo Braudy (eds), *Film Theory and Criticism: Introductory Readings*, fourth edition (New York; Oxford: Oxford University Press, 1992): 165.

[10] Brian Henderson, "Toward a Non-Bourgeois Camera Style", in Bill Nichols (ed), *Movies and Methods: An Anthology* (Berkeley; Los Angeles; London: University of California Press, 1976): 425. Emphasis in original.

[11] Alain Robbe-Grillet, *Pour un nouveau roman* (Paris: Minuit, 1963).

[12] Margulies: 37.

[13] "Chantal Akerman on *Jeanne Dielman*", *Camera Obscura* 2 (autumn 1977): 118. Emphasis in original.

[14] Rich: 27.

[15] Ibid: 28.

[16] A recent exception to this is Margulies, who gives a certain amount of space to Akerman's relationship to a "Jewish aesthetic", linking Akerman's use of language to Kafka's "deterritorialization" of meaning as discussed in Deleuze and Guattari's *Kafka: Toward a Minor Literature*; however, this

aspect of Akerman's work still remains for the most part unexplored.

[17] Chantal Akerman, "On *D'Est*", in Halbreich and Jenkins (eds): 20-21.

[18] Ibid: 21.

[19] Trinh T Minh-Ha, "Not You/Like You: Post-Colonial Women and the Interlocking Questions of Identity and Difference", in Gloria Anzaldúa (ed), *Making Face, Making Soul/Haciendo Caras: Creative and Critical Perspectives by Feminists of Color* (San Francisco: Aunt Lute Books, 1990): 371. My understanding of identity and difference owes a debt to this work.

[20] Ibid: 373.

[21] Akerman in Halbreich and Jenkins (eds): 17-23. Emphasis in original.

[22] Ibid: 28.

[23] Jean-Luc Godard, *Alphaville*, screenplay translated by Peter Whitehead (London: Lorrimer Films, 1966): 68-69.

[24] Margulies: 11.

[25] Jonathan Crary, "Unbinding Vision", *October* 68 (spring 1994): 21-22.

[26] Ibid: 25n7.

[27] Ibid: 27.

[28] Quoted in Burch: 483.

[29] Philippe Lacoue-Labarthe, *La communauté désœuvrée* (Paris: Christian Bourgeois, 1990).

[30] Catherine David, "*D'Est*: Akerman Variations", in Halbreich and Jenkins (eds): 61.

[31] Cited in Margulies: 43.

Filmography
Selected bibliography
Contributors
Index

Filmography

The following abbreviations have been used:

ad	art director	m	minutes
bw	black and white	*m*	music
CA	Chantal Akerman	p	producer
col	color	pc	production company
d	director	ph	cinematographer
ed	editor	s	story
ep	executive producer	sc	scriptwriter

Unless indicated otherwise, all films are directed by Chantal Akerman.

Saute ma ville
Blow up My Town
1968 13m bw 35mm
ph René Fruchter *ed* Geneviève Luciani *cast* CA

L'Enfant aimé ou je joue à être une fenmae mariée
The Beloved Child, or I Play at Being a Married Woman
1971 35m bw 16mm
cast Claire Wauthion, CA, Daphna Merzer

Hotel Monterey
1972 65m col 16mm silent
pc Paradise Films (Brussels) *sc* CA *ph* Babette Mangolte *ed* Geneviève Luciani

La Chambre 1
The Room, 1
1972 11m col 16mm
pc Paradise Films (Brussels) *sc* CA *ph* Babette Mangolte *ed* Geneviève Luciani

La Chambre 2
The Room, 2
1972 11m col 16mm silent
pc Paradise Films (Brussels) *sc* CA *ph* Babette Mangolte *ed* Geneviève
Luciani

Le 15/8
1973 42m bw 16mm
pc Paradise Films (Brussels) *d* CA, Samy Szlingerbaum *sc, ph, ed* CA,
Samy Szlingerbaum

Hanging Out Yonkers 1973
1973 90m col 16mm [unfinished]
pc Paradise Films (Brussels) *sc* CA *ph* Babette Mangolte *ed* Geneviève
Luciani

Je tu il elle
I...You...He...She
1974 90m bw 16mm
p, sc CA *pc* Paradise Films (Brussels) *ph* Bénédicte Delsalle, Charlotte
Slovak, Renelde Dupont *ed* Luc Freché
cast CA, Niels Arestrup, Claire Wauthion

Jeanne Dielman, 23 quai du Commerce, 1080 Bruxelles
1975 200m col 16mm
p Evelyne Paul, Corinne Jenart *pc* Paradise Films (Brussels)/Unité Trois
(Paris) *sc* CA *ph* Babette Mangolte, Bénédicte Delsalle *m* Beethoven
ed Patricia Canino
main cast Delphine Seyrig, Jan Decorte, Henri Storck

News from Home
1976 85m col 16mm
p Alain Dahan *pc* Unité Trois (Paris)/Paradise Films (Brussels) *sc* CA
ph Babette Mangolte, Jim Asbell *ed* Francine Sandberg
cast CA (narrator)

Les Rendez-vous d'Anna
Meetings with Anna
1978 127m col 35mm
ep Alain Dahan *pc* Hélène Films (Paris)/Unité Trois (Paris)/Paradise
Films (Brussels)/ZDF (Germany) *sc* CA *ph* Jean Penzer *ed* Francine
Sandberg
main cast Aurore Clément, Jean-Pierre Cassel, Helmut Griem, Magali
Noël

Dis-moi
Tell Me
1980 45m col 16mm

Toute une nuit
All Night Long
1982 89m col 35mm
p Marilyn Watelet *pc* Avidia Films (Paris)/Paradise Films (Brussels)
sc CA *ph* Caroline Champetier *ed* Luc Barnier
main cast Aurore Clément, Samy Szlingerbaum, Natalia Akerman

Les Années 80
The Eighties
1983 82m col video/35mm
p Marilyn Watelet *pc* Paradise Films (Brussels)/Abilene Production
(Paris) *sc* CA, Jean Gruault *ph* Michel Houssiau, Luc Benhamou
ed Nadine Keseman, Francine Sandberg
main cast Aurore Clément, Magali Noël

Un jour Pina m'a demandé
One Day Pina Asked Me
1983 57m col 16mm
Made for the French television series *Repères sur la danse moderne*
pc INA, Antenne 2, R.M. Arts, RTBF *sc* CA *ph* Babette Mangolte, Luc
Benhamou *ed* Dominique Forgue

L'Homme à la valise
The Man with the Suitcase
1983 60m col 16mm
p Yves Valéro *pc* Institut National de l'Audiovisuel (Paris) *sc* CA
ph Maurice Perrimont, Luc Benhamou *ed* Francine Sandberg
cast CA, Jeffrey Kime

J'ai faim, j'ai froid
I'm Hungry, I'm Cold
1984 12m bw 35mm
Segment for the omnibus film, *Paris vu par, 20 ans après*
ep Marc Labrousse, Jean Santamaria *pc* JM Production/Films A2 *sc* CA
ph Luc Benhamou *ed* Francine Sandberg
cast Maria de Medeiros, Pascale Salkin

New York, New York bis
1984 8m bw 35mm [film lost]

Lettre d'un cinéaste
Letter from a Filmmaker
1984 8m col 16mm
Made for the French television series *Lettre d'un cinéaste*
pc Paradise Films (Brussels)

Golden Eighties/Window Shopping
1986 96m col 35mm
p Martine Marignac *pc* La Cécilia (Paris)/Paradise Films (Brussels)/
Limbo Film (Zürich)/in association with Ministère de la Communauté
française de Belgique and Ministère de la Culture (France) *sc* CA, Leora
Barish, Henry Bean, Pascal Bonitzer, Jean Gruault *ph* Gilberto Azevedo,
Luc Benhamou *ed* Francine Sandberg *m* Marc Herouet, CA
main cast Delphine Seyrig, John Berry, Jean-François Balmer, Myriam
Boyer, Fanny Cottençon, Charles Denner, Lio, Pascale Salkin, Nicolas
Tronc

La paresse
Sloth
1986 14m col 35mm
Segment for the omnibus film, *Seven Women, Seven Sins*
cast CA, Sonia Wieder-Atherton

Le marteau
The Hammer
1986 4m col video

Letters Home
1986 104m col video
pc Centre Simone de Beauvoir (Paris) *pb* Luc Benhamou *ed* Claire
Atherton
cast Delphine Seyrig, Coralie Seyrig

Mallet-Stevens
1986 7m col video
pc BRT *ph* Luc Benhamou
cast Sonia Wieder-Atherton, Coralie Seyrig, CA

Histoires d'Amérique
American Stories/Food, Family, and Philosophy
1989 92m col 35mm
ep Bertrand van Effenterre, Marilyn Watelet *p* Bertrand van Effenterre
pc Mallia Films (Paris)/Paradise Films (Brussels) *sc* CA *ph* Luc Benhamou
ed Patrick Mimouni *m* Sonia Wieder-Atherton
main cast Judith Malina, Roy Nathanson

Les trois dernières sonates de Franz Schubert
Franz Schubert's Last Three Sonatas
1989 49m col video
pc La Sept/INA
cast Alfred Brendel

Trois strophes sur le nom de Sacher
"Three Stanzas on the Name Sachet" by Henri Dutilleux
1989 12m col video
pc Mallia Films (Paris)/La Sept/Arcanal/CGP
cast Sonia Wieder-Atherton

Nuit et jour
Night and Day
1991 90m col 35mm
ep Martine Marignac, Maurice Tinchant *p* Pierre Wallon, Marilyn Watelet *pc* Pierre Grise Productions (Paris)/Paradise Films (Brussels) *sc* CA, in collaboration with Pascal Bonitzer *ph* Jean-Claude Neckelbrouck *ed* Francine Sandberg, Camille Bordes-Resnais *m* Marc Herouet
main cast Guillaine Londez, Thomas Langmann, François Négret, Nicole Colchat, Pierre Laroche, Christian Crahay, Luc Fonteyn

Le déménagement
Moving In
1992 42m col 35mm
pc Le Poisson Volant (Paris) *sc* CA *ph* Raymond Fromont
cast Sami Frey

Contre l'oubli
Against Oblivion
1992 110m col 35mm
pc Les Films du Paradoxe *d* various
[CA directed one short segment of this omnibus film]

D'Est
From the East
1993 107m col 35mm
ep Marilyn Watelet *p* François Le Bayon *pc* Paradise Films (Brussels)/ Lieurac Productions (Paris) *sc* CA *ph* Raymond Fromont, Bernard Delville *ed* Claire Atherton

Portrait d'une jeune fille de la fin des années 60 à Bruxelles
Portrait of a Young Girl at the End of the 1960s in Brussels
1993 60m col 35mm

pc IMA Productions (Paris) *sc* CA *ph* Raymond Fromont *m* Yarol *ed* Martine Lebon
cast Circé, Julien Rassam, Joelle Marlier, Cynthia Rodberg

Un Divan à New York
A Couch in New York
1996 109m col 35mm
p Regine Konckier, Jean-Luc Ormières *pc* Les Films Balenciaga *sc* CA, Jean-Louis Benoit *ph* Dietrich Lohmann *ed* Claire Atherton *m* Paolo Conte, Sonia Wieder-Atherton
main cast Juliette Binoche, William Hurt, Stéphanie Buttle, Barbara Garrick

Chantal Akerman par Chantal Akerman
Chantal Akerman by Chantal Akerman
1996 64m col video
p CA *sc* CA
main cast CA

Sud
South
1999 71m col video
p Xavier Carniaux *pc* AMIP, Carré Noir, Chemah I.S., INA, La Sept-Arte, Paradise Films, Radio Télévision Belge Francofone, Yleisradio
ph Raymond Fromont *ed* Claire Atherton

La Captive
The Captive
2000 118m col 35mm
p Paulo Branco *pc* Centre National de la Cinématographie, Gimages 3, Gémini Films, Le Studio Canal, Paradise Films, arte France Cinéma *sc* CA, Eric De Kuyper, from the novel *La prisonnière* by Marcel Proust *ph* Sabine Lancelin *ed* Claire Atherton *m* Imogen Cooper, Sonia Wieder-Atherton
main cast Stanislas Merhar, Sylvie Testud, Olivia Bonamy, Liliane Rovère, Françoise Bertin, Aurore Clément, Vanessa Larré, Samuel Tasinaje, Jean Borodine

Selected bibliography

Akerman, Chantal. *Les Rendez-vous d'Anna* (Paris: Editions Albatros, 1978).

——————. *Un divan à New York* (Paris: L'Arche, 1996).

—————— and Eric De Kuyper. "Le Manoir", *Cahiers du Cinéma* supplement to issue 400 (October 1987): 8.

Alemann, Claudia and Heike Hurst. "interview mit chantal akerman", *Frauen und Film* 7 (March 1976): 32-37.

Apon, Annette. "Chantal Akerman, onderweg naar de autonome vrouw", *Skrien* 84 (February 1979): 28-31.

Aranda, Iván and Andreas Pagaolatos. "Entrevista con Chantal Akerman", *Contracampo* 20 (March 1981): 55-61.

Arnaud, Catherine. "Toute une nuit", *La Revue du Cinéma/Image et Son/ Écran* 377 (November 1982): 28-29.

Aubenas, Jacqueline (ed). *Chantal Akerman* (Brussels: Atelier des Arts, 1982).

Baecque, Antoine de. "Letters Home de Chantal Akerman", *Cahiers du Cinéma* 399 (September 1987): ii.

Barrowclough, Susan. "Toute une nuit (All Night Long)", *Monthly Film Bulletin* 51: 603 (April 1984): 103-104.

——————. "Chantal Akerman: aventures in perception", *Monthly Film Bulletin* 51: 603 (April 1984): 104-105.

Bassan, Raphaël. "Nuit et jour: Nomadisme des passions", *Revue du Cinéma* 474 (September 1991): 26-27.

Bergstrom, Janet. "*Jeanne Dielman, 23 Quai du Commerce, 1080*

Bruxelles by Chantal Akerman", *Camera Obscura* 2 (autumn 1977): 114-118.

Carbonnier, Alain. "Golden Eighties", *Cinéma* 360 (June 25, 1986): 3.

Champetier, Caroline. "Rencontre avec Chantal Akerman: 'Les Rendez-vous d'Anna'", *Cahiers du Cinéma* 288 (May 1978): 53-61.

Chantal Akerman (Madrid: Filmoteca Nacional de España, 1977).

"Chantal Akerman on *Jeanne Dielman*", *Camera Obscura* 2 (autumn 1977): 118-121.

Cook, Pam. "Golden Eighties", *Monthly Film Bulletin* 54: 638 (March 1987): 67-68.

Creveling, Christina. "Women Working: Chantal Akerman", *Camera Obscura* 1 (autumn 1976): 136-139.

Daney, Serge. "Toute une nuit: Chantal Akerman", in *Ciné journal 1981-1986* (Paris: Editions Cahiers du cinéma: 1986): 131-132.

Danton, Amina. "Tout ou rien", *Cahiers du Cinéma* 447 (September 1991): 62-63.

Dawson, Jan. "News from home", *Monthly Film Bulletin* 46: 546 (July 1979): 150.

Delavaud, Gilles. "Les chemins de Chantal Akerman", *Cahiers du Cinéma* 322 (April 1981): v-vi.

Deleuze, Gilles. *Cinema 2: The Time-Image*, translated by Hugh Tomlinson and Robert Galeta (London: The Athlone Press, 1989).

Doane, Mary Ann. "Woman's Stake: Filming the Female Body", *October* 17 (summer 1981): 23-36.

Dubroux, Danièle. "Le familier inquiétant (*Jeanne Dielman*)", *Cahiers du Cinéma* 265 (March-April 1976): 17-20.

—————————————, Thérèse Giraud and Louis Skorecki. "Entretien avec Chantal Akerman", *Cahiers du Cinéma* 278 (July 1977): 34-42.

Elley, Derek. "All Night Long", *Films and Filming* (May 1984): 35.

Fischer, Lucy. "Shall we Dance? Feminist Cinema Remakes the Musical",

Film Criticism 13: 2 (winter 1989): 7-17.

Forbes, Jill. "Les Rendez-vous d'Anna", *Monthly Film Bulletin* 47: 558 (July 1980): 139.

——————. "Histoires d'Amérique: Food, Family and Philosophy (American Stories)", *Monthly Film Bulletin* 57: 673 (February 1990): 40-41.

——————. "Conservatory blues: *Golden Eighties*", *Sight and Sound* 56: 2 (spring 1987): 145.

Gabanelli, Milena. "Cronache: Akerman, Duras, Eustache a Bologna", *Cineforum* 20: 3 (March 1980): 85-86.

Godard, Jean-Luc. "Entretien sur un projet: Chantal Akerman", *Ça Cinéma* 19 (1980): 5-16.

Halbreich, Kathy and Bruce Jenkins (eds). *Bordering on Fiction: Chantal Akerman's* D'Est (Minneapolis: Walker Art Center, 1995).

Hoberman, J. "Jeanne Dielman: Woman's Work", *The Village Voice* 29 March 1983: 1, 48.

——————. "Once More with Feeling", *The Village Voice* 14 May 1985: 60.

——————. "Mall Flowers", *The Village Voice* 21 April 1992: 51.

Indiana, Gary. "Getting Ready for *The Golden Eighties*: A Conversation with Chantal Akerman", *Artforum* 21: 10 (summer 1983): 55-61.

Ishaghpour, Youssef. *Cinéma Contemporain: De ce coté du miroir* (Paris: Editions de la Différence: 1986).

Johnston, Claire. "Towards a Feminist Film Practice: Some Theses", in Bill Nichols (ed), *Movies and Methods, volume II: An Anthology* (Berkeley; Los Angeles; London: University of California Press 1985): 315-327.

Kaja. "L'homme à la Valise", *Variety* 29 August 1984.

Katz, Alyssa. "True Lies: Working the Space Between Fact and Fiction", *The Village Voice* 23 May 1995.

Kinder, Marsha. "Reflections on 'Jeanne Dielman'", *Film Quarterly* 30: 4 (summer 1977): 2-8.

Kinder, Marsha. "The Subversive Potential of the Pseudo-Iterative", *Film Quarterly* 43: 2 (winter 1989-90): 2-16.

Kruger, Barbara. "*Les Années 80*", *Artforum* 22: 4 (December 1983): 84-85.

Kuhn, Annette. *Women's Pictures: Feminism and Cinema*, second edition (London; New York: Verso, 1994).

Kwietniowski, Richard. "Separations: Chantal Akerman's 'News from Home' (1976) and 'Toute une nuit' (1982)", *Movie* 34/35 (winter 1990): 108-118.

Lakeland, Mary Jo. "The Color of Jeanne Dielman", *Camera Obscura* 3/4 (summer 1979): 216-218.

Len. "Paris Vu Par... Vingt Ans Apres", *Variety* 25 July 1984.

"Les rendez-vous d'Anna", *Revue Belge du Cinéma* 11 (October-November 1978): 76-77.

Levieux, Michèle. "Du Côté de Chez Kafka", *Écran* 78: 75 (15 December 1978): 45-46.

——————. "Propos de Chantal Akerman", *Écran* 78: 75 (15 December 1978): 47-51.

Levy, Emanuel. "D'Est (From the East)", *Variety* 11 October 1993.

Loader, Jayne. "*Jeanne Dielman*: Death in Instalments", *Jump Cut* 16 (1977): 10-12.

Longfellow, Brenda. "Love Letters to the Mother: The Work of Chantal Akerman", *Canadian Journal of Political and Social Theory* 13: 1-2 (1989): 73-90.

McRobbie, Angela. "Passionate uncertainty", *Sight and Sound* 2: 5 (September 1992): 28-29.

——————. "Nuit et jour (Night and Day)", *Sight and Sound* 2: 5 (September 1992): 54-55.

Magny, Joël. "Les Rendez-vous d'Anna: Le 'non' de l'auteur", *Cinéma* 78: 239 (November 1978): 92-93.

Mairesse, Emmanuel. "A propos des films de C. Akerman: un tempsatmosphère", *Cahiers du Cinéma* 281 (October 1977): 60-61.

Margulies, Ivone. *Nothing Happens: Chantal Akerman's Hyperrealist Everyday* (Durham, NC; London: Duke University Press, 1996).

Martin, Angela. "Chantal Akerman's films: a dossier", *Feminist Review* 3 (1979): 24-47.

Martin, Marcel. "Les Rendez-Vous d'Anna", *Écran* 78: 75 (15 December 1978): 51-52.

Maupin, Françoise. "Entretien avec Chantal Akerman", *La Revue du Cinéma/Image et Son* 334 (December 1978): 99-103.

Mayne, Judith. *The Woman at the Keyhole: Feminism and Women's Cinema* (Bloomington, IN: Indiana University Press, 1990).

Morley, Meg. "Les Rendez-Vous d'Anna (Chantal Akerman)", *Camera Obscura* 3/4 (summer 1979): 211-215.

Mulvey, Laura. "Guest Appearances", *Time Out* 475 (25-31 May 1979): 19.

Narboni, Jean. "La quatrième personne du singulier *(Je tu il elle)*", *Cahiers du Cinéma* 276 (May 1977): 5-13.

Nesselson, Lisa. "Nuit et jour (Night and Day)", *Variety* 9 September 1991: 65.

Paskin, Sylvia. "Waiting for the Next Shot – Chantal Akerman", *Monthly Film Bulletin* 57: 674 (March 1990): 88.

Patterson, Patricia and Manny Farber. "Beyond the New Wave: I. Kitchen Without Kitsch", *Film Comment* 13: 6 (November-December 1977): 47-50.

Perlmutter, Ruth. "Feminine Absence: A Political Aesthetic in Chantal Ackerman's [sic] *Jeanne Dielman, 23 Quai De [sic] Commerce, 1080 Bruxelles*", *Quarterly Review of Film Studies* 4: 2 (spring 1979): 125-133.

——————. "Visible Narrative, Visible Woman", *Millennium Film Journal* 6 (spring 1980): 18-30.

Philippon, Alain. "Fragments Bruxellois: Entretien avec Chantal Akerman", *Cahiers du Cinéma* 341 (November 1982): 19-23.

——————. "Nuit torride", *Cahiers du Cinéma* 341 (November 1982): 24-26.

Pym, John. "Jeanne Dielman 23, Quai du Commerce 1080 Bruxelles", *Monthly Film Bulletin* 46: 543 (April 1979): 72.

—————. "Je tu il elle (I...You...He...She)", *Monthly Film Bulletin* 46: 547 (August 1979): 175.

Reynaud, Bérénice. "Toronto's 'Festival of Festivals'", *Afterimage* 13: 4 (November 1985): 20-21.

Rich, B. Ruby. "Up Against the Kitchen Wall: Chantal Akerman's Meta-Cinema", *The Village Voice* 29 March 1983: 1, 51.

Rooney, David. "Portrait of a Young Girl At the End of the 1960s in Brussels (Portrait d'une jeune fille de la fin des années 60 à Bruxelles)", *Variety* 5 December 1994.

—————. "A Couch in New York (Un Divan à New York)", *Variety* 12-18 February 1996: 81.

Rosenbaum, Jonathan. "Jean-Luc, Chantal, Danièle, Jean-Marie, and the Others", *American Film* 4: 4 (February 1979): 53-56.

Silverman, Kaja. "Dis-embodying the Female Voice", in Mary Ann Doane, Patricia Mellencamp and Linda Williams (eds), *Re-Vision: Essays in Feminist Film Criticism* (Frederick, MD: University Publications of America, 1984): 131-149.

Squire, Corinne. "Toute une Heure: Corinne Squire Talks to Chantal Akerman", *Screen* 25: 6 (November-December 1984): 67-71.

Taubin, Amy. "A Woman's Tedium", *Soho Weekly News* 25 November 1976: 31.

—————. "Laughter in the Dark", *The Village Voice* 5 July 1989: 60, 64.

—————. "The Sound & the Fury", *The Village Voice* 12 May 1998: 123.

Treilhou, Marie-Claude. "Chantal Akerman: 'La vie, il faut la mettre en scène...'", *Cinéma* 76: 206 (February 1976): 89-93.

Tremois, Claude-Marie. "Chantal Akerman: 'A partir de quelques images de mon enfance'", *Télérama* 14 January 1976: 66-68.

Contributors

Jennifer M Barker teaches at Northwestern University and is a doctoral candidate in the Department of Film and Television at UCLA. Her dissertation takes a phenomenological approach to the tactility of the cinematic experience.

Janet Bergstrom teaches film history and theory at UCLA. A founding editor of *Camera Obscura,* she has published essays on emigre directors Jean Renoir, Fritz Lang, and F. W. Murnau, as well as Chantal Akerman, Claire Denis, and Asta Nielsen. She is the editor of *Endless Night: Cinema and Psychoanalysis, Parallel Histories* (1999) and the author of a monograph on Chantal Akerman (forthcoming) and is currently engaged in a study (for DVD and for print), *Murnau in America: Sunrise to Tabu.* Her essay "Keeping a Distance: The Innovators 1970–1980: Chantal Akerman" appeared in *Sight & Sound* in November 1999.

Kristine Butler is an assistant professor of French at the University of Wisconsin–River Falls. Her primary areas of research are early cinema and turn-of-the-century French literature. She has published on the films of René Clair, on Spanish filmmaker Pedro Almodóvar, and on early French serial films. She is currently developing research in problems of ethnic and cultural identity in early French cinema and is working on a book-length manuscript entitled "The Aural Flâneur," which discusses the ways that urbanization and the development of technologies such as the phonograph changed the way French narrative developed in the late nineteenth century.

Sandy Flitterman-Lewis is an associate professor at Rutgers, the State University of New Jersey. A founding editor of *Camera Obscura* and of *Discourse,* she has written over fifty articles on feminist theory and cultural studies. She is the author of *New Vocabularies in Film Semiotics*

(1992). Her current work is on childhood, the family, and anti-Semitism in Occupation France, on which her forthcoming book, *Hidden Voices,* is based.

Gwendolyn Audrey Foster is an associate professor in the Department of English at the University of Nebraska. She is the author of a study of postcolonial women filmmakers entitled *Women Filmmakers of the African and Asian Diaspora: Decolonizing the Gaze, Locating Subjectivity* (1997) and *Captive Bodies: Postcolonialist Subjectivity in the American Cinema* (1999).

Catherine Fowler finished a PhD on Chantal Akerman in 1995. She is reader and course leader of the MA in independent film and filmmaking at Southampton Institute of Higher Education. She has published on feminism and film, experimental cinema, and Belgian cinema.

Ivone Margulies is an associate professor in the Department of Film and Media Studies at Hunter College (CUNY). She is the author of *Nothing Happens: Chantal Akerman's Hyperrealist Everyday* (1996) and the editor of the anthology *Rites of Realism: Essays on Corporeal Cinema* (2003). She is currently at work on a book on reenactment and exemplarity on film.

Judith Mayne is a professor of French and women's studies at Ohio State University. She is the author of many volumes in film studies and women's studies, including *The Woman at the Keyhole: Feminism and Women's Cinema* (1990) and *Cinema and Spectatorship* (1990).

Maureen Turim is a professor in the Department of English and the Program of Film Studies at the University of Florida. She is the author of *Abstraction in Avant-Garde Films* (1985), *Flashbacks in Film: Memory and History* (1989), and *The Films of Oshima Nagisa: Images of a Japanese Iconoclast* (1998), as well as many other articles on feminism, cinema, and the avant-garde.

Ginette Vincendeau is a professor of film studies in the Department of Film and Television Studies at the University of Warwick. She is the author and editor of numerous critical essays and monographs, including the *Encyclopedia of European Cinema* (1995), *The Companion to French Cinema* (1996), *Pépé le Moko* (1998), and *Stars and Stardom in French Cinema* (2001).

Index

197